T0285425

Unheard Witness

The publication of this book was made possible by the generous support of the Louann Atkins Temple Women & Culture Endowment.

Kathy Leissner Whitman and her husband, Charles Whitman, Easter, 1964. Private archive of Nelson Leissner.

Unheard Witness

THE LIFE AND DEATH OF
KATHY LEISSNER WHITMAN

Jo Scott-Coe

University of Texas Press Austin

The Louann Atkins Temple Women & Culture Endowment is supported by
Allison, Doug, Taylor, and Andy Bacon; Margaret, Lawrence, Will, John, and
Annie Temple; Larry Temple; the Temple-Inland Foundation; and the National
Endowment for the Humanities.

Requests for permission to reproduce material from this work should be sent to:
    Permissions
    University of Texas Press
    P.O. Box 7819
    Austin, TX 78713-7819
    utpress.utexas.edu

♾ The paper used in this book meets the minimum requirements of ANSI/
NISO Z39.48-1992 (R1997) (Permanence of Paper).

Library of Congress Cataloging-in-Publication Data

Names: Scott-Coe, Jo, 1969– author.
Title: Unheard witness : the life and death of Kathy Leissner Whitman / Jo
Scott-Coe.
Description: First edition. | Austin : University of Texas Press, 2023. | Includes
bibliographical references and index.
Identifiers: LCCN 2022056014 (print) | LCCN 2022056015 (ebook)
    ISBN 978-1-4773-2764-7 (hardcover)
    ISBN 978-1-4773-2765-4 (pdf)
    ISBN 978-1-4773-2766-1 (epub)
Subjects: LCSH: Whitman, Kathy Leissner, 1943–1966. | Whitman, Kathy
Leissner, 1943–1966—Correspondence. | Whitman, Kathy Leissner, 1943–
1966—Death and burial. | Whitman, Charles Joseph, 1941–1966—Family. |
Abused wives—Texas—Austin—Biography. | Abused wives—Social aspects—
United States. | Mass shootings—Social aspects—United States.
Classification: LCC HV6626.22.T49 S368 2023 (print) | LCC HV6626.22.T49
(ebook) | DDC 362.82/9209764—dc23/eng/20230317
LC record available at https://lccn.loc.gov/2022056014
LC ebook record available at https://lccn.loc.gov/2022056015

doi:10.7560/327647

This book is dedicated to anyone,
living or deceased,
who did not know where to turn.

If you or someone you know is experiencing relationship
abuse in any form, help is available.

The National Domestic Violence Hotline provides free,
confidential support 24/7/365.
Text START to 88788,
call 1-800-799-SAFE(7233),
or chat online at TheHotline.org.

Contents

Introduction

THE NARRATIVE OF THIS BOOK BEGINS and ends with
two catastrophic public events: Hurricane Carla in 1961 and
Charles Whitman's Tower massacre in 1966. As devastating
as Carla was when it struck the Gulf Coast, people understood the danger and united ahead of time. Whitman, by
contrast, was an insidious threat, charming for an audience
but a bully in private long before he shot strangers from the
University of Texas clock tower, killing fifteen and wound-
ing thirty-one.[1] Just as Carla was the worst hurricane to hit
Texas in more than half a century, Whitman's rampage was
the deadliest public shooting covered "live" by media, long
before the term "mass shooting" became part of our weary
vernacular. As brutal as he revealed himself to be under
a bright blue sky, there seemed at the time no method for
tracking—never mind interrupting—his pathway to public
violence. He was white and blond, handsome and well liked,

ideally suited to navigate a society that enabled him to pass as harmless and well intentioned. In the wake of his Tower rampage, and for more than fifty years afterwards, many Americans preferred to frame his story as one of sudden, unthinkable, horrific surprise.

The woman married to Whitman lived a lonely reality between these two storms. Kathleen "Kathy" Leissner arrived at the University of Texas at Austin one day after Hurricane Carla devastated the region where she had grown up. Within less than one year, at the age of nineteen, she wedded the man who would stab her to death in bed after first killing his own mother. More than five decades later, Kathy's voice emerges from a vast private correspondence to illuminate the domestic abuse that, according to data available in 2022, precedes public shootings nearly 60 percent of the time. "Tell everyone hello for us," she wrote her parents as problems surfaced in the early days of her marriage, "and explain what happened."[2]

Until her eldest surviving brother, Nelson Leissner, came forward as a traumatized family member and fierce guardian of documents saved from accidental purging even through years when he was not sure how or when he would allow them to be shared, Kathy remained a two-dimensional victim. Inside the canon of the Tower shooting history, both in official records and secondary retellings, her husband was simultaneously demonized and elevated as the sole "author" of the event, whose acts, words, and explanations shaped our attention. Meanwhile, reduced to a pretty teacher's portrait and a grisly crime scene photograph, Kathy became romantic background in retellings that repeated and sentimentalized her husband's twisted logic: that he killed Kathy, his "most precious possession," because he "loved" her and wanted to do her "a favor." After her murder Kathy was thus subjected to what Sylvia Hubel calls "epistemic smothering," a rhetorical structure that precludes (whether from habit or intention) new testimony or analysis from entering the record.[3]

I have spent twenty years examining the troubling line we draw between private patterns and public displays of violence. Time and again, throughout my work as a writer, teacher, and mentor, in my own life as well as those of friends and colleagues, students, and my family, I have experienced firsthand how disorienting it can be to discover or describe trouble without any ready audience, or with an audience that invalidates. Herein lie the earliest narrative fragments—truly the "first" responses prior to any public report—preemptively scrapped or simply unsought by investigators, journalists, or other authorities because nothing that (yet) ranks as a crime has transpired, because the most obvious crime appears to be solved, or because observers second-guess their own voices. Racism and prejudice about gender, sexual identity, and class too easily sideline testimony in commercial media as well as in courtrooms. And within these implicit "hierarchies of victimization," those closest to the perpetrator remain among the least "ideal victims," more likely to be stigmatized or blamed when hurt by a loved one, whether they report or not.[4]

As the fiftieth anniversary of the Tower shooting approached, Nelson granted me first-time and exclusive access to 215 letters written and received by Kathy during the period spanning from June 1962, just before her engagement, through July 1966, two weeks before her murder. This was a substantial sample, but Nelson was always clear that there were many more. When he sent the first tenderly packed boxes (containing photographs, family documents, and other primary materials in addition to the letters), I was astonished and humbled. His purpose remained unequivocal: he wanted the full humanity of Kathy to be respected, and he wanted others to benefit from the sharing. "If it can save just one life," he said repeatedly, "that is what I want."

I was completing another book at the time, *MASS: A Sniper, a Father, and a Priest* (2018), tracing the social, cultural, and religious influences that contributed to Whitman's formation as a predator, including his close association with a priest identified in 2019 as "credibly accused" of abusing children. That sobering work well-prepared me to comprehend the milieu wherein Kathy, like so many women, faced unspeakable cruelty and dysfunction in places where they were supposedly most safe—in their churches, in their families, and in their closest relationships. Kathy's humanity was threatened immediately by a relationship with a man whose notions of "love" had been warped by childhood trauma and profoundly twisted by ideologies of ownership, objectification, and abuse. Unlike most victims, he perpetuated the damage.[5]

A child of the "silent generation," raised in a small Texas farming community southwest of Houston, Kathy came of age during a decade of post–World War II prosperity and entered the University of Texas just as the social conformity held at such a premium during her teenage years was beginning to be actively questioned. Rather than experiencing active-shooter drills in school, Kathy knew the duck-and-cover drills of the Cold War. In a world without the Internet, social media, or twenty-four-hour news cycles, the pace of communication was much slower. By 1960–1961, during Kathy's senior year of high school, women in Texas were organizing politically to challenge sexist state laws even as many communities dragged their heels on full racial integration of schools and businesses. She lived during the height of the civil rights movement and its violent backlash, through John F. Kennedy's election and assassination, and the steady uptick of war in Vietnam. Her married life began as Latina

In the early 1950s, American schoolchildren follow their teacher in a duck-and-cover drill to prepare for nuclear war. AP Photo/Dan Gross.

nurse Polly Abarca fought to secure sex education and birth control among rural and lower-income families in South Texas, but before the Supreme Court rulings of *Griswold v. Connecticut* (1965) and *Eisenstadt v. Baird* (1972) protected contraceptive access as a constitutional right.[6] Kathy was killed before the women's movement or anything called "sexual liberation" had taken full flight: three years before *Our Bodies, Ourselves* appeared in print, three years before the Stonewall Riots, eleven years before the National Women's Conference in Houston, and twenty-four years before Ann Richards was elected as the second woman governor of Texas. *Playboy* was a mainstream influence in popular culture, while *Ms.* magazine had not yet published its first issue. Kathy was murdered the year Barbara Jordan became the first Black woman elected to the Texas state senate. The Civil Rights Act of 1964 and the Voting Rights Act of 1965 had passed, but interracial marriages were still prohibited by anti-miscegenation laws, and the safest place to be anything but heterosexual remained a closet.

More than fifty years later, here I am—a California transplant and former military brat by way of the Midwest, a white writer from Generation X, an English professor, a stray Catholic, an aunt to many and mother to none—documenting the story of a Texas woman dead three years before I was born. At the beginning of this process, I read her letters one at a time, often late into the night after days of teaching, carefully opening envelopes and unfolding pages where Kathy composed her thoughts at the same age as most of my students, from eighteen to twenty-three. After my first journalistic portrait of her, "Listening to Kathy," appeared in *Catapult* in 2016, I realized that the letters deserved deeper and more sustained attention.[7]

I signed the contract for this book weeks before the COVID-19 pandemic hit, and when I shared the news, Nelson agreed to grant me access to all remaining letters. At the end of a rainy weekend in Galveston, he and I gathered around his dining room table, collating batches by year and by author, bunching them gently with loose rubber bands. I packed them into every available space of my carry-on bag, cautiously easing through the metal detectors at Hobby Airport and bringing them to California. The lockdown restrictions came as I began this manuscript, and my connection with Kathy's struggle amplified the physical realities of my own anxious confinement. New layers of meaning passed through me, sharpening what I had learned from reading and transcription, writing and lecturing for nearly five years. While I was safe in my home, the quarantine exacerbated unsafe conditions for others: those living with dangerous partners or family members whose abuse is already well concealed even when the entire world is not sheltering in place. In 2020 the *New England Journal of Medicine* identified intimate partner violence (IPV) as the "pandemic within a pandemic." The Texas Council on Family Violence (TCFV) reported a 22 percent increase of women's IPV deaths statewide in 2020, with 228 people killed and the highest number of women's fatalities since 2010.[8]

Pulling the book into shape, I felt often like an intruder who needed to earn and re-earn a sacred trust. Even as I had to distance myself in the examination of historical and literary material, I also felt deeply a sense of "being with" Kathy during an adulthood when she so desperately sought a loving reader.[9] For many reasons beyond COVID, I identified with her invisible isolation, recognizing how her letters can serve as an essential contribution to the histories of discarded voices, what counts when we speak of violence, whose testimony we gather, and how we respond.

THE STUDY OF LETTERS OR EPISTOLARY material (what scholars also call "life writing") is an intimate and sensory process, especially in an electronic age, and it invites interdisciplinary analysis. I have relied heavily on my training in disciplines of literary criticism as well as composition and rhetoric, drawing on theories of interpretation that emphasize women's agency, subjectivity, and discounted knowledge inside apparent gaps or silences (consider Hélène Cixous's *écriture féminine*, Cynthia Enloe's "feminist curiosity," Julia Kristeva's intertextuality, and bell hooks's practice of epistolary witness). The expertise of archival scholars such as Maria Tamboukou and Margaretta Jolly offered useful insights for examining groups of letters across time, among authors, and within historical and social contexts.

Access to a private archive of this size, density, and scope (roughly six hundred letters written and received within four years) is a particular treasure, especially as the papers of "ordinary women" tend to be discarded. Archivist Svanhildur Bogadottir notes how even as women traditionally play the role of family documentarian, gendered social barriers tend to undervalue women's materials unless their creators are deemed famous. Referencing historian Gerda Lerner, Bogadottir adds that the result is a "systemic exclusion of women from society's memory tools and institutions."[10] Further complicating preservation efforts, surviving relatives, spouses, or lovers may heavily censor information even if the original writer composed with an eye towards future publication (consider Ann Frank's diary) or if documents do not reflect well on a prominent living individual (consider poet Sylvia Plath's unpublished letters to her therapist, alleging abuse by her husband Ted Hughes). In the wake of racial violence, geographical displacement, and missing or destroyed records, descendants may take years to restitch histories together, as Cassandra Lane explores in her 2021 memoir, *We Are Bridges.*

A full consideration of Kathy's correspondence cannot change the reality of her murder, but it can alter the context within which we respond to stories of mass violence as well as private abuse. Kathy reached for a future that was brutally torn from her before the terminology of domestic violence and IPV had yet evolved. Lenore E. A. Walker had not yet published her formative work on the syndrome of gender-based violence. Diana E. H. Russell had not yet published her study of sexual assault in married relationships, a topic that remained essentially taboo. Evan Stark had not yet defined coercive control as a practice of calculated and highly gendered subjugation, a crime against women's liberty akin to hostage taking—more prevalent as legal systems attuned to overt violence.[11] Abuse in the home tended to be portrayed in extreme terms (as wife beating) or downplayed, conflated with normal marital disputes (e.g., *The Honeymooners*), or absurdly comedic misunderstandings (as in *I Love Lucy*'s "black eye" episode). The "power and control wheel" had not yet been developed to identify pervasive forms of abuse beyond obvious physical injuries. Seven spokes of the original wheel (which continues to be adapted to address different relationship contexts and abuse patterns) can help readers visualize what Kathy experienced with her husband: intimidation, emotional abuse, isolation, minimizing/blaming, asserting male privilege, economic abuse, and coercion and threats. An eighth category, the use of children, also applies to Kathy as a nonmother: her partner pressured constantly about pregnancy, fixated on future children, and monitored her body obsessively even as she dreaded conceiving. "I am so thankful we don't have any children nor any on the way," she wrote in late 1963. "[Y]ou can't raise children in conditions as unstable as ours."[12]

Kathy did not anticipate that five years after high school graduation she would be murdered by the man she married. As a vibrant, socially intelligent, and unguarded personality, she developed ways to subvert and challenge her husband's domination and his brittle attitudes about gender roles and sex. But her self-confidence wavered as her husband's behavior took a cumulative toll on every aspect of her well-being, instilling hesitation and hypervigilance over time. In hundreds of pages and thousands of words, Kathy maneuvered between declarative, interrogative, and subjunctive voices, reaching for what might be possible, where, when, and *if only*—in contrast with her husband's imperative and conditional statements, evasions, hollow reflections, scripted compliments, and repeatedly threatening and dangerous actions. Being white, being pretty, coming from a working and prosperous middle-class family with two college-educated parents, securing her own college degree "on time" within four years, and earning a teaching certificate—none of it protected her from the realities of abuse. At each turn, Kathy's conscientiousness and decency, alongside the privileges of her identity, were weaponized into self-blame and exploited to elicit compliance as well as secret-keeping.

Most often, testimony comes from those who survive. Kathy's letters trace a hidden and ultimately fatal struggle in all its ordinariness, in real time, in lived language, before anyone else was paying attention. By witnessing her story—in all its granularity, minutiae, and vulnerability—I hope to guide readers towards an understanding that need not elude us as we try to imagine interventions for "normal" horrors unfolding offstage, years before the gun goes off.

THE LAST FRIEND TO SET FOOT in Kathy's home before her murder was Elaine Brazzell (formerly Fuess). She and her then-husband, Larry, dropped by the evening of July 31, 1966, and they visited with Charlie alone because Kathy was finishing the second half of her split shift at Southwestern Bell. Years later, motivated to understand how anger could contribute to such violence, Brazzell became a licensed professional counselor. When we spoke by phone, she described a dinner visit several months before that last day. As the two women prepared food in the kitchen, Kathy mentioned quietly that Charlie had aggressive and mean moods and that he sometimes frightened her. "I didn't have the skills at the time to get that she was describing a problem," Brazzell said. "I wish we had just stopped and sat down, right there, and talked about it."[13]

Kathy may well have shared more at that moment. But we also know now that victim-survivors often halt or hesitate their testimony, even as they begin to test the waters of telling. Brazzell's recollection, among others, demonstrates how in the last year of her life Kathy was starting to question what Walker identifies as "sex-role socialization," recognizing that Charlie's psychological state was not her responsibility, despite his insistence to the contrary.[14] In hushed comments to a trusted friend, she was temporarily disrupting an external image of domestic peace or tranquility, and, in her own time, she was permitting herself to acknowledge that her husband was as capable of cruelty as he was of being, or seeming, loving.[15] Kathy possessed significant expertise that she did not yet entirely trust, and her language did not readily or confidently translate into recognizable words signaling emergency.

But the story never starts, nor does it truly end, when the shooter on the Tower—or at the school, church, nightclub, mall, or [insert your setting here]—opens fire and is put down. Jane Monckton Smith's stunning book, *In Control: Dangerous Relationships and How They End in Murder* (2021), traces how systems of justice face a serious limitation in their design to address incidents rather than to connect patterns of interaction.[16] Close-reading of language—and of interactions as texts—remains an underestimated skill (diminished as soft or feminine). Even the word used to describe advance warnings from a violent perpetrator is a passive one: "leakage."[17] As the highly masculine field of law enforcement has become more militarized, officer training and education in recognizing coercive control has not kept up with research, a limitation Stark analyzes within broader social and policy contexts. The impact of unofficial witnesses can also be transformed through bystander intervention strategies specifically related to IPV.[18]

This book documents Kathy Leissner Whitman's experience trying to love, and to leave, a dangerous man. I centered her story and perceptions within historical materials, newspaper reports, and relevant secondary sources. To contextualize her detailed responses, it was critical to summarize and quote selectively from letters she received from her mother and certainly her husband. I omitted most names not already identified in the public record. To maximize page space, I did not preserve line breaks from transcripts as I wove them into narrative. I corrected misspellings or typos that would distract readers, but I retained errors that contributed insight to the material.[19] I also preserved two recurring words in Kathy's idiosyncratic usage and spelling without correction because they render the sound of her voice: she often used "mabe" (for "maybe") and "sometime" (for "sometimes"). I have done my best to honor Kathy's language without trying to manicure her to fit some arbitrary standard of perfection, which would only mimic her husband's pattern. I sought to respect the dignity of her life without sentimentalizing her pain or judging her struggle.

We face a strange paradox: even as we recognize the human role in natural disasters, we seem to accept the daily accumulation of mass shootings as a natural, perhaps unavoidable, hazard. Our attitudes about IPV remain similar: 62 percent of college students across a spectrum of identities still experience abuse from a partner.[20] With numbers like these, Americans are more likely to know—or to be—a victim or perpetrator in private than to succumb to a mass shooting. In Kathy's time there was nothing like a public radar system to track first signs of danger behind closed doors. In our time, as experts seek to marshal national resources to recognize and connect red flags more effectively to prevent public violence, an interior view of one woman's history with a future killer can help us refine new maps and new pathways to disruption.[21]

Unheard Witness

Danger, 1961

IN NEEDVILLE, TEXAS, A SMALL FARMING community roughly one hour from the Gulf coastline, Kathy Leissner was packing for college. Imagine the bureau with drawers hanging loosely open, a cosmetics case near the vanity mirror, closet doors flung back, a few cardboard boxes on the floor. Clothing folded gently, arranged across the bedspread in semi-tidy mounds sorted by style, fabric, and occasion. A pile of hangers. Perhaps one hand smoothing creases along a new cotton shirtdress. Kathy and her mother had created many new outfits in the previous weeks: each stitch and pleat, zipper and button, a product of their summer sewing frenzy.

Her teenage brother, Nelson, kept talking about the cars. Starting the weekend of September 9, an unusual stream of traffic plowed north out of Freeport along Highway 36 into Fort Bend County, eventually slowing to a logjam that cut

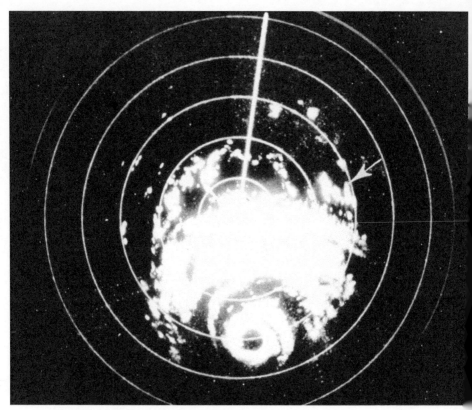

A radar image shows the outer storm bands and eye of Hurricane Carla coming into view as it filled the Gulf of Mexico in September 1961. National Oceanic and Atmospheric Administration (NOAA).

Needville into two uncrossable halves. The tanks at the town gas stations ran dry after a few hours.[1] Kathy could have trudged through the wide yard behind the house and less than half a mile across small fields and pastures to witness the urgent evacuation herself, in advance of Hurricane Carla's projected landfall. As the calm gray sky grew heavier and the humidity bore down, hundreds of men, women, and children passed through, determined to survive. Improvised containers were strapped to trunks, roofs, or flatbeds for whatever precious cargo folks salvaged in a hurry. Dogs poked snouts from windows. There was an occasional chicken.

Kathy had been born near Freeport, and her life would have looked quite different at this moment if the Leissners had not moved on. She and Nelson, with their little brother Ray, would probably be riding with their parents and pets in a vehicle along this very road, trunk and footwells packed with essentials, heading away from the natural force that would not take no for an answer. But as her younger sibling now chattered on about Chevrolets and Pontiacs, station wagons and livestock trailers and pickups, Kathy trusted the refuge of the large brick ranch-style home her parents, Raymond and Frances, had built on the east side of the highway two years earlier. She was less anxious about safety than the potential disruption Carla posed to her immediate plans at the University of Texas, where she had been accepted as a pharmacy student. Carla's arrival would overlap with registration, and classes were set to begin on September 18.[2]

Fortunately, her father had already completed his rice harvest, and in the days before the storm he took no other chances. He and Nelson had gone to the fields and driven three diesel tractors, a short-bed trailer, and two trucks back to the house, parking them alongside the outer walls and windows to guard against blowing debris. Tearing up the lush lawn with heavy tires was a small price to pay for protection. Raymond even squeezed a neighbor's Volkswagen next to his wife's Volkswagen inside the two-car garage, then somehow managed to sandwich his own truck inside as well.[3]

Kathy's parents had been reading the papers, of course, as everyone had. Before long, continuous KHOU television broadcasts made the situation visually clear. By two p.m. Sunday, September 10, Carla's eye crept into shadowy view on a radar screen, and reporter Dan Rather pointed the tip of a pencil to indicate the approach of the northern storm bands, an ominous white eyebrow. A voice warned viewers how deceptive the quiet, "near calm" inside the eye would feel after the first, worst strike of the storm. Anyone caught inside the eye would need to brace for the next, inevitable part of the cycle or risk being caught by a deadly surprise: another brutal attack of wind and rain always came from the opposite direction.[4]

The cars on Highway 36 were long gone when Carla struck Texas as a Category 4 on Monday, September 11. The Leissners could count themselves among the lucky as landfall occurred roughly ninety miles southwest, between Port O'Connor and Port Lavaca, while the family hunkered down with neighbors. When electricity flickered, Nelson's battery-powered radio became the most reliable source of updates. During the worst, first hours of the storm, they sat for breakfast as winds raged outside. An empty horse trailer broke the spell of normalcy, flying across their yard like a giant tin can and shattering a neighbor's pasture fence, thankfully injuring no one.[5]

Kathy had just turned eighteen. To mark the milestone, her grandmother Leissner had deposited $100 in an account opened under her name at the First State Bank. Hurricane or no hurricane, Kathy knew the meaning of this support even as she longed for more independence. A loving family cared for her as she learned to be responsible and look out for herself. Kathy had written her first checks at dry goods stores and shoe shops, splurging at Early's ($16.94 for shoes) and Wonder Fabric Center ($13.27)—all in the happy preparations for moving to Austin.[6]

Frances had a knack for guiding her children without hovering too much, and she knew her daughter's adjustment to this stage of adulthood would be gradual. After all, as Raymond might have put it, Kathy was not going to French Canada or Mexico or even New York City. She would be able to visit home when she wanted. She was bright and friendly, eager to trust and to learn. It mattered, too, that both her parents, especially Frances, had college diplomas.

As Carla's winds raged outside the sturdy Leissner walls, the two women braced their nerves, making final choices on clothes.[7] It was a steady, hopeful pace: take this, leave that— for now. Do not forget this umbrella. Remember the sewing basket. Kathy would have been able to hear her brothers in the den, her father clattering dishes in the kitchen. If the eye moved overhead, they would wait to endure the second wave together. There was no reason to panic.

Country Life, Only Daughter

KATHY'S MOTHER, FRANCES HOLLOWAY, WAS RAISED with her only brother eighty miles north of Houston in Trinity, a small town named after the Trinity River and a station for the Great Northern Railroad in the East Texas Timberlands region. Her father was a railroad agent, and her mother was a housewife who also worked as a teacher. A family of modest means, the Holloways put a premium on education for both children, and Frances at a tender age grew accustomed to adult responsibilities. During a period when her brother required extended hospitalization in Houston, Frances routinely collected his books from school and caught a train into the city to deliver his lessons. Frances thrived in her own studies as well, and by age sixteen, she enrolled at Sam Houston State Teacher's College in Huntsville, where she majored in chemistry and accounting, working in the cafeteria and mopping floors to pay for expenses as a resident in the dorm.[1]

Kathy's father, Raymond Leissner, was three years older than Frances. He and his two siblings, a brother and sister, grew up in and around Needville, raised by cotton and corn farmers. Raymond graduated from Rosenberg High School and subsequently enrolled in the University of Texas with the intention of becoming a dentist. However, when his father could no longer afford the expense, Raymond enrolled at Sam Houston as a student of vocational agriculture. Frances often told the story of meeting Raymond at a campus water fountain and having an instant attraction. When they married on November 30, 1939, in a ceremony performed by a justice of the peace, Frances had already earned both a degree and a teaching certificate. Shortly afterwards, Raymond received his own diploma.[2]

It took some time for the couple to settle. Raymond first took a job with Dow Chemical, and the couple moved to the town of Velasco, just five miles from the Gulf of Mexico. At the time, Velasco's economy and population was rebounding after roughly fifteen years of decline, aided by Dow's regional development and the diversion of the Brazos River into a functional shipping channel. Velasco was soon annexed into Freeport, which was fast transforming into a company town—or boomtown —built around the corporation that relied on coastal geography and labor. On days when the winds shifted from the north, the salty sea breezes mingled with the sharp or sour chemical smells not ideal for families whose livelihoods depended upon the source of the pollution. Raymond worked in Dow's brand-new plant, built in 1940 as a war plant to mine the ocean for magnesium in support of the Allied war effort. Kathleen Frances (Kathy) was born at Dow Magnesium Hospital on the evening of July 12, 1943.[3]

ABOVE: *Kathy Leissner, first grade portrait. Private archive of Nelson Leissner.*

LEFT: *Raymond Leissner holds his daughter, Kathy, c. 1944. Private archive of Nelson Leissner.*

When Kathy was two years old, her father left Dow. Determined to redirect his career, Raymond took his young family to stay with an aunt in Navasota, Texas, while he enrolled in classes at the University of Houston. He worked nights in a machine shop, hoping finally to qualify as a dental student in a Navy program.[4] In his temporary absence, Frances delighted in her first child and updated details in baby books. One, inscribed in light blue muslin, a gift from friends, was titled "Life Begins." The other, "Baby's Own Book," was covered in pink taffeta. Frances jotted entries in both books. Like so many women of her generation, she was a creative family documentarian.

Each baby book included a full family tree in Frances's blue cursive, tracing all the way back to great-grandparents on both Holloway and Leissner sides of the family. She recorded the names of both doctor and nurse at her daughter's birth (W. L. Galloway and Miss Purdue), along with Kathy's birth weight (nine pounds) and height (one foot, ten inches), and her dark brown hair and blue eyes. For remarks, Frances added, "No birthmarks. One curl on top of head. Dimples in cheeks. Tiny feet and hands." Dates and ages are recorded for Kathy's first smile, first tooth, first sitting and standing up, first day in highchair, first flight of stairs. For first crawl, in both books, Frances wrote with determined pride, "Walked first."

Frances likely backfilled memories as they struck her. In the pink book, Frances reflected at length on her daughter at five weeks old with maternal amusement: "Kathy's very first time to leave the house at 314 Bay St., Freeport, Texas, was to go to the doctor's office for a checkup on August 21. She was dressed in a little gown and pink 'flapper' shoes knitted with the toes out. She slept the entire time, rousing only once when Dr. Galloway examined her mouth and throat, which she resented highly! Waaa! (Everyone agrees she is beautiful and couldn't be doing better.)" The blue book lists every health milestone: inoculations against diphtheria and whooping cough, dates when upper and lower teeth appeared, the progress of heights and weights.

Many entries are idiosyncratic. Frances noted, "Very slow about cutting teeth. Had fever and was cross with first ones." About Kathy's aptitude for movement, Frances observed, "By the time she could stand alone she attempted to dance to the radio, could keep time amazingly well." Illustrating her talent as a seamstress, Frances trimmed small, perfect loops of her daughter's hair at three weeks, one year, two years, and three years old—from dark brown to golden, each tied with a tiny blue or pink ribbon and carefully stored in miniature plastic pockets. Her wry humor appeared on the

birth announcement card where, on the line for "Parents,"
she first filled in her husband's name, "R. W. Leissner," but
finding no room left for her own name, she added underneath "(alone?)."[5]

Meanwhile, contrary to his hopes, Raymond was turned
down for the Naval dentistry program because, at twenty-
nine and a half, he was considered too old. He took Frances
and baby Kathy to Houston where they lived for a time at San
Felipe Courts, housing built in the 1940s for white defense
workers.[6] When he secured a new position as an operator
making gasoline at Crown Central Petroleum Corporation,
the family purchased a new house in Pasadena. There, they
splurged on studio portraits of Kathy as a toddler. Posing
in ribbons and a jumper, Kathy at age three appeared in a
newspaper advertisement for Walker Studio with the slo-
gan, "Don't Take Chances on Something as Precious as Your
Baby's Picture."

After a severe explosion at the petroleum company, Raymond decided to quit the chemical industry for good. He
worked selling fabrics for a silk company until his second
child, Nelson, was born, and then decided his future lay
in farming. The Leissners returned to Fort Bend County,
where in partnership with his brother, Raymond managed
just over three hundred acres of his father's land in Needville. In 1951, the land was divided evenly and deeded to
the brothers individually, and Raymond rotated his portion
annually between rice and cattle for market.[7]

Although Kathy's father decided rice would net a better
return than other crops, he also knew it was labor intensive
and required significant water supply. Muscle memory from
growing up on a farm, combined with studies of agriculture
and animal husbandry at Sam Houston, contributed to Raymond's success, but even the wisest farmer and rancher
could not anticipate every problem. One year he bought

twenty-two heads of Black Angus cattle and, without any clear rhyme or reason, almost all died. A farmer couldn't belabor an event like that. He had to learn limits, cut his losses, and move forward.[8]

The Leissners first lived in small houses on the west side of Highway 36, a short walk from the center of town but a fair distance from the rice fields and cattle pastures. By the time Kathy entered first grade, her place in the small community was socially and financially secure. A photo likely snapped by Frances shows her squinting into the sunlight with a friend on her first day of school. Even as the family settled successfully into the seasons of farming life, Frances was a rare woman among her in-laws and neighbors: she was married with children and had a college degree, and she worked outside the home as an elementary school teacher. Calm and down-to-earth, she nevertheless faced jealousy and suspicion from some locals who retained their prejudices about a woman's place. She retained her sense of humor, writing on the back of one photo of Kathy and Nelson as toddlers playing in the yard, "The way the kids usually look—muddy!"[9] Soon Frances was pregnant again and gave birth to a second son, Ray.

Kathy's parents joined Needville's First Methodist Church, where Raymond attended regularly and sometimes taught Sunday school. The church provided community for children—picnics and food drives, hayrides, Bible camps. A photo from the early 1950s shows Kathy among a group of children gathered to sing in the sanctuary. Frances directed her attention to support behind the scenes. Her mathematical savvy came in handy during late nights with the church's large ledger books splayed across the kitchen table.[10] She knew that no matter how much people prayed, no matter how many Bible verses they quoted, dollars and cents added up or they didn't. In the red or in the black, a church budget was no place for false hope or fuzzy logic. A person had to own the losses and debts and always take proper care of the yield.

By the 1950s racial and economic segregation remained visible in the small community of roughly six hundred people, with Highway 36 serving as an informal dividing line.[11] Whites lived and moved freely on the eastern as well as western sides of the highway, but Black families established homes on the west side and rarely crossed over except for employment or when conducting business in town—at the grain elevator, the dry goods store, the post office, the bank, the drugstore, or the doctor's office.[12] The old, once-segregated movie house now stood empty, but the office of Dr. Joe Yelderman retained its back entrance for Black patients (reportedly due to insistence of one prominent local resident) even as "Dr. Joe" made house calls regardless of race. Black farmers stored their harvests in the central grain elevator with white farmers. Ladd's Market and packing house butchered and stored meats in the freezer for Black as well as white customers, although social events, schools, and houses of worship remained segregated.[13]

After five years Raymond purchased eight city lots of residential land at Kneitz and Antonia Streets, on the east side of Highway 36. There, he and Frances designed and built the house where they would spend the coming decade, joining a small development where their closest neighbors were among the town's most well-known community members, including the local banker, lumberyard owners, a pharmacist, and an attorney. Raymond himself supervised the laying of the concrete slab and the brick-and-mortar masonry. He planted trees for shade and for growth before they broke ground for the slab. Pecan trees came first, then water oaks, tallow trees, and pines. The family moved into their new house around Thanksgiving 1959, the middle of Kathy's junior year of high school.[14]

Raymond and Frances were prosperous but not extravagant, and they afforded their children structure as well as room to grow. Frances made sure that the desk built into her sons' bedroom accommodated Nelson's left-handedness alongside Ray's right-handedness. Even before there was much furniture in the family den, the room often bustled with Kathy and her classmates playing records and dancing, enjoying slumber parties and birthdays. The Leissners hired workers for the farm (and later to help with childcare), but they made certain their children were not exempt from labor. At a young age Kathy and her brothers worked in the rice fields in spring and summer, driving tractors, tending the levees, and helping with the harvest. In the fall and winter they learned to drive and feed the brown-and-white Herford cattle, spraying for fleas and ticks in preparation for market.

During sweltering summers the children also explored the countryside. Guns were an ordinary part of life, but they were not fetishized. Boys learned early the proper way to handle guns, plinking cans along fences, hunting rabbits and eventually deer. Both Kathy and Nelson rode the cattle horses barebacked—bridle and reins only, no saddle—and they sometimes raced across the fields, jumping over the rice levees. There were beehives in the tall grass that a horse could step in, unawares. They learned to recover from being thrown.[15]

In their father's fields, just off Meyer Road, they could follow the canals on a hot day to enjoy the fresh, cool waters of the artesian well. Kathy and her girlfriends skinny-dipped sometimes when they were alone, or when they thought they were. An inscription in Kathy's yearbook joked about the rice canals as a local gathering place—"for swimming, cutting feet on bottles, and meeting anyone you don't want to see."[16] Kids improvised ways to scare off water moccasins, tossing rocks into the center of the water and watching the surface shiver as the snakes slithered away. Snakes could strike by surprise, so it helped to know the farmer's cure for a bite: a thick poultice of chewing tobacco. But what if you were alone when you got bitten? What if you didn't chew tobacco?

Accidents sometimes happened: a car crash, a drowning, a misfired bullet. If nothing else, farm children learned, a misstep or an unlucky day could teach you to pay better attention.

FROM HER THIRTEENTH BIRTHDAY IN 1956 until her sweet sixteenth, Kathy gathered tokens of memories inside a large, premade scrapbook, peppered with commentary, running jokes, and coded reminders. Bound with string and sporting a heavily padded, preprinted cardboard cover, *Things and Stuff* was likely a birthday present, its broad brown construction paper pages ready for photographs and clippings. Now tattered and brittle, its binding long separated from years in storage, *Things and Stuff* provides a time capsule of Kathy's transition from girlhood through puberty in 1950s rural Texas. At times Kathy jotted notes to her future self or to the friends she often trusted to peek at her pages, to be shared the way a teenager now might share text messages or images on social media: "Bet you can't guess what this is HA! HA!"

On the first page Kathy pasted a blue ribbon from the Consolidated Youth Fair, a birthday card from a friend, and a handwritten caption that appeared to comment on a boy she liked: "What a character." Subsequent pages brim with taffeta spirit ribbons from pep rallies for football, baseball, and basketball games: "Hold those Tigers," "Trap the Gators," "Roust the Rebels." She saved a candy bar wrapper ("World's Finest Milk Chocolate") from a band fundraiser, adding a record of her contribution: "I sold 8 bars." Underneath foggy black-and-white photos from her thirteenth birthday party, she offered play-by-play captions of hijinks, describing who drank how many Cokes and who was pouring what soda on whom.

Kathy's personal treasures demonstrate the range of her early enthusiasms. She kept programs from cattle shows and school band concerts, party invitations, club rosters, bowling score sheets, and clippings from regional bathing beauty pageants. She taped or glued many souvenirs—flattened paper straws and cups, flower corsages clustered with tulle, and ribbons from parties. From the auto races at Playland Speedway in Houston, Kathy penned a sidenote in all caps: "MY EARS ARE STILL RINGING." She also kept a mimeographed batch of pages titled "What's Cooking??" with the purposes, degrees, by-laws, and recreational opportunities of Future Homemakers of America (FHA). On a page she titled with faint pencil, "From FHA Summer Party," Kathy listed club "to-dos": "Try to get the tennis courts finished. Taking fruit baskets to sick people in the hospitals. Bondfire [sic] the night before Homecoming."

Kathy improvised pockets to store special notes from friends and relatives. She saved a letter sent by her grandmother Leissner on a trip to Mount Rushmore. She kept a letter from a cousin in Huntsville who detailed an outbreak of flu in October 1957: "We nearly had to close school about three weeks ago. 30% of our high school was absent (me included)." Sometimes Kathy annotated the letters she saved, as when she circled one line in a classmate's reassuring note on blue stationery: "I don't like John as a boyfriend."

Kathy dedicated a special page to letters from her parents during a trip to Washington, DC. Frances penned one of these on lime-green letterhead from Joy Motel in Maryville, Tennessee: "I surely hope you are getting all our cards and letters—sometimes I have to mail them in the funniest places," she wrote. "The last 'batch' I put in a little basket in a café-filling station in the mountains. . . . Guess what we saw today—a real wild black bear sitting on the side of the road!" She composed another on stationery imprinted with the stately brown logo of Brick House Tavern in Williamsburg, and her message implied the depth of two-way communication among family members. "It's surely a relief to know that everything is working out well," Frances wrote. "This is a very good arithmetic paper, Nelson—just keep it up. I'm glad 'we' won the game, too, Kathy, and thanks so much for the little handprint of Ray. Daddy really enjoyed that." On plain notebook paper, from a cabin in Rockaway Beach, Missouri, after a drive through the Ozarks, Frances urged her children to behave with relatives: "Don't forget to make your beds, keep your things put up, and anything else you can do. I know that if you just stop and think you can do lots of things to make things easier. And for goodness sake, don't fuss." Raymond finished the note to his kids with a wry comment on the weather: "A norther blew in tonight so imagine it will be colder from here on. If it snows, I'll send you a snowman."[17]

Even with supportive family, many friendships, and cheerful temperament, Kathy recorded her insecurities. She tucked away two Modess menstrual calendars—both torn in fourths—into handmade pockets. Occasionally, she kept notes she drafted but reconsidered, as when she tore up a letter to a boyfriend, paper-clipped it back together, then jotted nearby: "Did not send off thank goodness." Next to a handwritten notecard for a classroom speech, she added a self-deprecating commentary about her own performance, writing, "I didn't say a word right."

Perhaps most touching are Kathy's notes from slumber party conversations and weekend heart-to-hearts, as with an unsent letter she composed with a friend for an advice column. Folding together two drafts on watermarked typing paper, labelling them in green pencil, "My Problem," Kathy recorded the date as June 21, 1958, the summer after her freshman year:

> Dear Editor, I believe you will find my problem very hard to cope with. I am fifteen and will be a sopho-more next year in high school. I'm not very pretty and my figure could stand a little attention. I run around with the most popular crowd in my class. I have been elected to many class offices and have always had all the dates I've wanted. Well, now that you know where I stand as far as popularity is concerned I will try to explain . . .

At first glance, this letter paints a portrait of an anonymous girl who, despite social and academic success, doubted her imagined physical flaws. But as the convoluted ins and outs of the scenario continue from this point, a comical tone emerges, mimicking the overdrawn, melodramatic lone-ly-hearts columns of the mid-twentieth century. Written not in solitude but with a trusted friend, the letter was edited, recopied, and left unfinished—likely because the situation the girls sought to capture became a source of absurdity in the moment, easily disrupted by a favorite song on the radio or the appearance of Nelson in the doorway, smiling with a lemon in his mouth. Kathy's preservation of this text shows how she managed self-doubts through friendship and collaboration.[18]

Every small joy she could find, she tended. In fall 1958 she recorded a football game for which she had worn a special party dress and walked a boyfriend off the field. She preserved mud from her shoes that night in a packet she made from wax paper, scribbling a title nearby: "The most wonderful night of the year." Other inspirations remain mysterious, as with a folded sheet of cream-colored paper embossed with a faint, silvery swirl pattern—wrapping salvaged from an unidentified gift, something she had opened carefully to avoid tearing.[19]

Like her mother Frances, Kathy at an early age demonstrated an affinity for connecting and creating, an eye for patterns and decoration. As she matured, one of her most enduring qualities would be making do with whatever materials came to hand.

When Kathy attended Needville High School (NHS), the campus still contained an upper and lower school, from seventh through twelfth grades. The original complex of school buildings with their yellow brick walls, wooden floors and hallways, clustered together on the east side of Highway 36, five miles south of town, between Fritzella Street and North Stadium Drive. The original NHS had a separate science building, a gym and a football field with bleachers, and housing for the principal as well as the superintendent. Set in an idyllic clearing surrounded by trees and creeks, the campus provided the central gathering place for young white teenagers whose families often lived miles apart. When Kathy walked in graduation commencement the evening of May 29, 1961, there were just over fifty students in her class, and the school's combined enrollment was roughly four hundred. Yearbook photo captions document German and Eastern European surnames mingling with occasional Hispanic names—Polak, Lopez, Chaloupka,

*Kathy was crowned
Needville Youth
Fair Queen in 1960.
Private archive of
Nelson Leissner.*

Janicek, Figueroa, Wenzel, Zatopek, Villareal—but the school would not be fully integrated until 1966. Even seven years after *Brown v. Board of Education*, Black students still had to take a separate bus to their own school in the town of Kendleton, eighteen miles northwest.[20]

The photographic record provides overwhelming documentation of how much Kathy embodied local aspirations. The first full-page photograph in her senior yearbook is a stately portrait of the superintendent. But the opposing page, the one that draws the eye, contains a photo of Kathy in a floral party dress made by Frances, standing with a handsome young man, both identified in the caption as "Mr. and Miss NHS." Kathy was also voted Valentine Sweetheart and "best all around" for her class, and the *Blue Jay Chatter,* the school newspaper, listed her as "Ideal Girl" in the quality of "personality." She stood on the homecoming court as a junior, and in 1960 was crowned Needville Youth Fair Queen.[21]

With her broad range of interests, Kathy had a knack for

picking things up, more for camaraderie than competition. It is difficult to find any school activity in which she did not participate. She played on the first string of the volleyball squad as "set up" for three years, and she was head twirler for the high school majorettes. She played tenor saxophone in the concert band as well as the stage band, earning a blue-and-white chenille letter N for her participation. She served as secretary and vice president for the band club and was vice president of FHA after three years of membership. As a writer and designer, she was a columnist for the commercial club, art editor for the school annual, and a contributing editor for the school newspaper. For the science club, she served as an officer and club reporter. She performed in the senior play, *The Funny Brats*, as well as a more serious role in a civil defense program.

The candid shots rather than the posed photos capture Kathy's sense of fun and irony, even introspection. One snapshot, taken during a homecoming skit, shows Kathy on the set dressed as a barmaid in high heels, bare legs, and a short skirt—the only character who turns a saucy eye to the camera. The bright gold seal on Kathy's diploma indicated her academic achievements as a member of the National Honors Society, but the group portrait caught Kathy in a rare moment of separation from her classmates. She sat withdrawn on a step in the shadows with a frown of deep concentration on her face, not posing for anyone.

As a girl coming of age during a decade of conformity and increasingly commercialized femininity, in a rural area where folks harshly sorted "good girls" from "girls with reputations," Kathy faced her share of unfair scrutiny. Her father sometimes assigned her to drive the rice truck from the fields to the rice dryer in town, and she made the most of the task by working on her summer tan with bare shoulders and shorts. Grown men sometimes noticed her. Exercising any

ABOVE: *Kathy (center) clowns in the locker room with two high school friends and volleyball teammates after losing the district championship in 1961. As art editor for the school annual, Kathy made sure this photo made the cut of snapshots. Needville High School yearbook, private archive of Nelson Leissner.*

RIGHT: *Kathy relaxes at the counter of City Drugs in Needville, Texas. Private archive of Nelson Leissner.*

freedom as a young woman, whether out for an ice cream cone or running a simple errand, could draw gossip from judging eyes. Thankfully, Kathy had a steady and practical ally in Frances, who did not shrink to the expectations of busybodies.[22]

Like her mother, Kathy was self-sufficient as well as social. Many class parties and celebrations were hosted in the Leissner home. A recurring motif—in photos and in family movies—is Kathy slicing and serving cake. Friends would pile with her brothers into the car for day trips down Highway 36 to the beautiful shores of Galveston Island or to visit a classmate who was seriously ill.[23] There was nothing in Kathy's life to prepare her for anything other than an adulthood where education, work, parenting, and a social life could coexist. Although she certainly had to monitor her behavior as a young woman, she had no experience with social injustice. Her sexual education was limited, but her cheerful spirit had not been forced into back door entrances, restricted by segregated schools and bus seats. Her small rebellions had blossomed for the most part without fear and inhibition.

Still, Kathy did not romanticize Needville or the school where she availed herself of many opportunities and outgrew them all. In spring 1961 Kathy and her senior classmates took a bus trip to the tree-lined streets of Austin, the Texas capital that was also home to the state's flagship university, the campus where her father had first taken classes, and now the beacon of her own unfolding dreams. One can see how her mind longed to stretch in a bigger place with new people, where she could experience the world beyond the fields. She was excited to become a Longhorn at "dear ole TEXAS" as a pharmacy student—a woman in what remained a very male-dominated field. A younger friend had been inspired by Kathy's example, inscribing a yearbook note in purple ink, "It would take a book to tell you how much I think of you and how much you have helped me." Another joked, "If you ever get homesick just think about me and [friend] and thank God you're not here."[24]

In late summer Kathy and her mother made a shopping trip for school supplies and clothes, and Kathy wrote a check for $35.48 at Fed Mart, a large discount store. The day after that excursion, Frances deposited $150 into Kathy's account, shoring up her finances for the inevitable expenses in the transition to university.[25] The countdown to her future began just as a tropical depression formed in the Southwest Caribbean Sea. The *Victoria Advocate* and the *Corpus Christi Caller-Times* were soon reporting about the powerful tropical storm headed straight for Texas and brewing into a hurricane. Gulf Coast residents in the hurricane's path soon realized they had two options and limited time to decide: evacuate to higher ground if necessary, shelter in place where they could.[26]

There were no signs of a different threat on the horizon—a handsome young man wearing the uniform of a United States Marine and making his way from Florida to the UT campus. Before long, Kathy would bring this stranger home to meet her parents and brothers, and before her sophomore year, she would marry him: the man who would kill her.

Pulled Off Course

ADVANCE WARNING ABOUT CARLA SAVED THOUSANDS of lives, and the Highway 36 gridlock through Needville gave Kathy and her brothers an up-close view of survivors in freeze-frame. Initial reports estimated that 250 thousand people left their homes for refuge inland. (Later tallies put the figure even higher: between 350 thousand and half a million people.) At the time the exodus was considered the largest weather-related peacetime evacuation in American history. Remarkably, 465 injuries and 46 fatalities were reported afterwards—low numbers in proportion to the power and scope of the storm. The Great Hurricane of 1900, by contrast, had killed between six and twelve thousand, virtually obliterating the island of Galveston.[1]

Multiple systems of postwar technology and infrastructure converged in 1961 to give advance warning about Carla's grave threat. In July NASA had launched its Tiros

A Texas woman stands in the wreckage of her home in Carla's aftermath. Shel Hershorn Photographic Archive, e_sh_0011, Dolph Briscoe Center for American History, The University of Texas at Austin.

III satellite, which made the storm visible on September 7, just as it began to gather power near Mexico's Yucatan Peninsula, six hundred miles from the Texas coastline. The new land-based radar device at Galveston's branch of the United States Weather Bureau, the WSR-57 console with a 250-mile range, tracked the storm minute-by-minute as it inched closer to Texas. Dan Rather, who had just celebrated his first year as a newscaster on KHOU-TV, took his crew to film onsite at the Galveston weather bureau office. On live television, he asked a meteorologist to place a transparent map of the Gulf of Mexico across the radar screen so that viewers could watch Carla slowly take shape—at its largest point almost entirely filling the Gulf. The urgency of Rather's message was unequivocal: Carla's threat was not to be minimized.[2]

Emergency responders wasted no time. The civil defense headquarters in Austin sent empty buses southward to assist with evacuation, and the Red Cross arranged a reported 178 pop-up shelters as inland hotels were overwhelmed. In Houston, within twelve hours the population of domestic refugees in public shelters jumped from seven thousand to fifty-five thousand. Many people pushed much further north, towards Austin.[3]

As Carla knocked out an estimated 166,000 telephones, severely disrupting essential communication systems, switchboard operators worked overtime to connect worried loved ones and dispatch real-time assistance. (There was no 911 system yet.) The switching center in Houston alone reportedly managed a record 800,000 calls. Southwestern Bell sent women operators by plane and Greyhound buses from Missouri, Kansas, Oklahoma, and Arkansas to relieve their Texas sisters, many of whom had not left their posts for three or four days.[4]

Tornadoes followed Carla, with two twisters striking Galveston the early morning hours of September 12. Even as the winds calmed and the waters receded, real property and environmental damage yielded a ruinous economic toll for thousands of families. Photos of the aftermath document heartbreaking wreckage and displacement: victims picking through smashed remains of homes and barns and public buildings, dead livestock strewn across fields, young mothers wandering with children. There were demolished boats and shattered docks, cars upside down in roads, toppled powerlines, and massive uprooted trees. Live wires and high water made a terrifying combination. The flight of rattlesnakes *en masse* to high ground added yet another hazard to the recovery process.[5]

Aerial photos revealed how the entire coastline was left blackened and bruised. As far as 130 miles northeast of

Carla's direct hit, homes and vegetation were mercilessly scoured from the beachfront at Rollover Pass on the Bolivar Peninsula. The surge of waves onto Mustang Island cut a new cliff into dunes fifty yards from the previous shoreline. Matagorda Air Force Base was pummeled beyond recognition. Port O'Connor, according to one report, was reduced to "a pile of sand." Many cattle, rice, and cotton farms were wiped out entirely. Water contamination in Port Aransas was so dangerous that nearly two thousand people received free shots for typhoid and were instructed to boil drinking water. Total damages statewide exceeded $2 billion in today's dollars.[6]

It was in the wake of this catastrophe—just hours after tornadoes passed through Galveston—that Kathy left home. She loaded her boxes and bags into the car with help from her brothers and parents, who stayed behind to assist in the local recovery effort. Frances and Raymond ensured their daughter would travel with a trusted escort, and she waved farewell from the white Chevy Impala driven by her high school sweetheart, Lawrence. A cancelled $5 check recorded one stop at Foley's Dry Goods, perhaps a final layaway payment on a dress. Under her signature, Kathy wrote her new address: "2101 Nueces, Austin, Tex," the Bradfield boarding house three blocks from the heart of the UT campus.[7]

The couple headed northwest along the highway that one day earlier had been described as "a giant unmade bed" where hundreds of families camped and cooked on both sides of the grassy shoulder, resting on their way to safety. The roads told a story of Carla's damage with careening telephone poles, stripped billboards, uprooted trees, and flooded ditches. Steering into Austin that late afternoon, the car merged into heavy traffic—heavier than usual for the first week of registration. Hundreds from the diaspora had taken refuge in the City Auditorium as well as the City Coliseum, near the southern shore of Town Lake. Survivors

Kathy would never meet had tucked themselves into motels and hotels, on cots in auditoriums and gymnasiums and church halls, or with relatives and friends. Like them, she had emerged from the storm, but unlike anxious thousands, unsure of what awaited them at home, she knew that her family and their livelihood were safe. At least for now.[8]

And at the end of the day, there was Lawrence: handsome in his crew cut, his goodbye kiss before the Chevy melted out of view around a distant corner. Kathy had worn his promise ring on a necklace for a long time. The theme song of their graduating class—"Where or When?"—still posed its melancholy question: Whom would they each remember, and whom would they forget?[9] With dangers averted and the future at her fingertips, Kathy smiled and lifted pretty eyes to the porch of her new home.

KATHY HAD ENTERED COLLEGE AT AN important historical moment in the United States, as women's enrollment in higher education began its unstoppable surge. The National Center for Education Statistics (NCES) documents that in 1961, Kathy's first semester at the University of Texas at Austin, the total percentage of female high school graduates enrolling in college was 41.3 percent, up from 37.9 percent in 1960—an increase of 52,000 female students nationwide in a single year.[10]

In 1961 UT Austin was not only the largest of twenty-two accredited universities in the entire state, but it was also still the only campus of the University of Texas System. As such, it attracted students of very different communities, from Dallas and Houston to Baytown and Lubbock, as well as many international students. Headcount enrollment figures for the fall semester show that Kathy Leissner was one of 6,507 women on a campus with 13,889 men. Enrollments were not yet racially disaggregated, but other records document

A coed walks up the mall at UT Austin. The Cactus yearbook, di_04231, Dolph Briscoe Center for American History, The University of Texas at Austin.

that Black students were a tiny minority at the time—about two hundred, or roughly one percent.[11]

Throughout the week of September 11, local newspapers, including the university's own paper, the *Daily Texan*, reported record-breaking registration lines at Gregory Gym. Kathy's new home at Bradfield stood three blocks from the campus border of Guadalupe Street (known locally as the

Drag), and only a few more steps from the Littlefield Fountain and the Tower mall lined with oak trees. For the first time ever, Kathy was truly on her own, surrounded by a historic natural disaster recovery effort mingled with the frenetic energy of students. Local agencies such as the Austin Police Department and the Austin Civil Defense agency rallied to assist a reported eight thousand refugees from the coast. Sororities, fraternities, and other UT clubs also volunteered alongside the Red Cross to set up and manage shelters. A few women's residences had opened on Sunday, September 10, to accommodate students fleeing their homes in Galveston, Corpus Christi, and Freeport.[12]

Despite Carla's lingering rains, thousands of drenched students lined up under umbrellas and waited to proceed into the hot, humid gym to draw registration cards and talk to advisors about schedules.[13] By midweek, as the skies cleared, student organizations and clubs swarmed new registrants outside the gym offering information about the Athenaeum Society of debaters, the Tai Kwan Do Club, the University Religious Council, and student political organizations. Petitioners were also seeking signatures for the full racial integration of university athletics.[14]

Kathy was among a reported 5,400 freshmen and transfer students eligible for new student orientation. The rush of these activities concluded Wednesday after a battery of proficiency tests in algebra and English, a screening of *This Is Your University*, and a dance at the student union with music by the Mello Tones. Convocations for men and women were held separately. As a pre-pharmacy student, Kathy enrolled in a standard mixture of general education and major preparation classes: general biology, general chemistry, English composition, Introduction to Economics I, and college algebra. She also had to fulfill a no-unit health and physical education requirement.[15]

Bank records allow a glimpse of Kathy's first steps in Austin as she managed money for day-to-day expenses. She made a purchase at Hemphill's Bookstore the day she arrived, spending $6.32 on books and supplies. The most interesting exception to school-related expenses came Saturday before classes began, when she spent $7.12 at E. M. Scarbrough & Son, the art deco department store on West Sixth Street.[16]

As a new student in a male-dominated institution of higher learning, Kathy's life and roles became more explicitly gendered than in Needville. Like all women students, she was now commonly referred to as a coed. Newspaper photos of registration crowds as well as checkout lines in the basement of the University Co-Op show how women were outnumbered in the spaces they navigated. On the one hand, any woman would have her pick of male companions, but depending upon her comfort level and experience, she could also feel surrounded.[17] As a white woman in science courses (in contrast with general education), Kathy would have found herself in a smaller minority, alongside an even tinier cohort of Black women students who faced intersecting sexual as well as racial prejudice about their abilities.[18]

Some women were gaining recognition for their accomplishments, such as student journalist Pat Rusch, who was highlighted in the *Daily Texan* for her groundbreaking coverage of Carla's damage to Texas City. University officials were making visible efforts to reach out to women students who were white. Kinsolving Dormitory, for example, which housed eight hundred white-only female residents on the north edge of campus, launched Operation Knowledge, a series of speakers and programs to enhance the intellectual, cultural, and spiritual development of women students. The new dean of students, Dr. Dean Barrett, delivered a talk on "the role of the woman in education."[19]

NEEDVILLE, TEXAS Sept. 14 19 61 NO.

FIRST STATE BANK 88-1801

PAY TO THE ORDER OF The University of Texas $ 114.18/100

One Hundred and Fourteen & 18/100 —— DOLLARS

Kathy Leissner
2101 Nueces, Austin, Tex.

HILL—WACO

NEEDVILLE, TEXAS Sept. 16 1961 NO.

FIRST STATE BANK 88-1801

PAY TO THE ORDER OF The University CO-OP $ 13.01/100

Thirteen and 1/100 —— DOLLARS

Kathy Leissner
2101 Nueces Austin, Tex.

HILL—WACO

D.L. 506 5792

NEEDVILLE, TEXAS Sept. 16 1961 NO.

FIRST STATE BANK 88-1801

PAY TO THE ORDER OF E. M. Scarbrough & Son $ 7.12/100

Seven and 12/100 —— DOLLARS

XR 6-8831 Kathy Leissner
2101 Nueces Austin, Tex.

HILL—WACO

Kathy Leissner's first checks at UT Austin, including her first tuition payment. Private archive of Nelson Leissner.

These maneuvers rang hollow in contrast with the gla-
cial pace of structural changes. Few instructors at UT were
women, and it would be nearly three years before the university opened dorms to Black students and hired two—just
two—Black faculty members. During her first semester
Kathy would have witnessed interracial social activism for
the first time. In October 1961 three Black women staged
a peaceful protest at Kinsolving, refusing to leave the lobby
and visiting friends on the upper floors, an act that infuriated
the Board of Regents as well as wealthy donors. Students
remained undeterred, organizing sit-ins at lunch counters
and "stand-ins" outside movie theaters, and businesses
responded as the university dragged its heels. The popular
landmark hangout, the Night Hawk, was the first to integrate
on the Drag, and its owner Harry Akin led collective action
for racial integration among Austin restauranteurs. Full integration at UT would not occur until spring 1964.[20]

Although Kathy had no racial restrictions on where she
could live, interact, or shop, UT was visibly a man's campus,
with coeds commonly viewed less as intellectual peers than
as prospects among male competitors; they also bore the
brunt of sexist humor. Women had to sign out when leaving
their dorms and were required to meet an eleven p.m. curfew
or face probation for breaking it. They were not yet allowed
to wear pants on campus, and they could also be punished
for "unsatisfactory housekeeping." During Kathy's first week,
one article in the *Daily Texan* attempted to decipher the various cues of female availability, as if this were a matter to
be settled by fraternity brothers rather than women themselves: "Drops, Pins Not Necessarily Final Word on Girls'
Eligibility."[21]

Little Man on Campus, a nationally syndicated single-
panel comic by artist Richard Bibler, regularly appeared on
page two of the campus paper, portraying women students

as interchangeable objects of ridicule. The registration day strip showed a freshman advisor haplessly counseling a coed in a sexy bridal gown about her second semester schedule "just in case." While the comic certainly skewered many layers of absurdity in university life, it consistently rendered women as cluelessly vain and objectifiable, also portraying sexual harassment—or even assault—as an understandable hazard for curvaceous girls who dared to interact with male professors or visit the library stacks on their own. Newspaper entertainment pages included showtimes for a range of dramas, comedies, and thrillers—from *Gidget Goes Hawaiian* to *Scream of Fear* and *A Cold Wind in August*—all alongside "adults only" banners promising racier features at the Capitol Theater on West Sixth Street. Like wallpaper, such ads reflected the heterosexual postwar *Playboy* culture, where women's freedom was constructed mostly in terms of appeals to Madison Avenue men and the bachelors who craved to emulate that image.[22]

As sexualized consumer targets, women could be easily distracted from academics without guidance from mentors, clubmates, or wise sorority sisters. Articles in the *Daily Texan* devoted space to fashion advice for "clothes conscious university girls" who needed to "keep up with Forty Acres 'dos' and 'don'ts.'" Casual was in, and dressy was out—sweaters, skirts, dark cottons, loafers with socks, and tennies or "fruit boots" (a homophobic reference to tennis shoes) were essential. Kathy would have distinguished proper attire for class attendance, sports events, church and cultural gatherings, and parties or formals. Earrings while wearing loafers were taboo. Cocktail dresses were more fashionable than long formals.[23]

Ads for safe and "approved" university housing were also everywhere, targeting young women based on affordability and location as well as exploitation of fear. The Friday before classes began, the top headline of the *Austin American-Statesman* referenced an arrest of a window peeper who was reported by a "level-headed coed" who lived close to campus.[24] The second day of classes, the Austin Police Department published a warning against peeping Toms, recounting numerous complaints the previous year, mostly from women's dorms and rooming houses. The story did not address sexual harassment or violence, implying mostly that peeping was an inevitable risk on a coeducational campus. Rules of prevention offered by police were not directed to male students, witnesses, or potential perpetrators, but to women: they should keep their shades down, never undress in a lighted room, and never panic if glimpsing a peeper because discovery would scare him away.[25]

Such messages—girls were responsible for their own safety, while "boys would be boys"—would have been nothing new for Kathy or for her female classmates, whether they came from large cities or small country towns. She would later write about jogging at night, but only with friends "so we won't get picked up or raped or anything."[26] More broadly, myths of stranger-danger and racist stereotypes shaped suspicions about criminality, blinding women to handsome, well-dressed, white dangers in plain sight.

Sometimes trouble did find good girls. Kathy's first week at UT, the *Austin American* and the *Austin American-Statesman* covered a grimly sensational three-day trial that finally hit the front page on September 15. Father John Feit, a white Catholic priest, had been on trial in Austin for an attempted rape in March of Maria Guerra, a Hispanic coed, three hundred miles south, in Edinburgh, Texas. Because of concerns about local jury bias, the trial had been relocated to the capital. The details seemed unthinkable: Guerra testified that she had been kneeling at the altar rail in the church sanctuary when the priest attacked from behind. She had wrestled away and reported the incident to local authorities. Another witness testified that she had seen a man matching Feit's description around the time of the alleged assault. In photos, the priest looked affectless in his religious collar and hornrims, sometimes with a cigarette.[27]

The story would have made no sense at all: a girl assaulted while she was praying in church, by a man whose very job was to be holy? As a Methodist, Kathy did not know much about Catholics, but she knew families who belonged to the only Catholic parish in Needville, and no friends had spoken of problems remotely like this. The Austin jury deadlocked, so the judge declared a mistrial. Perhaps for some jurors it was simply easier to believe that two Mexican girls had lied than to believe that one white priest was guilty.[28]

It is doubtful that Kathy heard much about the case. The *Daily Texan* included only a small update many months later, when Feit pleaded guilty to a lesser charge of aggravated assault and paid a fine of $500 plus court fees. Kathy would not live long enough to learn that the priest had not only attacked Guerra, but a few weeks later had also raped and murdered a second woman, Irene Garza, and left her body in a ditch. It would take nearly sixty years for the second crime to be adjudicated, with Feit finally convicted and sentenced.[29]

Such gruesome tales would have seemed a world away from Kathy's worst imaginings. Free and unattached, she did not know that she was about to enter the disorienting mystery that would end her own life. Waiting to cross the Drag on her way to classes for the first time, Kathy would stand on the corner in view of one of the popular men's dormitories, Goodall Wooten, where her future husband had moved into his room on Sunday, September 10, after attending mass.

When the semester began the former Eagle Scout and Catholic altar boy had been in town for nearly two weeks and had called his own priest confidant in Houston.[30]

For now, Kathy simply walked past Goodall Wooten those first glorious days in Austin, disappearing into the thrum of chatter and foot traffic, drawn by the pull of gravity into the center of the university. With her new friends and roommates, there she was—twinkling with effortless charm, unworried by fate—daring to believe that education and romance could coexist. And as the young women together turned up the broad walk alongside the oak-lined mall towards the Tower, the young men sharing smokes and jokes at the Littlefield Fountain had no reason to hide that they were looking.

KATHY PACED HER ADJUSTMENT TO COLLEGE with occasional weekends at home. At the end of her first week she purchased a Greyhound bus ticket for $5.39, presumably to cover roundtrip fare to Needville. From her perch in a window seat on the bus heading south, retracing the route she had taken with Lawrence, she would have had a clear view of the massive post-Carla cleanup along the roadways and ditches and rest stops. A cancelled check dated Saturday, September 23, shows that she returned to one of her favorite stores, Wonder Fabric Center, presumably for materials to enhance her wardrobe.[31] Talking to her family was clearly a priority: her largest expense in October was the phone bill to Southwestern Bell. She purchased another Greyhound ticket on October 20, suggesting another trip home or an outing with friends.

Kathy's phone bills decreased in November and December, reflecting the Thanksgiving and Christmas breaks as well as a growing social life. Jack's Party Pictures on the Drag took photos at all the Greek society parties and official

Kathy toasting at a fraternity party in October 1961. Jack's Party Pictures, private archive of Nelson Leissner.

UT functions, and each Monday Jack's displayed a selection in the front window of their shop, where students lined up to order the most recent "flicks" from the weekend. In October 1961 Kathy was among the customers. She picked up dry cleaning and got her hair done at Mr. Pat's Coiffures on Friday, October 27, likely preparing for a formal hosted by Pi Kappa Alpha fraternity (the Pikes)—still counted among the six most prestigious fraternities at UT. The following week Kathy wrote two checks to Jack's and saved one photo for herself.[32]

This photo and a passing mention in a much later letter are the only traces that Kathy sampled the rituals of Greek life. While she was temporarily curious about the networks they afforded, she would not have needed a sorority to maneuver socially. Even though she worried occasionally about being viewed as what she termed a "hick," she had plenty of social confidence and little patience for snobs.[33] She was also adept at the gendered highwire act: being a good girl without getting tagged as a schoolmarm, being fun without getting labelled as wild. Why decline any opportunity to enjoy a party if she was invited?

Some flirtatious fun beneath the Cold War surface may have been less enjoyable—at least less mutual—than portrayed in the moment. The civil defense warning systems in Austin tested their sirens monthly, maintaining vigilance about a possible nuclear attack and publishing regular alerts, as reported the first week of November in the *Daily Texan*. In the same issue a reporter for the paper wrote gleefully about a "birds-and-bees college rite," a massive panty raid conducted after a false fire alarm on the night of November 2, when a mob of 2,500 men swarmed women's dorms and boarding houses chanting, "We want girls." As some men climbed window railings and scaled walls, women responded by tossing "flimsies" to the grass or by cutting the lights and slamming windows shut.[34] Women giggling at windows or gathering on rooftops were reportedly amused. No other interpretation was solicited. To be fair, a woman could more easily laugh at such a scene when the front door was locked, when police were watching, and when she did not face the onslaught alone.

CHARLES "CHARLIE" WHITMAN WAS ALREADY AT ease in male-centered institutions. Although Austin was larger than the coastal town of Lake Worth in southeastern Florida, where he had grown up until he ran away to join the Marines, the environment would nevertheless have felt familiar. Even though he was the first to attend college in his immediate family, Charlie already had implicit status

as a white male and a southerner. Both of his parents origi-
nated in Savannah, Georgia. His father, C. A. Whitman, was
a working patriarch who built a successful plumbing and
septic cleaning business but shamelessly terrorized Charlie and his two younger brothers, Patrick and Johnnie Mike,
as well as their mother, Margaret, at home—behavior that
alienated neighbors even as it went largely unchallenged,
leaving the family isolated. With a devoutly Roman Catholic
mother, Charlie had experienced twelve years of parochial
school, trained to be an altar boy, and grown up as a Catholic
Boy Scout, earning Eagle Scout status at the tender age of
twelve. He had a great deal of formal and informal interactions with clergy, both in school and in scouting.[35]

Self-conscious as he was about his father's trade, Charlie
found himself in three exclusive groups atop the proverbial
food chain: as a US Marine, a recipient of the Naval Enlisted
Science Education Program (NESEP) scholarship, and a
student of engineering. All his visible and invisible privileges, combined with the damage they concealed, inflamed
his sense of entitlement. Emboldened by new freedoms on
campus, he could play the good Catholic boy or the good
soldier when he wanted, but he also liked to bend and challenge rules, and he pushed against consequences when they
came. One of his English composition professors, a woman
instructor at UT, reported how pleasant Charlie could be
as long as grades were going his way. (He unsuccessfully
contested a D on a paper and struggled to make a C in the
course.) She observed that he did best when regurgitating
others' ideas and struggled to develop his own thoughts
well.[36] Mirroring skills enabled him to pass among WASPs
when socially necessary or convenient, and it helped to have
enablers—friends, authorities, or older men—who would
vouch for him and laugh at, or bless, his bad choices.

Notations in Charlie's At-a-Glance Diary his first week at

Charles Whitman relaxing in uniform, January 1962. Private archive of Nelson Leissner.

UT recorded a phone call as well as a likely intended visit "for advice" to see his mentor and former scoutmaster from childhood, Father Joseph "Gil" Leduc. Transferred as a seminarian in 1952 from Florida to Texas, Leduc was ordained for the Diocese of Galveston (now Galveston-Houston) in 1955, serving at multiple parishes and taking on the role of Sam Houston area chaplain for Catholic scouting. Newly assigned to a fledgling, makeshift parish on the south side of Houston where he offered mass in the adjacent garage of a two-story house, Leduc had recently purchased a private cabin in the remote Chocolate Bayou of Liverpool and cashed out a large promissory note (roughly one hundred thousand in today's dollars) against the value of the property. Through his freshman year, Charlie had a great deal of contact with Father Gil, despite the nearly three-hour drive between them.[37]

Charlie also recorded that he wore his USMC uniform on September 19, the second day of classes. It would be several weeks until Kathy met him on a cool night in November, through introduction by a friend. Preparing for that evening, she trimmed and shaped her fingernails, polishing them red. He would remind her—three years later—that the color had not been to his liking.[38]

Kathy would have appreciated that Charlie came from a working family rather than easy money. With his buttery blond crew cut, he looked a bit like a choirboy, except for the smirky little side-smile with a naughty edge. She observed how he could sit at a piano anywhere and charm the keys. Kathy could read music herself, and she had enjoyed records of the popular pianist Van Cliburn, the tall Texan from Kilgore who had risen to fame after winning the first International Tchaikovsky Competition in Moscow.[39] But Charlie was so much sexier than Van Cliburn. And on the doorstep of her boarding house, saying goodnight after a long talk, she savored his kisses. If his fingertips wandered just that little bit, perhaps teasing the waist of her cardigan near the spine, it would have been thrilling. Later, she would recall how quickly he talked seriously of marriage—unaware how rushed courtship could be a warning sign.[40]

Kathy's dorm phone number soon appeared on the upper front corner of Charlie's At-a-Glance Diary. In late November, not long after their first date, Charlie headed with two friends and their guns towards the Lyndon B. Johnson ranch, deep into the beautiful Hill Country, where they jacklighted, shot, and killed a deer on the roadside and loaded it into the trunk of their car. The young men stopped at a service station on the way home so that Charlie could clean the blood from his hands and arms. Once back in Austin, they dragged the carcass on a tarp through the halls of Goodall Wooten, leaving a bloody trail to their rooms on the seventh floor. Two reports emerged: Someone at the service station had taken note of Charlie's bloody hands, and in the hills a person had observed the deer hanging from the trunk of the car and reported the license number. Charlie was skinning and butchering the animal in the shower when the game warden and police officers arrived to confront the young men. Despite being charged with unlawful possession of a deer in Texas—no small deal—the young men's penalties were relatively light: a $100 fine each plus court fees, and no jail time.[41] Even let off easily, Charlie filed a week later for a new trial.

A judge summarily dismissed Charlie's brazen request. But the game warden commented on the young man's likeability. Father Gil recalled the incident as a prank, while others remembered that Charlie wanted to send his father deer meat for Thanksgiving. The explanations—real and pretend—would not really matter. For his friends and their immediate circle, which had now expanded to include Kathy, the whole story was hilarious, such an escapade. After all, it was only a deer.[42]

Whirlwind

KATHY BROUGHT FRIENDS AND BOYFRIENDS HOME before Charlie. One young man drove a Bonneville convertible that caught Nelson's attention as it rolled into the circular driveway, but she assured him that it was nothing serious, a couple of dates. By February 12, 1962, Kathy and Charlie were officially "dropped": she was wearing a bespoke tag pendant and would never date anyone else again. When the popular pianists Ferrante and Teicher played a concert on Valentine's Day at the Municipal Auditorium, Charlie likely took Kathy. An album by the entertainers would later signify nostalgic memories from before their marriage.[1]

As the months unfolded, Charlie was not always on his best behavior. Kathy was in the car during at least one flash of disturbing aggression. Heading to a firing range with Kathy and friends, he yelled racially pejorative remarks at a pedestrian and flashed a pistol before speeding off again. She and

Kathy Leissner with Charles Whitman on February 27, 1962, fifteen days after she was "dropped." Note the bespoke tag on a chain at her neck. Private archive of Nelson Leissner.

the other passengers reportedly chided him. Charlie was also a brash gambler. After a poker game where he lost $200 to two known Austin criminals, he put a stop-payment on the check he wrote. When it bounced, the men confronted him at knifepoint. For a time afterward, Charlie reportedly wore a .357 Magnum—not a small weapon—under his coat when attending classes. The situation led Kathy and another of Charlie's close friends to press him to stop playing cards, and he appeared to listen, at least temporarily.[2]

That was the thing: sometimes Charlie stopped—or seemed to stop—when Kathy confronted him. He knew how to look contrite. When they were alone kissing in a clover field along a road in the Hill Country or parked in a friend's Corvette on the cliffs that overlooked Mansfield Dam and Lake Travis, Charlie could seem tender, even nervous or fragile.[3] But his pranks—such as dangling by one arm from his seventh-floor balcony to get her attention—could be dangerous. At this early stage, he could easily downplay or conceal the extent of his substance use or pornographic fixations.[4] Any problems he seemed to have, at least the ones Kathy could see, appeared a matter of immaturity and harsh environment rather than intractable patterns of behavior or character. All she knew of his family background were the stories he told her about his father's domineering temperament, and Kathy felt deep compassion about that. One could understand how a boy under those conditions might grow to be tough or angry, at least until he met a good woman. Charlie was very good at telling her she would keep him straight.

Caught up in the adulation, Kathy was dazzled by the promise of the man she thought Charlie was becoming. Indeed, the officer in training, the future engineer, and the altar boy who played piano offered good cover for the narcissistic hoodlum, the gambler, and the bully with a violent temper.

KATHY'S INTERESTS THAT SPRING OTHER THAN Charlie are untraceable and her world narrowed considerably in comparison to her active high school years. Meanwhile, the campus welcomed an historic visitor who encouraged the steadfast press for full university integration. Civil rights leader Martin Luther King Jr. addressed a crowd of twelve hundred in the Texas Union Ballroom on March 9. There is no record that she attended.[5]

Kathy's largest expense that semester was documented by a $40 check dated May 22, her notation "for car damages" in the memo line. The actual damages were not clear, but Kathy's payment indicated that she accepted some responsibility, perhaps preemptively. The only other surviving record of the accident is an odd, improvised communication among four men, dated one day after Kathy's check.

Inside an unaddressed envelope labeled to Kathy's father, "Mr. Leissner," Charlie composed a handwritten statement for the other driver of a 1961 Falcon to sign, releasing "R. W. Leissner from all claims for damage done to my automobile . . . on Friday 18 May 1962 by his daughter Kathleen F. Leissner." The statement was signed by the other driver and two witnesses (Charlie and yet another man). In the chivalric social pretenses of the time, Kathy was an unnecessary signatory even though she had been driving, and her handwriting appears nowhere on the page, a harbinger of future erasures. On the one hand, the letter cast Kathy as a woman driver in the position of incompetence, with Charlie acting as paternalistic savior-rescuer. But the incident also demonstrates how he already portrayed himself as a knight who could intimidate or threaten other men; he was certainly angling to impress Kathy's father.[6]

In that aspiration, Charlie was mistaken. Although Kathy likely found his gesture romantic, the manipulative note appeared to have zero substantive impact. Her payment to the other driver cleared the bank, putting her account into temporary overdraft, closely followed by a deposit from her father. A few weeks later, in June, Kathy informed Charlie in a letter, "You might know that the character that hit me the other day hasn't a thing to his name and no liability insurance as he said he had. Now we can't get the car fixed. Mother is only a little bit angry." She added a joking line—in hindsight, an excruciating irony: "I'm such a jinx, you had better think twice about asking me to marry you."[7]

At sixteen, Nelson did not buy Charlie's act at all. On his first visit to Needville, Charlie offered a big handshake and gameshow grin, bragging how he was going to be an engineer and how he worshipped the ground Kathy walked on. Nelson was appalled by the way Charlie waltzed into the den of the Leissner home, commenting on its impressive size and asking how much the house had cost. Raymond did not take kindly to casual disrespect, and his calm and pointed answer, while polite, offered a subtle warning of displeasure.[8] Meanwhile, Nelson could not understand why Kathy had broken with Lawrence, whom he liked and trusted. When he asked his sister, she answered that Charlie was very special to her. The letters she wrote in the summer of 1962 bring her hopes into vivid focus before her fate changed forever.

BY JUNE 10, FOLLOWING SPRING FINALS, Kathy returned home, recovering from an appendectomy. (Charlie much later would remind her how he "bathed her forehead" and tried to ease her pain after surgery.) Although she was madly in love, she was not so sure that she would be returning to UT her sophomore year, and she summarized the situation for Charlie in a typewritten letter, fitting as much detail as possible onto the small page:

> [W]e got my grades and I was terribly shocked to
> find I made a D in Chem. and Eng. when I thought
> I had a C. Mother and Dad are not too hep on send-
> ing me back to Texas. I told them I didn't want to go
> anyplace else because I would lose all those D hours.
> They both want me to change my major to educa-
> tion. Daddy doesn't blame me for the grades but he
> came out and asked me to level with him on just how
> much in love I am with you. He said that although he
> knows we didn't spend a lot of time together I was
> thinking about you when I was trying to study. Some-
> how Mom or Dad said something about your asking
> me to marry you and I said you had. . . . Mother said
> that might be the best thing to do since we can't
> seem to study now. Daddy said something about it

was up to me or us if we thought we could live on
your salary. He seems to have the attitude that it's my
life and he can't control it so he's leaving it up to me
and hoping I'm wise.

Kathy intuited encouragement as well as a hint of pressure
from her father even as she acknowledged that her relationship had been a significant distraction. If she took on the
adult role to marry, it would be her responsibility to make
the marriage work. Her longing for a positive resolution was
palpable. "Everything that happens reminds me of you and
sure does hurt," she said.[9]

Kathy was far from isolated as she weighed educational
plans alongside a future as a wife. Many discussions about
Charlie, especially with her father, took place in the open.
"We had another big round at dinner," Kathy wrote. "It's getting so I hate to go to the table." Despite the disagreements,
Kathy was reflective on the mode of interaction as well as
the subject matter. "They aren't all lectures but discussions!"
she observed, continuing, "Daddy thinks he can read the
mind of every young man under 23 and all he is after is sex! I
made a joke out of the whole thing and laughed at him. I told
him that if you were going with me for what you could get,
you were certainly spending a lot of time doing it." Another
element did not sit well with her father. She wrote, "He said
that if you really loved me, you'd let me finish my education
before we get married."[10]

Kathy concluded that the true crux of her parents' concern was that she would no longer live near home. Her parents had been more accepting of Lawrence, she reasoned,
because he would likely remain in Fort Bend County. But
she was not insensitive to the impact of her choices. After
witnessing her mother crying alone in her room, Kathy

worried that she was the source of the tears. "I really feel bad honey," she wrote to Charlie. "I hate to hurt Mother so."[11]

Romance was not her only focus. She enrolled in summer school at Wharton Junior College, retaking trigonometry and an English literature course in order to make up credits. She learned that money, not grades, might impede her return to UT. "Mother doesn't feel we can afford it," Kathy wrote, the evening before finishing a theme outline for a paper in her English class. "She thinks that I could go to Sam Houston for about 2/3 what I spend at Texas." Interestingly, Frances soon committed to funding Kathy's education herself no matter what lay ahead, an assurance that Kathy eagerly reported: "Mother said that she would pay for my tuition + books should I decide to get married before getting my degree." She added, "Be glad when we can talk about it with them and get things out in the open + cleared up."[12]

Charlie made two visits to Needville in June: one for his birthday the weekend of June 23–24; and another the weekend of June 30–July 1 for a serious talk with Kathy's father. The first visit was a source of considerable tension, as Raymond and Frances had already planned a weekend trip to San Antonio in advance of the most labor-intensive phase of the rice harvest. Raymond did not want to change his plans, and he also did not approve of Charlie staying with no chaperone in the house.

Kathy wrote to Charlie after a trip to the beach in Galveston, where an otherwise beautiful day was marred by a massive influx of seaweed that "bloomed" along the shoreline, an unforeseen consequence of Hurricane Carla from the previous year. "It's supposed to be costing the Galveston beaches about a million dollars," she said. Kathy began with a recap of the latest family disagreement, but in the end there was no question that Charlie should come as planned for his birthday: "Daddy + I had a big round. (Mom's on my side.) It seems this is the last weekend before Daddy really has to start almost living with the crop. They both hate to not be here when you come, but it can't be helped." Charlie could arrive Saturday, but he would have to spend the night at a neighbor's house. Kathy was making a special dress, planning meals and a birthday cake, and Charlie planned to take Kathy into Houston to meet his mentor, Father Gil.[13]

THE WEEK AFTER CHARLIE'S BIRTHDAY, KATHY earned an A+ on her trigonometry exam, and her father confirmed that she could return to UT. A box of Florida mangoes, a present from Charlie's parents, also arrived at the Leissner house. As the couple considered wedding dates in January or June 1963, Kathy carpooled to Austin with a friend on June 28. Notably, she made a deposit for a room at Grace Hall, the historic Episcopal women's dorm, clearly planning to be single for the upcoming term, if not the entire year. She was in love, but she was not panicked to marry.[14]

That plan changed abruptly when Charlie returned home with Kathy to speak man-to-man with Raymond. This time he spent the night. After he left, Kathy effused to Charlie, "You have no idea how much better things are here at home since you talked to Daddy." Two days later, her father's turn-around was remarkable. "Mother said something about waiting until next June and Daddy said he didn't see why we don't get married this summer. He said, 'If you're going to get married, why wait until next January.' I almost fell out of my chair."[15]

The whirlwind was in full force. By July 10 the wedding date was set for Friday, August 17, Charlie's parents' anniversary. Kathy admitted that she was stunned: "I'm still not over the initial shock of our getting married in 6 weeks," she wrote to her fiancé after a trip with her mother and friends to Neiman Marcus. "I have already asked my attendants and yesterday . . . I bought a dress and veil + all. I even got my wedding night nightgown set. It sure is pretty. I can't wait to wear it for my honey." Her formal engagement portrait soon appeared in the *Fort Bend Herald Coaster*.[16]

KATHY HAD PLENTY OF COMPANY DURING this period. She took country drives with friends, attended summer baseball games, went swimming, shopped in Rosenberg and Houston, and chauffeured neighborhood kids back and forth to Little League games in her mother's Volkswagen. Several friends were planning weddings of their own, and classmates from high school as well as former roommates from UT visited her. The Leissners hosted a huge corn roast. Kathy also had a near-miss driving when a man side-swiped the VW as she made a turn near Johnny's Gas Station. The incident was not only a reminder of aggressive drivers on the road but also of how her surgical incisions were still healing. "Mother just knew I had broken apart my stitches + everything," she wrote. "I guess I'm getting used to accidents!"[17]

As wedding preparations intensified, Kathy turned to her mother and to married confidantes for support. She not only browsed through bridal books for pictures of dresses and table settings but also gathered feedback about real-life subjects—from financial costs ($4.80 a month for birth control pills and $12 a week for groceries) to personal privacy and bathroom habits, as well as sexual compatibility. Kathy delighted in these intimate chats. "I really enjoy talking to her," she wrote of a visit with one newlywed friend. "I get so tickled at her and some of the odd things they do. It was hard (and sometimes I had to stop myself) not to reveal exactly how much I know about my Honey." After sharing

In a light blue dress with white trim, Kathy cut the cake at a bridal shower hosted by family friends on July 26, 1962. Private archive of Nelson Leissner.

what another married friend told her about sex, Kathy also found a way to validate Charlie's apparent expectations and, less directly, to balance them with her own. "Do you know that they only make love about every three days!" she wrote. "I can't imagine being married to someone who only desired me 2 or 3 times a week. Oh, yes, and she desires him most during her period and that's when he won't make love to her. He must not be very considerate."[18]

Neighbors, aunts, and longtime family friends organized not one but two wedding showers for Kathy, including a luncheon at the Normandie Restaurant in Houston. Kathy ordered the wedding invitations topped with a black "KWC" monogram engraved inside a blind-embossed seal. Kathy even purchased the wedding bands, ordering a sentimental inscription inside each one—"Until the 12th of Never"—in part, a reference to the Johnny Mathis song. Writing to Charlie on one of her new postmarriage thank you cards, Kathy shared a warning from one of her friends: they should hide the car during the reception to make sure their getaway was not interrupted.[19]

Despite all her resources, Kathy still had difficulty securing contraception. Not even a longstanding family friendship with the local doctor—and an official wedding date—guaranteed Kathy a prescription. "I saw Dr. Joe in the drug store today," she wrote to Charlie in mid-July. "[H]e asked me if I was coming in so he could tell me a 'little story'! I just laughed and said yes! I sure hope he approves of the pills." The next day Kathy was surprised that Dr. Joe had refused. "Instead he gave me some kind of cream," she wrote. "I told mother I was going to some Dr. who would give me the pills. I'll tell you about the cream later. It doesn't sound bad at all."[20]

Dr. Joe's resistance was emblematic of the ways in which male authorities still exercised default control over women's choices at the time, even in the most intimate aspects of their lives.[21] However, as her letter indicates, Kathy did not take his refusal as the final word. While she had been socialized to take for granted that women needed male approval for wedding dates and medical treatments, she had not entirely discarded her ability to question and advocate for herself—at least when it came to her own body.

Charlie was already quite comfortable deploying his privileges, and the engagement emboldened his paternalism. Kathy's mirroring of his rhetorical cues at this time, even in passing exchanges, illustrates her acculturation to an expectation of female deference to men, especially when it came to money or subjects where her knowledge and experience were limited. At almost nineteen, Kathy knew the social code well, and her partner—only three years older than she—expected nothing less than full compliance. Antihomosexuality, for example, was central to Charlie's social standards. He rebuffed Kathy's connection between "Walter," the name he used for his penis, and a nineteenth-century American poet she had recently read. "Hey!" Kathy wrote, celebrating the connection. "He's named after Walt Whitman!" Charlie responded tersely, hinting at his own homophobic anxieties. "Walt was a queer and Walter is not, let's hope so at least," he responded. Kathy was quick to take his word and promptly apologized.[22]

Some of Kathy's accommodations were not passing echoes but permanent changes of behavior. After receiving Kathy's first long letter in June, Charlie critiqued its typed format, his disapproval both possessive and parental: "[I]f I want to read typewritten paper I can find plenty over at the ROTC building. Honey, I'd sure appreciate it if you'd *write* my letters. They seem to be a little more like my Kathy than when you type them."[23] She never did so again.

Kathy also received early doses of Charlie's emotional manipulations. "Boy I feel lousy," he wrote in response to her father's skepticism about his intentions. He added melodramatically, "I feel like I've had my heart kicked out. It'd be different if I were trying to have relations with you. But here that is the last thing I want to do and yet I get accused of it." He asserted his expectation that Kathy would defer to him after the wedding: "[I]f you marry me I'd expect you to go with me. . . . [M]y home is Fla. and if I go into business with my Dad that is where we'll live." Revisiting the subject of staying at the Leissner house, Charlie pouted that he didn't want to "impose" by staying with a neighbor, adding, "If I'm going to cause a fuss I'd rather not come." Later, following his man-to-man with Raymond once the wedding date had been set, Charlie spoke as if he had won a victory over Kathy's father, referring to her as if she were one of the prize cattle prepared for market: "Your Daddy is sorta getting stung isn't he. Getting you ready to give to someone else."[24]

While signals of her early accommodation are unmistakable, Kathy also directly and indirectly resisted Charlie's whims. Before their engagement, he had already fixated on the precise moment when he got the "drop" on Kathy, counting down as if it were a moment of capture: "How's it feel to be tied down to the same fellow for 4 months, 1 day, 23 hours, and 35 minutes?" he asked. "I am sure glad I tied down that little dropper of mine." Although Charlie believed from that moment Kathy belonged to him, she did not share his fixation, noting her own reflection that he was physically out of reach. "Happy four months anniversary a little late," she wrote. "If I knew where to reach you, I would call."[25]

Charlie did not present Kathy any ring—not even a borrowed or repurposed token, such as a family heirloom or modest birthstone. The bespoke tag drop was all she would receive. Since the couple would be wearing wedding bands weeks before they returned to UT, there might have appeared no practical need for an engagement marker. But the omission did stand out. Charlie's At-a-Glance Diary from fall 1961, prior to his meeting Kathy, suggested no aversion to spending money on jewelry. In his first semester at the university, he recorded expenses for a Texas pin as well as a ring that alone cost $49, roughly three and a half times the price of a pistol he purchased around the same time.[26]

Charlie left the traditional groom's purchase of wedding bands for Kathy, a task she seemed happy to embrace.[27] But this also meant she purchased the rings up front, with him promising to "get straight" with her for the cost afterwards. Meanwhile, he dedicated significant funds to a down payment on a new car, a 1962 Chevy Corvair Monza. He emphasized to Kathy how quickly the car and insurance payments had drained his account: "Just think this AM I had $720.00 and now I only have $46.00. But at least I have some receipts to show for it."[28] The flashiness of this expenditure for a young man about to start married life may have indicated a deep immaturity, but Charlie's accounting here was early evidence of how he used prices and costs to emphasize loss as much as to inflate self-importance—even as most if not all of his financial security still came from his father. Kathy, by contrast, never commented on wedding-related expenditures, even though she kept receipts for flowers and other items.

To some of Charlie's subtle manipulations, Kathy responded with clarity. After a drinking bender on July 4, a few days after his big talk with Kathy's father, Charlie sent Kathy a cryptic letter in which he said he was hungover and needed to talk to her about his "state of mind." Bothered by his evasiveness here as well as in a subsequent phone call, Kathy began by addressing the subject directly: "I'm worried about you. . . . I know it's no fun being 150 miles apart but we just have to put up with it. Honey, what is it you want to tell me. I'm curious! I hope it's nothing bad." She went on to encourage him about a chemistry quiz he had taken, but then her tone became somewhat frantic, writing, "Please write me about what's wrong. I can't wait until next Friday. Please!" As she concluded, her mind was still not at rest. "The more I think about it," she wrote, "the more I hope that my honey is feeling better than he was when he wrote that letter."[29] The unresolved exchange foreshadowed in miniature Kathy's future struggles to communicate with Charlie during his darker moods. It also demonstrated how he manipulated her social intelligence and sensitivity to corner attention and stoke worry.

Even at this early stage, Charlie had expectations for Kathy's body—harbingers of much more explicit and obsessive rules to come. Trying to head off expenses not covered by his military insurance coverage, he urged her to "get [her] teeth in good shape" so they would not have a dental bill after the wedding. Kathy herself referred playfully to physical activity in terms of Charlie, as when, three weeks before the wedding, she described "exercising for my honey." But in the same letter, Kathy also pushed back against Charlie's latest, strange assertion that she should consult the new edition of *Modern Bride* for an article about "the need for a premarital exam." Such exams were midcentury code not only for a pelvic examination of a young bride-to-be (including verification of virginity) but also as "medical preparation" for intercourse. Not skittish about sex, Kathy was baffled for a simple reason: she had already visited the doctor. "Honey, are you worried about me or something?" she began. "Why are you so concerned about my examination? I promise there is nothing wrong with me, other than being *love starved.*"[30]

After Charlie selected the Austin apartment where the couple would live after the honeymoon, he spent a great deal of time telling Kathy how much cleaning it would need, asserting that he would not have time for the more menial chores. He sent Kathy the apartment key in a letter, explaining that he had already bought "a chain lock + a lock for the bedroom door" along with Ajax, sponges, and a bucket; he pledged to caulk around the sink and lavatory pipes. However, he was worried that the apartment would not be clean enough for his family's arrival prior to the wedding. "I don't think I should take the time. I really need to get after my studies," he wrote, adding, "You think about it and let me know if you can possibly come sometime to clean it like you want."[31]

Kathy did not blindly take the bait. She was excited to receive the apartment key, but she brushed past his suggestion that housekeeping would fall to her alone, listing necessary tasks as collective actions. "[W]e can clean the apartment, talk to the doctor, and anything else that needs to be done," she wrote. Twelve hours later, following a phone call where Charlie had been complaining, Kathy tried to lighten his mood. She was incredibly busy herself: finishing summer courses at Wharton, driving the rice truck for her father as the harvest started, spending afternoons polishing silver for their reception, and handling nearly all material details of the wedding with zero help from her fiancé. "Sweetheart," she said, "I just want you and not a big ceremony and all. Oh! Well, it's almost over with." In a flirty letter where she also teased him about their upcoming honeymoon, Kathy urged him to study hard, as she knew the results would affect his scholarship—and their future together. "You have to make some real top notch grades," she wrote, "so 'we' will still be here next fall."[32]

In her final letter before taking vows as a married woman, Kathy described finishing the wedding invitations despite frustration about missing addresses for select invitees. She was excited for a fabric shopping trip to Rosenberg, so that she could sew "something for the honeymoon and that I can wear to school too," the new clothes suggesting the easy blend she envisioned between school and marriage. For Kathy's final preparatory visit to Austin, Nelson served as a chaperone, accompanying her by bus and staying with the couple in the apartment. Her last check as a single woman was dated August 13, four days prior to her wedding: $4.00 for a doctor's visit in Wharton.[33]

THERE WAS ONE SIGNIFICANT DETAIL THAT Kathy did not arrange: the ceremony itself. Customarily, weddings were held in the church of the bride and her family, which in this case would have been Needville's First Methodist Church. But if Charlie wanted to remain a Roman Catholic, according to church rules of the day he needed a bishop's formal permission (called a dispensation) to marry any Protestant, who would either convert to Catholicism or take a minimum of six lessons before signing an agreement to raise children in the faith. Even when undertaken in one's home parish, such marriages generally required significant advance planning in order to secure dispensation, to allow time for the instructional period, and, in the last weeks prior to the ceremony, to publish public marriage banns listing the couple's names.[34]

Kathy was the first Leissner to marry a non-Protestant, and such a mixed marriage remained a big deal in her family. Sensing Protestant suspicions, Charlie conveniently downplayed the role of his religious background even as he insisted on a marriage in the Catholic Church, ostensibly to appease his mother.[35] Kathy herself was not one to agonize over theological rules. The closest Kathy came to expressing subtle reserve about the church was in her passing wish to marry without any "big ceremony"—perhaps glossing a degree of Protestant skepticism about the elaborate rituals of Catholicism and its priesthood.

In this area she seemed much like her mother: people-oriented rather than doctrinaire when it came to religion. It would have seemed charming and uncomplicated that Charlie introduced her to Father Gil, whom he had known from childhood back in Florida. (It would not have occurred to her to question why he had transferred to Texas.) The priest served as a fixer for complex processes in a diocese where Charlie had no history, including securing permission from the pastor of St. Michael's Church in Needville to grant access for the ceremony. Father Gil was supposed to communicate arrangements the first week of August for Kathy's religious instructions, just two weeks before the wedding. With strange ease, he did not slow the process even a little bit for this couple who had known each other a matter of months, whose families had never met. Kathy gained no time to reflect or learn more.[36]

Charlie's last letter before the marriage included a direct request about whether she would attend an early morning mass with him before their ceremony—not a standard inquiry for a lapsed believer. Her response is not recorded. Reflecting on the symmetry of their wedding date with his parents' anniversary, Charlie had noted, "I have to get them a card."[37] Such a mention would have seemed to Kathy a lovely commemoration with no need for analysis.

The couple took their vows on a hot and humid Friday afternoon, August 17, seeming to begin a life where education, family, and profession would readily intertwine. A photo taken from the organ loft in the back of St. Michael's Church casts a wide angle down at the friends and family members in the pews, a spotty gathering of men in well-fitted suit jackets and women whose heads are covered by stylish hats. In her white dress and veil, Kathy kneels in the center, on the second step at the foot of the altar, with Charlie kneeling next to her in his slim white jacket and exposing the scuffed outer soles of his shoes. His two brothers flank either side— Patrick as the best man at Charlie's right and Johnnie Mike in the white surplice a step above, to Kathy's left. Looking down on them all is Father Gil, an open prayer book in one hand, blessing the hasty union.

Kathy had no way of zooming back to see herself in this moment: how she had taken her place as a young woman on an altar flanked by men inside a complex lineage she did not grasp. Like the most faithful members of this religious tradition so new to her, she had no way to imagine the darker underbelly of any church with its pristine white altar and Gothic arches and candlesticks. The priest's solemn words mismatched his elfin appearance, his ready smiles

Kathy's wedding ceremony at St. Michael's Catholic Church in Needville, Texas, August 17, 1962, Rev. Joseph "Gil" Leduc presiding. Private archive of Nelson Leissner.

and joking, the ostentatious blue convertible he had driven into the parking lot. But as strange as the priest might have seemed, he was merely a functionary whose influence she expected to recede, just as he disappeared without offering any prayer at the reception. Kathy could not know that more than half a century later, the priest whom her new husband seemed to trust so deeply would be named as "credibly accused" of abusing children.[38]

At the far edge of the wedding party, Nelson considered questions his own handsome smile belied. He still distrusted Charlie, and he was about to witness—too late—exactly what kind of family his sister had joined.

AT THE RECEPTION ON FRIDAY EVENING, the Leissner home bustled with guests and well-wishers. The den filled with presents as the photographer snapped pictures. In the dining room the cake was a traditional three-tiered tower standing on four single-layer cakes at the base. Buttercream ribbons and clusters of wedding bells topped each cake. Kathy changed into her honeymoon suit and a netted pill-box hat, and her mother pinned the going-away corsage on her jacket: a large orchid nestled in wisps of tulle. Someone attached streamers to the car and painted messages across the windows, including Kathy's name in white block letters on the passenger side. She rolled the window halfway down to wave, her smile and fingers blurring as the car pulled away, shadows of well-wishers and the outline of a warm and welcoming house vanishing in the background.

It was dark when the couple arrived at the Las Vegas Motor Hotel on South Main Street in Houston where they stayed one night. In her honeymoon letters Kathy traced her first impressions of newlywed life. Using letterhead snatched from the hotel, she wrote her first short letter from the road. Postmarked in New Orleans, her message is a straightfor-ward flutter of bliss and postwedding family business:

> This is really just a note not saying anything but just
> to let you know we are fine and as my new husband
> would say, "happier than the devil." I hope that
> Granny is fine and makes the trip to Hunstville fine.
> Please see to it that Vickie, Ronnie, and Mrs. Otto get
> their gifts, I left above the T.V. Oh—and please find
> out what our pattern of stainless steel is and send
> it to Fla. We may order the rest of it. I told Charlie
> about the $25 from Aunt Kitty and what we are doing
> w/it. He is satisfied. We ought to hit New Orleans
> about 6:00 or 7:00. We're going out tonight and I'm

Kathy waves from the Corvair as she leaves for her honeymoon. Private archive of Nelson Leissner.

getting all excited. Mother, tell everyone "thanks" again tell them all "hello" for us. Charlie said to tell his new "Mom + Dad" hi and ask Daddy about the crop!

Two days later Kathy jotted a quick update to her parents on a bright postcard advertising the neon marquee, luxury buffet tables, and double swimming pool of the Candlelight Inn, one of "The Gulf South's Most Luxurious Motor Hotels and Resorts."[39]

She saved her fullest account of the trip for a long letter penned after she had settled in at the Whitmans' home in

Florida. "We haven't had a min. rest since we got here," she wrote, referring to the steady queue of relatives. The letter included two wedding clippings from local newspapers ("one of the pictures is pretty good and the other is terrible") as well as two short notes added at the end, by her new father-in-law and by Charlie. Kathy included mixed messages about how Nelson was doing. He had traveled ahead to Florida with Charlie's parents and two younger brothers, Patrick and Johnnie Mike. On the one hand, Kathy wrote, "Nelson is having a nice time and the only trouble is with Mr. Whitman." But she quickly offered her initial impression that any conflict was beneficial: "I think the way he is treating Nelson is helping him because he has to take a lot of bull and give him his share back." She added that her brother was teaching Charlie's mother how to dance, and that he was getting along with Patrick, even though Patrick's lost glasses had put a crimp in their activities. "They went to the show and had to sit on the front row and look up," she wrote.[40]

Kathy highlighted her litany of newlywed adventures, starting with details of the first night in Houston: "I got a big kick out of calling you. Oh! Charlie bought or ordered a fifth of champagne and we didn't even drink 2 full glasses of it. I saved the bottle." Her second night of marriage was her "big night on the town" in New Orleans, where local officials had been reportedly executing vice raids for two weeks in the seedier tourist traps. Charlie eagerly introduced Kathy to Bourbon Street, where they "saw a strip-tease show, ate steaks, and really just walked up and down looking at all the shows." The night concluded with a visit to the My-O-My Club, a female-impersonator club located at the time on Lake Pontchartrain. "Have you heard about it?" she wrote. "Mom, I can't wait to tell you about it! You really won't believe it!" Sunday included more quotidian adventures for honeymooners: a Mississippi steamboat cruise, dinner at an Italian restaurant, a visit to the French Quarter where Kathy had her portrait done by a street artist. The weekend concluded with a visit to Pat O'Brien's "for this famous drink called a hurricane," before they headed on to Florida. The couple had one last day alone together, in Silver Springs. Kathy embraced it all and kept her tone light, even as she unequivocally assured her parents where her heart belonged: "Fla. is fine for vacation," she wrote as she wrapped up her letter, "but give me Texas any day."[41]

Nelson had already been with the Whitmans for three days by the time Kathy arrived. The family had given him a tour of the regional sights, including a ride in a glass-bottom boat. Nelson had wanted to spend time at nearby beaches as well as the Lake Worth Lagoon, within walking distance of the Whitman home on South L Street. The trip would enable him to get acquainted with Patrick, also a teenager, whose plans to become a priest had recently changed, leaving him sullen and depressed. The two boys did not connect so well after all. Nelson was also jarred by the way Charlie's parents exchanged barbs in tense conversations, addressing themselves in the third person, as "Mother" and "Daddy." Worst of all, Nelson witnessed how dinners in the Whitman household could be open warfare, and Charlie's father had no inhibitions even with a guest at the table. He screamed at his wife and sons, in one fit of temper throwing a pan across the table and crashing it into a cabinet. The reaction—or lack of reaction—suggested a palpably dreadful routine. It became even more personal when Mr. Whitman said he wanted to "knock some sense" into Nelson's head.[42]

The disturbing visit added new alarm to his original doubts about Charlie, and Nelson worried how these dynamics would influence Kathy's future. But her arrival at the Whitman home presented a more immediate diplomatic issue. Nelson knew that his ability to confide in his sister would be limited not only by the crowded physical circumstances but also by the social conventions that now—just days after the marriage had been sealed—constricted them all. Her hours were filled with visitors who sought to meet her, deliver presents, and take the new couple out for picnics, dinners, and water skiing. It was a few days before Nelson managed to corner Kathy quietly on a shopping trip in an aisle of a grocery market. He shared his feelings about what he had witnessed, and he clarified his desire to leave, urging Kathy not to share details with Charlie. Nelson had brought some money with him, and to avoid any confrontation, he offered to get a plane ticket and head back to Needville with the excuse of helping their father finish the harvest.

But at this stage Kathy wanted total transparency with her husband, and she passed the report directly to Charlie. Predictably, the result was not good. Nelson recalled another big family blow-up as Charlie realized Nelson's mistrust. To make matters more challenging, Kathy was not simply dating this man—she had married him. One can imagine a gloating quality buried in the tension, as if Charlie had won a new victory. Disgusted as he felt, Nelson remained for the uncomfortable duration, with no choice but to accompany the couple on their drive back to Texas.[43]

Nelson recalled that the three of them left Lake Worth on September 8 in the late morning—an unwise time to start if their goal was to reach Texas in a single day. Mr. Whitman had provided the couple a cheap, two-wheel trailer to drag behind the Corvair. The trailer had simple plywood sides and a canvas tarp strapped across the top, to protect wedding presents and other belongings that did not fit in the trunk. Nelson himself held the brand-new television set, the couple's "nice" gift, on his lap in the backseat.[44]

Charlie's plan to make it without an overnight stop meant driving more than eleven hundred miles from the

South Atlantic coast. This required first heading northwest, towards the Florida panhandle, then due west across Alabama, Mississippi, and Louisiana before even glimpsing the Texas border. If they stopped only for bathroom breaks and ate sandwiches with Cokes and coffees in the car, the trip would take roughly seventeen hours at the wheel. Charlie was convinced that he could beat the clock, though it was unclear whom he was really racing.

It was cloudy, and the steamy afternoon would have been tiring even on a day without an overbearing sun. Kathy and Nelson wanted to take turns driving, but Charlie stubbornly refused. As night descended on the outskirts of a coastal town (likely Biloxi, Mississippi), the air thickened with mist and drizzle, making it more difficult to see. Charlie somehow drifted off the main freeway onto a feeder road and could not find his way back. As he guided the lost car along a bumpy neighborhood street, the trailer's tongue suddenly detached. The chain guard remained, leaving the trailer head to scrape and jostle wildly before it smashed into the bumper and tugged the Corvair into a dangerous zigzag. Some of the trailer boards split on impact, shattering a taillight.

Charlie stopped and the three surveyed the damage, horrified to realize that the tarp had flown off. Turbulence had strewn wedding presents and other belongings into the road and along the shoulder. Together they salvaged the remains and were lucky that a local man pulled his truck over to help. He offered a place to stay for the night, an efficiency room near his home.[45]

Early the next morning, the man helped fix the taillight, repair slats on the trailer, reload, and reorient the car back to the main road and the freeway. Needville was still six hours away. When Charlie finally pulled into the circular driveway outside the Leissner home—the home where they had waved their glorious goodbyes three weeks earlier—they made a pit stop and gathered up remaining belongings and new gifts. Then it was full steam back to Austin, yet another three hours. In a letter to Frances afterwards, Kathy's new mother-in-law made a passing reference to the accident with her son at the wheel. "Thank God that they weren't hurt," she wrote.[46]

On the surface, Kathy put the stressors of the trip behind her, but she was not oblivious to what had happened, and she would not forget what her brother had told her. Fifteen months later, in January 1964, in a letter to Charlie, she would reflect on her father-in-law's treatment of Nelson with unequivocal disdain. "I think Daddy W. actually makes problems for himself," she wrote. "Just like when he took Nelson to Florida. He was determined that Nelson and my daddy had some insurmountable problem that he was going to fix up. I'm sorry, honey, I just can't seem to understand those people as hard as I've tried."[47]

With time, distance, and an accumulation of experiences, Kathy would deepen that clarity of mind, that confidence to trust her own impressions. But the coming months would bring hurtful and confusing surprises that not only threatened her safety but undermined her achievements and undercut her best judgment.

Trouble Starts at Home

A CLUSTER OF MULTIUNIT TWO-STORY CLAPBOARD buildings (now called Park Place) stands virtually unchanged at Nelson and Ninth Street on the west side of Austin in the Clarksville area, roughly two miles from the university campus. After a nerve-wracking forty-eight hours of travel, Kathy and Charlie arrived here, pulling the rickety trailer late on Sunday, September 9, just as the first cold front of autumn brought lower temperatures, winds, and rain to the city. Slipping the key into the door of no. 104, they cozied up the modest rooms they had cleaned before the wedding, stocking empty shelves, cabinets, and drawers. They had new stainless utensils; cookware, dishes, and serving ware (including "a decorated chop plate" gifted by a friend in Green Bay, Wisconsin); yellow sheets and pillowcases; new towels.[1] They proudly displayed their modern-looking compact television set in the living room. Externally, at least, everything was in place for the newlywed sophomores to begin their life as a team.

Kathy and her husband had ten days to ease in before the fall semester began, and more changes were in the air. To accommodate growing enrollment at UT, an additional day had been added for registration. KLRN, an educational television station, had opened a studio on campus. Local activists continued to press recalcitrant local businesses on full integration, including at an ice-skating rink, the Ice Palace. In the coming months women's roles would be an open source of debate on campus. One guest, Dr. Lillian Gilbreth, spoke optimistically about the potential to integrate career, homemaking, and parenting—as long as women had "the full support" of "family and friends." But another speaker, Dr. Robert Ledbetter, addressed a campus women's group and suggested that a wife's financial success could wound a "fragile male ego."[2]

Kathy had something to prove to herself because of spring's lackluster grades. Cheerful September letters to family detailed her schedule and expenses: "You will not believe what I have to take. Geology, Astronomy, English (technical writing), Gov. and History. It took me $91.57 to register and I have bought $32 worth of books and I haven't even bought my History + Gov. books. You won't believe this, but I still have to buy 5 books that come to a total of $27 or $30." Kathy included her husband's contribution to the household. "Charlie built two bookcases," she wrote. "One for the bedroom and one in the living room." She took on the task of covering all their books with brown paper to protect them from damage.[3]

Predictably, there were odds and ends to resolve after the honeymoon, as Kathy wrote to her parents in advance of their much-anticipated October visit for a football game. "When y'all come down we would like for you to bring that crystal bowl and the Ferrante and Tiecher album we left there before we were married," she said. She also requested that her parents bring her party dresses and a pair of "wheat jeans" Charlie had left at the house and now needed for labs. It took the couple almost three weeks to secure a telephone.[4]

As she reentered university life as a married woman, Kathy had to navigate adjustments to her role and identity in ways that Charlie did not. When she joined a group for NESEP wives and attended a coffee, she seemed glad to make friends but noted that only one woman remained in college. Another had already graduated from the College of Pharmacy and now held a job in Austin, but most of her new married acquaintances were younger and already consumed with children. Kathy recounted an amusing mistake: "The funniest thing happened—I introduced myself as Kathleen Leissner in a name game and the place about cracked up." She was inspired to have her first course with a female professor, a technical writing course for science majors. "[G]oing to be a real jewel," she wrote. "My teacher is a woman and obviously believes in much work out of class."[5]

Kathy's effort to assert her individual identity within her married role—positive and lighthearted at the onset—was reflected in her language and style as well as the materiality of her letters. She did not yet have any personal stationery, and Kathy's first two notes were written on Charlie's UT Austin letterhead, with the university seal and his full name embossed at the top left—the same stationery he had used during their courtship. Following a November visit with her parents, Kathy inserted herself, scribbling "Mr. and Mrs." in the margin next to his name.

Her update in one Sunday letter presented a vivid portrait of their married routines and special outings, as well as a report about midterm grades. Rather than portraying subservient drudgery, her description emphasized the promise of mutual values, accomplishments, and the small pleasures of her new life in Austin:

> Charlie is doing his exercises. . . . I made an applesauce cake and put brown sugar icing on it. . . . Tonight we always take out an hour to watch "Bonanza" and [friends] are coming down to watch it with us. We alternate every other weekend. Hope the cake doesn't kill them. We splurged and went out this weekend. Friday we went to the Italian Village and ate Lasagna and then we went dancing to the Jade Room. We had a real good time. The game yesterday was pretty bad. We just don't like afternoon games and Texas looked as poor as ever. . . . Here are our grades so far:

Charlie	Me
M.E. –(88)	History (C)
(mechanical engineering)	Gov. (Don't know yet)
Calculus –(81)	Astronomy – 81 – B
History –(78)	Eng. –B
Gov. –(68)	Geology –78 & 88

> Sounds better than last year, doesn't it? . . . Next weekend (Nov. 10) is the Marine Corp Birthday. They are having a Marine Corp. Ball out at the Officers Club at Bergstrom. I don't know if we can go because Charlie doesn't have any dress blues and can't get into his greens. I sure hope he can figure something out.

While Kathy seemed to enjoy acting as primary correspondent at this point, signs were emerging that she had adopted the mantle of intercessor, a role that would soon become tiresome. For now, the cues were subtle. Towards the end of this letter, for example, Kathy explained that Charlie wanted to "drop a line" but could not interrupt his shaving.[6]

On a few occasions that fall, Charlie wrote his own letters to Kathy's parents, perhaps in response to her urging that he communicate directly with her family. But there were early flickers of a pattern that would continue, where Charlie's communication undermined or confused interactions between Kathy and her family. For now, regarding the Leissners' imminent visit to Austin for a football game, he jotted a short note apologizing directly to Frances for failing to secure good tickets despite a previous promise. He included this message with one of Kathy's letters, along with handwritten directions to the apartment. Frances afterwards penciled in corrections on Charlie's map.[7]

Charlie also assumed control over the couple's finances even though they continued to receive substantial financial support from both the Leissners and the Whitmans. In December he wrote his own short letter to Kathy's parents, opening obsequiously to praise Kathy's high grade on a geology quiz the previous week ("I married a smart little girl didn't I," he wrote), then cutting quickly to his central purpose. Knowing full well that Kathy's mother would be the first recipient of the letter, he made an explicit request for her to intercede with Kathy's father. Charlie wanted Raymond to put in writing that he would cover all her tuition and books, as well as fifty percent of their total living expenses, with the other half to be covered by his own father. He stated that the document was necessary because it would somehow enable Kathy to avoid nonresident fees the following semester—a cloudy rationale, since Kathy had always resided in Texas. Within a few days, Frances sent the letter as requested. A copy did not survive.[8]

BENEATH THE SURFACE, KATHY'S INTIMATE LIFE was not going smoothly. During fall 1962 she was managing ambiguous health concerns of a gynecological nature. She was not the first nineteen-year-old bride to deal with irregular or painful periods, an adjustment to birth control pills, and a new sex life. But Charlie, who styled himself as a sexual expert and as Kathy's teacher, tended to pathologize what he did not understand. (He thought it was abnormal, for example, for any semen to leave a woman's body after intercourse). One can only imagine his reaction if Kathy dared to express sexual dissatisfaction or discomfort in these early days. It did not help that her access to health care was determined by her husband's USMC status. "I have an appointment to see the base doctor out at Bergstrom AFB tomorrow," she wrote in September. "I sure hope everything is alright. I washed this afternoon and I found that it takes me 1 hr + 15 min."[9] The appointment passed by without a follow-up report, suggesting no urgent worry. Within a matter of weeks, however, the situation would be emblematic of Charlie's belief that something was "wrong" with Kathy.

There are no family letters during October, as the Cuban Missile Crisis frayed collective national nerves. President Kennedy's public television address on October 22 disclosed the discovery of nuclear weapons in Cuba and laid out his quarantine strategy to avert mutually assured atomic destruction, despite pressure from advisors to strike the island first. Through tense negotiations and back channels, Kennedy's administration managed to de-escalate the conflict even as bitter critics considered him guilty of "communist appeasement." Disagreement lingered afterwards: at what point was clever diplomacy better than direct confrontation with an enemy?[10]

At the same time, Charlie's family insinuated pressures into the newlyweds' household, both precipitating a crisis as

Kathy visiting with Granny Holloway in 1962. She died shortly after Kathy's wedding. Private archive of Nelson Leissner.

well as diverting attention from problems in the marriage. Charlie's father visited in November, taking a three-day hunting trip to Brackettville with his son. Kathy indicated to her family that Charlie's brother, Patrick, had undergone screening for a possible intestinal tumor, then appeared to be "doing fine" six weeks later, after a clear diagnosis.[11] She did not yet realize that Patrick was struggling deeply for more complicated reasons, which her in-laws took great pains to conceal.

November ended with the death of Kathy's maternal grandmother, Ida Lee Holloway, affectionately known to her family as "Granny." Kathy and Charlie joined her mother and relatives for a short visit to Huntsville and attended the funeral in Trinity. Frances's subsequent letters to the couple mingled details of the aftermath with holiday preparations. She recounted a long afternoon helping to clear out her mother's closets, then faced terrible weather on the way back to Needville. "It took us over four hours to get home. The fog was so thick we couldn't travel but about 35 or 40," she wrote. "Yesterday I felt like a truck had hit me—but today I'm just numb." Even in the grief and strain following her mother's death, Frances's voice communicated steadiness and grit. Focusing on how life continued, Frances wrote that Nelson had a cold, was "fighting with geometry," and had attended a Christmas party for the band that turned out to be "a dud." She was helping Ray and his friends study for a history test, noting, "I'm sure if it were an oral one, Ray could make 100." A busy teacher herself, Frances had volunteered to plan refreshments for upcoming teacher and student parties. She looked forward to getting a new car—a Dodge Palero—to replace her old Volkswagen, but she frankly admitted that after the work of a long semester, she dreaded the long drive for a family holiday trip to Mexico City. She praised Kathy's latest test score without creating any new pressure. "That *91* sounds beautiful to me!" she wrote. "Hope the others turn out as well—but don't push yourselves *too* hard."[12]

The holidays offered an uncomplicated respite before final exams, and Kathy marked the occasion to her family with a simple preprinted Christmas card depicting a snowman and snowwoman wearing hats, scarves, and mittens.[13] While the Leissners took the new car to warmer climes in Mexico City, she and Charlie traveled back to Lake Worth to spend a tense Christmas with his family. Kathy spent hours wrapping presents for her in-laws.[14]

At the end of the break, Kathy and Charlie returned from Florida to meet up with her family in Needville for a few days, celebrating the new year with stories of their respective travels. But the couple brought two additional passengers from Florida, both rescues from the Whitman house: Charlie's brother Patrick and a dog, Frosty. Patrick's presence seemed to have some urgency attached, but the reasons were cloudy. Patrick continued to face significant conflicts at home, and the trouble had intensified since he had left St. John Vianney Seminary and enrolled in public school. Meanwhile, Kathy had discovered what the Whitman family called Patrick's "problem"—his homosexuality—something her in-laws saw as shameful and wanted kept secret, even from her.[15]

How did suddenly taking in a depressed teenager struggling with sexual identity and parental shame become the responsibility of college newlyweds under the age of twenty-two, a couple who had barely started to live together? On the surface—bright, good-looking, married—they represented the perfect heterosexual ideal.

KATHY'S MOTHER DID NOT PUT HER concerns in writing at first, but they seemed to be keeping her awake. In a midnight letter addressing her daughter alone, written on mixed pages of pink and blue stationery, Frances perceived the challenges Kathy faced with her guests. Pets were not allowed at the apartment, and they were going to need more breathing room with Patrick. "Have you found a new apartment yet?" Frances asked. "Or is the 'cloak-and-dagger' bit with Frosty still working out?" She reflected warmly on their latest visit. "We were surely sorry to see you all leave Sunday—I don't know when I've been so lonesome," she wrote. She avoided posing questions and did not offer marriage advice. Instead, she commiserated with her daughter about the patience necessary for the new sewing machine, a present Kathy received at Christmas. Frances's advice read as gentle code for ordinary struggles faced by any young wife. "If you get started on that sewing for goodness sake don't get upset with that new machine—you have to get used to it. I remember quite well what I went through when I got mine—I would sew a seam on the new machine and go back to the old treadle—I got so disgusted with myself—oh brother! It's funny now, but then it was a terrible mess—ha!" In closing the letter, Frances included a wish that her daughter would get some rest.[16]

But Kathy had more than a new machine and a mess of fabric scraps to fit in a pattern, and the proverbial seams were not holding, no matter how she tried to sew them. As the first days of 1963 unfolded, Kathy found her top priority—studying for finals—compromised by extra duties as hostess. The couple and their new guests moved again, though not far, taking all the belongings they had unpacked in September to a new two-bedroom unit in the same complex. Their time and attention were even more divided, and expenses tightened as well. To add to the stress, Kathy knew that if Charlie did not meet the military's strict grade requirements, he could lose his scholarship, jeopardizing their immediate and long-term plans.

In early January, in a short note to her family, Kathy said she wrote at her husband's request. Her chagrin emerged as she explained about a bounced check: "We got [the check] back or rather Charlie went down and paid the drug store where he cashed it. We can't figure it out—because it says nothing about insufficient funds on it. . . . Charlie had already spent his Christmas money naturally and had to pay it out of groc. money." The couple were also apparently waiting for funds the Whitmans promised to send to offset Patrick's expenses. Most significant, however, was Kathy's suggestion that she was looking forward to time alone: "I have great news + mabe Charlie + Pat are going to Mexico during semester break + I can stay with you. I sure do miss you, Mother. Be sweet. You should hear from me tomorrow." She signed the letter with three names, "Kathy + Charlie + Pat."[17]

From a distance, Kathy's interpersonal labor is obvious, accounting for finances over which she retained no consistent control. She no longer had an independent bank account, and she was already explaining Charlie's missteps. Although her oblique explanations did not invite more inquiry, she seemed to trust her mother to read between the lines. At the very least, Kathy was tired of close quarters with two young men whose shared, unspoken, and troubled history was unfolding in plain sight, crowding out her voice, her needs, and any rational questions she dared to ask.

It is unclear whether Charlie did take Patrick away to Mexico as Kathy anticipated, or whether Kathy returned to Needville for time alone with her family. Surviving letters suggest, however, that she managed to find a private opportunity after exams to confide in her mother about the misery that had been brewing for many weeks. To make matters worse, Charlie refused any notion that he—or the terms of their marriage—needed to change. Instead, he redirected the source of trouble onto Kathy and had pressured her to see a psychiatrist.[18] In the last days of January 1963, Frances decided she could remain silent no longer, and an urgent letter arrived at the couple's apartment addressed directly to Charlie. Started January 28 and postmarked two days later, the seven-page letter on pale blue stationery had been written after a deeply fraught phone conversation about the state of the marriage.

In this nuanced and agonizing document, Frances made a compelling plea to her son-in-law. Because of its content and structure, the letter deserves to be read in full:

Dear Charlie,

This letter is probably going to be quite a shock to you even though we had quite a lengthy discussion Sunday. I honestly do not believe you heard a word I said. I don't know whether it's possible for me to reach you, but if I can at least get you to stand off and look at yourself and Kathy through someone else's eyes, then I have accomplished something.

I have a horror of hurting people—certainly I do not wish to hurt you, whom I have loved as a son. I don't believe Kathy was a bit happier nor more proud than I was on your wedding day. However, have no doubt that there is nothing, and I mean *nothing*, that I wouldn't do to protect my daughter's happiness.

I am a woman, just as Kathy is, and I know you feel that no woman can think logically. But I shall try—

You said that Kathy has changed. You are quite right. She is about the most miserable young woman—and she *is* a young woman, not a child, as you seem to think, who is trying to make a marriage work.

You say that you think Kathy needs to go to a psychiatrist. I disagree with you.

Kathy, until her marriage, has always been a normal, healthy, well-adjusted person with many friends and secure in the knowledge that she was loved and needed, a *person*, not a doormat.

You, as facts which you have told us would indicate, on the other hand, have been dominated by a father who wanted to mold you to his own pattern, building up frustrations and resentments that finally culminated in your leaving home to prove to yourself that you are a person, not a projection of someone else's personality.

Which of these two people would you logically assume to be the type of person who might conceivably someday need to go to a psychiatrist? Think a while.

I am in no way suggesting that *you* need to go to a psychiatrist—for, believe me, if I *did* believe it I would say so, quite frankly!

I do feel that both of you, together and separately, should go to a marriage counselor and as soon as possible.

You are an intelligent person. I dare say if you had some indication that you had some physical malignancy, you would immediately consult a physician. You both know you are not happy with this marriage. Then do the logical thing and go to someone who can help both of you.

You said you realized that bringing Pat to Austin was a mistake. I agree with you. He is a fine young man—or could be, if he weren't treated like a doormat, and I feel sorry for him, too. *But* no young married *couple* should be given the responsibility of straightening out seventeen years of someone else's mistakes. You need to be *alone* to work out your own problems—without pressure from *any* side—and I am certainly talking about *myself*, too.

I have no desire to interfere in your marriage. I can only pray that it works out for you both.

You said that you have no sympathy for someone who realizes he has made a mistake and doesn't rectify it. That is a rather harsh, cold statement and I would rather believe that you don't completely lack compassion.

By trying to completely dominate Kathy you are destroying the very things which attracted you to her in the first place.

I love you both very much, I am not a wise person—I do most of my thinking with my heart rather than with my head. It takes a lot of courage to really love someone—the more you give, the more you receive. I hope that someday you will really understand what I mean.

I love you.

Mother L.[19]

Neither a rant nor an attack, Frances's letter expressed fierce concern for Kathy's well-being and centered Charlie's responsibility. She expertly blended logical with empathetic appeals, suggesting a substantive grasp of the family trauma experienced by Charlie as well as his brother, and she challenged her son-in-law not to perpetuate the damage. Frances's emphasis on domination as a pattern rather than an isolated event also indicates a deeply perceptive insight well ahead of its time.

Although the details Kathy had confided remain unclear—whether she described her husband's temper or referred to any instances of physical force—it is indisputable that Frances was responding to a grave matter. At this early date, she was an unequivocal witness to serious trouble in her daughter's marriage, and her recommendation for individual as well as couple's counseling at the time was remarkable. Frances identified with Kathy in confronting Charlie's chauvinism, and she also attested to her daughter's sanity, refusing to dismiss Kathy's accounts of marital problems, however coded, as "hysteria" or "women's troubles." It is not difficult to picture Kathy later returning to the letter. Thick in its blue envelope, the document would have weighed heavily in the small palm of her hand, her mother communicating plainly: I see you are in pain. You deserve so much better.

TWO SUBSEQUENT LETTERS WITHIN A MATTER of days, both to her parents, indicate that Kathy and Charlie indeed discussed the contents of Frances's message. Kathy's identity begins to blur here, both as speaker and as intercessor, as "I" and "we." She composed her first response after spring registration and yet another family phone call, stating that she and Charlie would be visiting Needville for the weekend. She warmed up with details about their new course schedules, perhaps a bit too eager to signal renewed marital harmony and busyness. "We have history and government together and both are my old professors," she wrote. "I have 5 hours of laboratory and Charlie has 6. We get out of class at 1:00 on Mon + Wed, and Friday we both have a lab from 2–5." Fall grades had posted, and Kathy was proud of hers, writing, "I'm sure I can do even better this semester."[20]

The big news was that Patrick was leaving. Kathy understated her relief at his departure but stressed how much better she and her husband were getting along in his absence: "Everything happened so quick last week that I didn't even have time to write. We talked everything over Thurs. and decided that Pat was going to have to go back to Florida." She went on to make explicit reference to the impact of Frances's correspondence. "I think your letter sort of topped everything off. I hated to send Pat home but after we talked to the Whitmans they thought it would be best too." Kathy was especially hasty in her assurances that her troubles had ended. "Charlie and I are back to normal and we are getting along 100% better," she wrote. "We have had a couple more big talks and I think he realizes a few things about me and himself. . . . [W]e haven't had any arguments since Pat left." Charlie would later remind Kathy more than once of a moment during this tense period when she "told [him] the awful but powerful truth" and confronted him to do his part in the marriage.[21]

The letter may have partially reassured her parents, but new problems had already surfaced. Kathy did not include Charlie's grades as in a previous letter because she was worried. "Right now I have a horror of [him] being taken out of the program and we'll have to move again," she wrote. But she tried to keep the tone light. "We should find out today," she continued. "Just hope the Commandant had his morning coffee when he received the reports!" The latest phone conversation with her in-laws had been discouraging: "They made him mad as usual. He always seems to get the same ole lecture about what a disgraceful son he is and never any note of encouragement."[22] As much stress as her in-laws indeed contributed to her new life, they also served to camouflage Charlie's own behavior as a source of daily trouble.

Another reality complicated Kathy's mood, as the couple moved yet another time—for the second time in six weeks—retreating to a one-bedroom apartment at Park Place. "I'm so tired of moving I could die," she wrote. She noted that Charlie seemed to be trying to reconcile with her financially. "We are going down and spending the entertainment fund for the month on a new bedspread today," she said. "Charlie promised I could get a decent looking spread + make some drapes."[23] Rather than signifying substantive change, such "occasional indulgences" are hallmarks of coercive control.[24]

Now as later, Kathy would be drawn to curtains. They were easy to improvise and could quickly cover a dirty window, add cheerful color to a room, ensure privacy. But curtains could not cover every reality: Poor grades. Expectations from the Marine Corps. Mysterious conflicts in an extended family. A young woman's misgivings about the man she had married.

TWELVE DAYS PASSED, AND ON VALENTINE'S Day 1963, Kathy composed a long letter to her parents after yet another phone conversation about "bad news." She used tidy sheets of five-by-seven, three-ring, college-ruled notebook paper that mismatched the no. 10 business envelope she enclosed them in, and she approached the task in a more formal style than usual, with longer, more developed paragraphs—almost like a short essay. The impeccable penmanship and lack of edits suggest that Kathy may have copied the letter very slowly from a first draft, perhaps with a significant degree of input or supervision from her husband. After her standard salutation and an acknowledgment of the phone call, Kathy drove home the central point: Charlie's grades were insufficient to keep his scholarship, the Marines were calling him back to active duty at Camp Lejeune, and she was dropping out of college:

> [S]omehow I think it will be better. After all, you and Daddy didn't have it easy either when you first got married and I guess everybody has to do somethings the hard way. The only thing that will be hard on me is having to leave you, + Daddy, + Nelson, + Ray for so long. I guess it just shows how much of a kid I still am, but I sure do hate to leave Texas. I guess mabe I'm not grown up yet even if I am 19 years old. . . .
>
> I guess the main thing I wanted to ask or tell you is this. After Charlie talked to Daddy last night he said he thought that you + Daddy both regretted my marrying him, especially since it is his fault that I have to drop out of school. I can't make him believe any different, so it is up to you. I know you are disappointed in my having to quit school, but you also know that if at all possible I will finish sooner or later. It is true that if we hadn't gotten married I would still be free as a bird and be able to finish

Wednesday
Morning

Dear Mother & Daddy,

Sure was good to talk to you both last night even if we did have had news.

I don't really know what I want to say. Charlie was upset all day yesterday and I guess I was too. We really aren't disappointed with the way things worked out because it was really just fate. Charlie is still going to be able to take the re-exams even if we are in North Carolina by correspondance. Then he will have a 1.4 average and above what is necessary. He is going to take 30 hours of correspondance and try to get out of serving this extension until '66. We have figured out that we can still come out ahead because now he can finish in the corp and still graduate from Texas

Kathy's Valentine's Day 1963 letter to her parents, explaining that she was dropping out of UT and accompanying her husband to Camp Lejeune in North Carolina. The letter also included her official withdrawal slip. Private archive of Nelson Leissner.

school, but then also I wouldn't have that big lovable lug for a husband. I love him very much and I think he is and always will be a wonderful husband + someday father. I feel sure that both of you feel the same way even if you are disappointed and mad at him right now. Believe me he realizes his mistake more than anyone and knows just as well how much work lies ahead. I hope you will consider all this and make him feel that he's not considered the biggest louse in the world.[25]

Kathy urged her parents to come and visit—"if you can! next weekend!" Signed "with all my love," Kathy ended with her name only. She enclosed the somber white document indicating she had already withdrawn from UT. No similar record for her husband was included.[26]

After all she had done to improve her grades the previous summer and her first semester as a married woman, Kathy was now leaving Texas not because of her own lack of achievement, but because of Charlie. The letter emphasized her judgment and agency even as she made a plea on his behalf. I can handle it, she seemed to say. I can make it work, and the marriage will get better.

But Kathy would soon find herself more isolated than ever. Whatever she had confided to her mother about those first, early days as Mrs. Whitman, she was going to face more of the same, and much worse.

Mapping an Escape

WITHIN TWO WEEKS OF KATHY'S VALENTINE'S Day letter, the Corvair and trailer were loaded up and the couple was on the move again. On the way to Camp Lejeune in North Carolina, they took a southern detour through Florida to visit with the Whitmans for several days. As much as Kathy was determined to make the best of this abrupt personal sacrifice, she also had much reason to dread returning to visit the in-laws who had already stirred such confusion.

Kathy mailed her first letter to Texas from Lake Worth on March 1, 1963, reporting that she and Charlie had just purchased all new tires: "Now we don't have to worry about having a flat every 10 miles. We were real lucky on the trip to Fla." While Pat seemed to be doing much better, stress in the Whitman home felt inescapable. Despite earlier reports that the family dog, Frosty, had finally learned to sit up and shake hands, Kathy observed that he was actually "mean as the devil," a dynamic that oddly didn't bother the male inhabitants of the home: "Mom doesn't much care for him but the rest of the family is crazy about him. He picks on their other dog, 'Lady,' something awful but she's so old she doesn't have any teeth and can't bite back." A respiratory infection had afflicted the whole family. Kathy wrote, "Everybody here has a sore throat and cold including me."[1]

Collective illness did not slow the family down any, except that it subdued conflicts. "Everyone is getting along remarkably well," Kathy observed, "(probably because they're sick)!" She and Charlie went on outings with his family, although most brought disappointment or stress rather than pleasure. They bet on the dog races with his parents ("We had a good time but only cleared about $1.00") and went to the beach with his brothers ("John got bitten by a Man-o-War. It hurt real bad so Pat brought him home"). For some reason, the couple also shopped for trailers with Charlie's dad. "I don't think I'd like living in a trailer any way you look at it," Kathy wrote. "They were really pretty but you just feel too closed in." More discouragement arrived when the base denied Charlie's request for living quarters: "[I]t was just another kick in the rear. . . . At least we know now that we definitely don't have a place on the base." Kathy did not hold back her feelings about the whole environment: "We have beautiful weather here, but I still can't stand Fla."[2]

On top of everything else, Kathy had missed a period, and she openly shared mixed feelings with her mother. On the one hand, she wrote, "Better cross your fingers cause if something doesn't give in the next few days you ought to be a Grandmother around Nov." She went on, "I still haven't started and if I don't by the time we get to Camp Lejeune I'm going to the Doctor + check. It's probably nothing but Charlie's about to have a fit and a half. That's all we need right now!" Two days later, writing on "Sunday afternoon, that lonely part of the week," Kathy reported that despite her desire to wait and visit a doctor the following month if necessary, she had been taken to the Whitmans' physician. "I got a shot Friday and some pills to clear my nose," she wrote. "The doctor gave me an exam and said he couldn't tell why I hadn't started but that I definitely wasn't pregnant. He said I was probably just off schedule because of the moving and all." She underscored the contrast in her own reaction compared to Charlie's. "Needless to say that husband of mine is disappointed and I'm relieved!"[3]

She was indeed lucky. In the coming weeks it would be hard enough dealing with her husband's pressure and violent temper without the complication of pregnancy, and there would be no one to intervene—no family nearby, no police to call. In fact, for the next several months, she would have no telephone.

IN TEXAS KATHY HAD KNOWN FARM and city life, but she knew nothing about residing near a giant military base. Once a quiet rural community along North Carolina's New River in Onslow County, Jacksonville was located due north of eleven thousand acres identified in 1939 as ideal for a massive amphibious military training facility. Congress approved the land allocation for the new base in 1941, quickly confiscating farms, tobacco barns, and homes, displacing more than seven hundred families—a second wave of displacement following the eighteenth- and nineteenth-century relocations of Native American populations. As World War II raged through Europe, construction on Camp Lejeune was swift, and Jacksonville became a military boomtown, its population quickly overwhelming available resources and housing. From 873 residents in 1940, the town grew to a population of 3,960 residents in 1950 and over 13,000 thousand in

1960, two years before Kathy and Charlie arrived. Resentments ebbed and flowed between civilians and the military men who vastly outnumbered the locals.[4]

The night the couple drove into Jacksonville, Kathy was exhausted. They had traveled straight through from Florida for ten hours, first taking a drive past the main gate of the base and then finding a motel. The next day she and Charlie rented a small furnished apartment at 111C Morton Avenue, where they settled in quickly. Charlie went for maneuvers three days a week, leaving Kathy to fend for herself Tuesday through Thursday. She had gone from being surrounded by Whitmans to being surrounded by strangers in a place that had rearranged its entire landscape and economy around the needs of the military. Local tensions had a sordid side, as well. The week of Kathy's arrival, the city council was engaged in an ongoing battle as the *Daily News* reported likely imminent closures of two "near beer" establishments downtown—the Beachcomber and Belmont Recreation Center—following the conviction of a local man for "prostitution and assignation" in the area. The mayor compared his rationale for the clampdown to surgical intervention to stop the spread of cancer. Meanwhile, chemical pollutants ("volatile organic compounds") in drinking water both on and near Lejeune went undetected for almost forty years, quietly poisoning servicemen and their families.[5]

On this disorienting Atlantic frontier thirteen hundred miles from home, Kathy began her job hunt and cheered up her latest humble living quarters, writing nine detailed letters to her family between March 9 and March 30, four of them addressed directly to her mother. She composed many letters on the paper that came most quickly to hand: her husband's new USMC stationery, embossed in gold foil at the top center of the page. Kathy's first message captured her dreary initial impressions:

I guess I'll start with the town. It is terribly dirty and
all Marines. The base is huge and the town just sort
of runs around it. . . . The commissary is just one big
barn. They don't even bother taking the groc. out of
the boxes. The PX is just a big dept. store and it is
pretty nice. . . . All you can say for our apartment is
that there aren't any holes in the walls. . . . We have
to pay $80 rent and I believe we must have one of
the nicest of all the accommodations even though it
is poor. . . . The complete perimeter is cement blocks
unfinished brown on the inside and the partitions are
varnished plywood. I really can't tell what color the
furniture is because it is so dirty. We think it's what
Charlie calls *shit* brindle brown! I have to get some
furniture shampoo and then I'll tell you what color it
is. . . . Mother, I'm not exaggerating—one out of every
3 women I've seen is pregnant. Both women on our
left and right in the apt's are very much so.[6]

In Austin Kathy's social circle had been baked in to university life. Even as a married student, she had her own classes,
friends, and professors. In Jacksonville she had to start over
among neighbors whose lives had taken different trajecto-
ries from hers.

After Charlie left the first time for field exercises, Kathy
reflected on the demands of his assignment as well as the
tension at the base. She hated being alone, and just five
months after the Cuban Missile Crisis had frayed American
nerves, fear of conflict hung in the air:

Charlie has been placed in the 2nd Batt. 2nd
Marines. In other words, he is in the fighting Marine
ranks. Things are really hot on the base and especially this outfit. They seem to think something is

going to break in Cuba and they will be the first to go. This wouldn't be so bad except that on top of being placed in 2nd Marines his 1st Sergeant thought he was so sharp and had such a good record, he placed him in the best, most gung-ho company. To top that off, the Sergeant Major put him in the charge of the machine gun squad. Mother, do you know that the life expectancy of a machine gunman is exactly 6 sec. after the 1st shot of the battle. That's the first thing you knock out, automatic weapons. Poor baby, he doesn't know anything about machine guns and they gave him a big technical book on them, he now calls his Bible.[7]

Kathy's first effort to locate employment on the base did not pan out when she failed a typing test. Observing how Charlie had struck up old military acquaintances again, Kathy decided to try her odds in the civilian setting downtown. "I'm beginning to learn my way around Jacksonville and the base," she wrote. "Charlie has seen several guys from Cuba in fact we are having a couple over for dinner. However, I haven't met one single person. I'm going to see if I can find a job in Jacksonville tomorrow. I'll only take a job off base if it's real good. Salaries on base are much better than in Jacksonville normally."[8]

For six weeks, in addition to applying for jobs, Kathy spent hours cleaning the apartment as well as making creative meals with an oven that was not ideal. (Among new recipes she attempted were lasagna—"I'll probably make a complete flop but I'm going to try"—and angel food cake.) She reported other choices, including setting up their bank account, with a sense of accomplishment and aspiration: "I feel real proud of myself. . . . I applied at a real big modern drug store and I'm hoping I can get on behind the cosmetic counter if I don't get on at the base."⁹

Daily rituals, even with her dry humor, seemed endlessly purgatorial. "[I]t seems that we have been here for a year already," Kathy wrote. "The days go by so slowly." She filled out fourteen job applications to no avail. The apartment floor was impossible to keep clean. "I have to scrape every little square with a knife. I've done about 10 squares and my arms are about to drop off. Do you know of anything that will take old old old wax off?" she wrote. "I'm going to try to use some ammonia and see if that won't loosen the stuff." Homemaking seemed overlaid with frustration, even for the sewing projects she usually enjoyed. "It's taking me forever to put the rick-rack on that dress," Kathy wrote. "I was working furiously . . . to finish [it] by tomorrow night and then I realized we haven't the money to buy the little patent leather belt I want to wear with it, so I guess I can slow down. I hate to disappoint Charlie, cause he bet me I wouldn't have it done." Some of her cooking tricks backfired, as when she tried a new method for making pancakes. "I was fixing them in a shaker instead of dirtying up my mixer," she explained. "I was shaking it like mad + the top came off and I had pancake batter all over the kitchen, myself, + all in my hair." She would not describe how Charlie cruelly picked on her in the kitchen.¹⁰

The Jacksonville washateria she liked ("everything is real clean and they have dry cleaning units, TV, free starch sink, 3 different kinds of washers, and 17 dryers") also happened to be a good location for composing letters: "I'm writing you on the back of a box of Cheer!" She seemed to be on perpetual laundry duty for Charlie, describing with some amusement how she starched, dyed, and ironed his underwear: "[H]e has inspection Friday and his underwear will look better laying out on his bunk if they are all ironed. Pretty funny! A couple of ladies looked at me like I was an idiot but I just kept on starching." She rose at five a.m. to fix his breakfast before departure on Tuesday mornings, made special suppers Thursday evenings when he returned, and spit-shined his boots in preparation for Friday inspections ("cause I promised I would if I didn't have anything else to do").

On the surface Kathy conformed to her wifely role, but she hinted at serious problems. One evening, for example, she downplayed Charlie's odd behavior while at the same time documenting it. Upon late return from work, he forced her into a strange activity: "[He] told me to put on one of his utility shirts and come in the kitchen. He had taken the mattress off the spare bed and put the kitchen table and chairs in the living room. Then he proceeded to show me all the new judo holds he had learned that day. I don't know why he thinks I need to know judo! I was so worn out I was in bed by 9:00." Such bizarre self-defense "lessons" would prove useless when Charlie struck her, as on one occasion in the Corvair when he injured her mouth.[11]

Kathy had dropped out of college for Charlie. She had vouched for him. He was not supposed to be laying hands on her. This unacceptable reality, underneath all obvious and rational explanations soon to be offered, would be a primary motivation for returning to Texas.

KATHY ACQUAINTED HERSELF QUICKLY WITH FAMILIES nearby. By the first week of April, she provided a rundown about three couples she had come to know the best, complete with names and ages of children. Most residents Kathy met had military connections, and the men came and went as duty (or bad habits) called, leaving wives or girlfriends to manage alone. Kathy shared limited leisure time by drinking "a glass of kool-aid" with a neighbor on warm afternoons, and she assisted with babysitting and childcare. Kathy even rolled a new friend's hair so she could look nice for her husband's special birthday dinner.[12]

As a recurring theme, Kathy expressed how surrounded she felt by pregnant women ("I'm really out of style! . . . This is the first town I've seen that has more maternity shops than dress shops! Ha!"), but she respected more than envied the challenges that real mothers faced day-to-day. Of one woman raising two little boys (at five and six years old, already "the terrors of the neighborhood") with her husband away in Knoxville, Kathy wrote, "The lady next door to me is a wonder. She had a baby that died during birth 4 days ago and she's out washing the car this morning. I don't know how she does it." When one of her boys "busted his mouth real bad," she wrote, "I had to rush him to the base hospital." Ten days later, the same woman began hemorrhaging in the middle of the night, so Kathy and Charlie rushed her to the base hospital. The next day, Kathy went alone to meet the woman's husband at the bus station. "He is a real *!* and not worth a plug nickel!" she wrote. "I sure feel sorry for [her]." Later, with another neighbor, she took the woman's boys to school and delivered personal belongings to the hospital.[13]

Emergency response in this location clearly depended on shared knowledge and cooperation among neighbors, especially the women. Charlie prevented the installation of a telephone, thus restricting direct lines of communication with family or anyone else. Kathy offered a neighbor's phone number and a contact number at Camp Lejeune to her parents "only for emergency," and tried to coordinate any conversations in advance, efforts further complicated by lag time between letters and the time zone difference.

Frances's letters were Kathy's lifeline that spring, along with other messages from aunts, uncles, and Grandma

("Mama") Leissner. With her usual chatty style, Frances kept Kathy up-to-date with Needville happenings: a day trip to Huntsville, a band boosters meeting to plan the annual banquet, a hypochondriac friend (who "can be practically dead with a rare ailment one day and well enough to go bowling, or card playing, or to dinner, whenever the occasion arises!"), a cousin's entrance into the Peace Corps, a dreadful teachers' meeting, and a high school classmate of Kathy's who was due to give birth any day.

Frances also sprinkled letters with details about Kathy's brothers and father. Ray had recently "made the highest grade in his class on a Science test—aren't you proud?" and was going to the rodeo with a friend. Nelson helped to decorate a friend's birthday cake, stayed out past 11:30 p.m. to catch a production of *South Pacific* at Wharton Junior College, and gave Frances rides home from her teaching job. Kathy's father was frustrated with a loaded truck that barely made it home ("It looked like *The Grapes of Wrath*," Frances wrote. "Ha!"), and he promised to write a letter. Frances also conveyed well-wishes from many neighbors, who "all send their love." She enclosed copies of the *Gulf Coast Tribune*, a poem from Ray, and batches of family snapshots.[14]

Recalling all too vividly the unhappiness her daughter had confided two months earlier, Frances offered validation at every turn. "Have you met anyone you can talk to?" she wrote. "The apartment sounds like a madhouse with all those children—sounds like an excellent location for a day nursery." Frances also addressed Charlie directly: "[I]f you have to be a fighting Marine, I'm sure you'll be a credit to the Corps. I can't think of a thing to say that doesn't sound trite or stupid. You know darn well that we are thinking of you constantly and pray you come back to us when this hitch is over. You both have a hard lot—I know Kathy is terribly lonely when you are on maneuvers." She also gently nudged against Kathy's domestic insecurities, reminding her that the family enjoyed her delicious cooking. "How did the lasagna turn out?" she asked. "I'll bet it was good! Nelson keeps wanting me to make your beef stroganoff—but I haven't tried it yet."[15]

Alarmed by the couple's limited phone access, Frances did not mask her exasperation at Kathy's vague explanations. Frances spoke directly on this point:

> By the way, *Mrs. Whitman*, you have ruffled my feelings! In fact, if I could get my hands on you, I would use my plastic fly swatter! Since when do I have to write you to call me! Don't you stupid people know that we would pay for a phone call, any *time*, any *place*, and for any *reason*—if only to hear your voices? In fact, if you want to do me a favor you'll get a telephone and I'll send you the money. . . . I think that's one of the main reasons I worry about you—I don't know how to call you. If you don't call next week I shall send the FBI around or report you to the NAACP (or whatever the initials are!).

Softening, Frances concluded by urging Kathy to keep writing ("it takes 3 days to get them by air mail") and added a gentle postscript: "Are there any nice stores in Jacksonville— Could you get some curtains there or could I send you some? What can you use—just let me know."[16]

Although Charlie's wages as a corporal were not clear, in Jacksonville, as in Austin, he maintained veto authority over the couple's budgetary priorities. Furthermore, Kathy reported that he had essentially laid claim to eighty percent of any income she would bring in once she landed a job.

"Charlie said I could have 20% . . . to spend on anything I want," she wrote, later stating that "maybe" they could afford a phone if she brought in a paycheck.[17]

With her husband actively controlling access to money as well as communications, Kathy expressed resistance where she could. After one phone call coordinated at the end of March, she wrote to Frances, "Ray and Nelson sounded real good but I didn't get to talk to Daddy as much as I would have liked to. That's kinda dumb to say though, cause I didn't get to talk to anyone as long as I'd have liked to." Two weeks later, after saying how much she appreciated the latest long letter from her mother, Kathy wrote, "It's funny, I've got so much to ask and say to Nelson, I don't know where to start. I feel like I'm being cheated out of my little brothers growing up." She praised Ray for his recent high scores and encouraged Nelson not to be discouraged that he had missed an A by one point on a test. "I always seemed to come out like that too," she wrote. "It's disgusting true, but it's still a good grade." She worried about her father "because he never sounds very happy. Is he just worried about how long we talk or is he not feeling well?"[18]

Kathy desperately wanted to return to Texas. Frances raised the subject in mid-March as part of a contingency scenario. As usual, while she addressed her daughter and son-in-law in the same letter on different points, she knew full well that both would have access to the entire text. Speaking to Kathy in a middle segment, she suggested an idea in the event of Charlie's deployment. "I'm sure I can pay your 'postage' by air," Frances wrote. "I don't see why you would need to stay there by yourself and you could keep the apartment if you wanted to—you wouldn't have any expenses here and I don't imagine you'll get a job that couldn't be taken leave of." She went on, "[O]f course, we'd *rather* have *both* of you but that's impossible. Besides, Daddy isn't getting any younger, you know, and he could use a good rice truck driver! And you might as well be miserable here as in North Carolina."[19]

A few days later Kathy confided to Frances that Charlie found the move threatening. "We have decided that unless he goes out of the country for over 6 mo., I'm going to stay here," she wrote, suggesting that her compliance was reluctant. "He has some fobia about me going home so to save the marriage I guess I'll stay." The following week, Kathy suggested that she might be able to reason with her husband if she focused on economics. "Charlie definitely doesn't want me to [come home], but mabe I can change his mind," she wrote. "If I could show him that it would be better if I did (financially that is)."[20] She clearly sought a rationale to cloak any motivation that might provoke him.

The couple's finances continued to strain as Kathy waited to hear about applications. She persisted at every turn, taking the Civil Service exam and applying for bank teller and sales positions. To improve her chances, she requested letters of reference from back home. She even considered night school at East Carolina College to study nursing, though based on Charlie's budgetary restrictions, she would have needed a job to afford the fees. Roadblocks appeared outside her marriage, too. After answering "a real promising ad in the paper" for a job that required no experience, she learned that the employer openly discriminated against married women. "They want a single girl because they have to train you and they have had too many experiences of married women getting pregnant and quitting," Kathy explained to her mother. "I guess you can't blame them but boy, it sure would have been nice. I did everything but tell them I was taking *Enovid*!"[21]

On March 31, in his first letter to Kathy's parents since December, Charlie reported he had retaken some exams for possible reinstatement at UT, adding that in the meantime he was going to apply to take a correspondence course in government. His main focus, however, was that Kathy had not yet secured a job. By contrast, even with his complicated schedule of obligations at Lejeune, Charlie volunteered that he had no trouble getting an offer: $35 for six days a week as a nightclub bouncer, from seven p.m. to eleven p.m. He dangled the prospect with feigned ambivalence, as if anticipating certain disapproval from his in-laws—and as if he could not be bothered to look further for different work. Where would additional money come from to cover their expenses? The pressure fell, once again, on Kathy.[22]

Not long after Charlie's letter about the nightclub job, Kathy asked her parents for a loan. While she had hinted at pinching pennies, she had not yet broken down to request money. She smuggled the information in the deep middle of a long letter sent around Easter. First, she thanked her mother for sending the certified recommendations that she could now include with applications. She stated that she had found common ground with the Protestant base chaplain, Captain Boone, who had come from Texas along with his wife. Her comments suggest that she had sought some counsel. "He is Baptist and is worried about Charlie + I being of different faiths," she wrote. After adding the latest updates about job inquiries, Kathy laid out the intricate background— three long paragraphs—for what could have been a straightforward ask.

Weeks before, on their way to Jacksonville, she and Charlie had gotten into an accident in South Carolina near a road construction site. ("The trailer again!" she wrote, calling back to their posthoneymoon calamity.) She offered a play-by-play of the domino effect among vehicles: "Charlie had to take the car off the road into the ditch to keep from slamming into the panel truck and then he dodged one of the dump trucks but by the time we reached the second dump truck the trailer was swinging us all over the place and we slammed underneath the rear of the truck. We weren't even scratched but the car looked bad." Notably, Kathy's downplay of the trauma does not square with her repetition of the word "slamming" and other drastic physical descriptions. ("[T]he truck mashed the front RH fender + the trailer squashed the rear left.")

Anticipating her parents' questions, Kathy continued. "We didn't tell anyone because you were doing enough worrying about us. Needless to say it put us in a tight bind for funds, in fact we are still feeling it." The total damages were $250, with all but $50 covered by insurance. Kathy laid out the financial premise but seemed hesitant or embarrassed to clarify an explicit amount of need. Even more sadly, her request for money seemed tied to a position she had not yet secured: "When I do get [a job], and if it's in a bank or office, I may have to borrow some money from you, if I can, to get some clothes until my first paycheck. I don't have anything for warm weather and I'll need something to get me started." Kathy avoided blaming Charlie, but her letter illustrated how alone she felt in her responsibility to manage hazards and economic stress.[23]

Her sustained efforts to bring in money finally bore fruit in mid-April. At first, Kathy had two job offers: one of them, behind the cosmetic counter at Howard's Drug Store, would pay $40 per week for a forty-eight-hour work week—roughly half the hourly rate Charlie had been offered as a bouncer. "Pay down here is terrible!" Kathy repeated. Then a third offer came from Liberal Credit in downtown Jacksonville ("the biggest pawn shop in town"), and she accepted that job—her first ever paid position—where she would "type statements and contracts." She was relieved to have found work, reporting her impression that Liberal Credit paid better wages than other off-base establishments. But her hours were also extreme, from noon to ten p.m. five days a week including Saturday. After taxes, her first paycheck cleared only "a flying $33 a week." Her husband did not assist with chores at home, and Kathy ended one letter summing up the doubleness of her labor: "I'm trying to get all my housework done before I start work."[24]

Kathy highlighted modest enjoyable activities on weekends and some evenings, at one point interjecting, as if to answer a lingering question, "Charlie and I have been getting along just fine." He had introduced her to the Non-Commissioned Officers (NCO) Club ("had a real good dance band"), and they hosted other couples for occasional dinners at their apartment. They took a day trip to Wilmington for the Azalea Festival, where they faced a deluge of traffic and arrived too late for the parade, instead catching a matinee of *To Kill a Mockingbird*. ("Don't miss that movie," she wrote.) Theaters provided reliably affordable entertainment, sometimes at the local drive-in that was free for military families. Kathy offered enthusiastic recommendations for lighter new releases, such as *My Six Loves* and *The Courtship of Eddie's Father*, but her favorite was the reprise of *Giant*, starring Elizabeth Taylor, Rock Hudson, and James Dean, a film that captured her lingering homesickness for Texas.[25]

From his desk on base duty one night while Kathy was working, Charlie reported to the Leissners about her first paycheck and thanked them for the loan they had apparently sent, as if he had been the one who requested it. "Her clothes sure do look good," he wrote, "even if I did pick them out myself." He mentioned that he and Kathy hardly saw each other due to their work schedules. He also asked Frances to send four textbooks he had left in Needville since he was considering enrolling in a class.[26]

Paid employment bolstered Kathy's confidence despite her husband's controlling paternalism. She had not been too proud to work in a pawn shop, but she informed her parents that she sought an even better position, especially as her results on the Civil Service exam came in with a high score of 93.3. She applied to operate a billing machine for an office at Camp Lejeune's Air Facility as well as a position at the telephone company. Of the latter, she knew any training as a phone operator would be portable, serving her well for possible employment elsewhere. She emphasized, "I really wouldn't mind having to quit to come home to Texas!"[27]

Working at Liberal Credit meant long hours of easy but monotonous labor, and the location of the shop, the center of Court Street, mattered a great deal considering Kathy's day-to-night schedule. She traveled to work on her own—by car or bus—arriving by noon and leaving after ten p.m. Charlie would not be able to drive her every day, and at the time, Court Street was not an ideal location for a young woman after dark. When the discount clothing stores, shoe repair shops, and cafés closed to local family business for the day, the atmosphere was dominated by Marines who flooded in from the base by busloads (nicknamed the "Vomit Comet") to blow off steam in the pool halls, tattoo parlors, and bars. There were plenty of striptease clubs—and one club Charlie frequented, Jazzland, dominated a corner intersection steps away from Liberal Credit. Kathy had an explicit dislike for the place. She was not squeamish or moralistic, occasionally indulging her husband's desire to take sexy Polaroids in the privacy of their apartment, but the divey scene did not sit comfortably with her. Well-aware of Charlie's appreciation for *Playboy*, she tolerated but did not enjoy seeing sex as simply another commodity.[28]

Kathy worked at Liberal Credit for roughly one month. Although she got along fine with her immediate supervisor— a woman who was credit manager—as well as the establishment owner, Kathy disliked another manager who barely

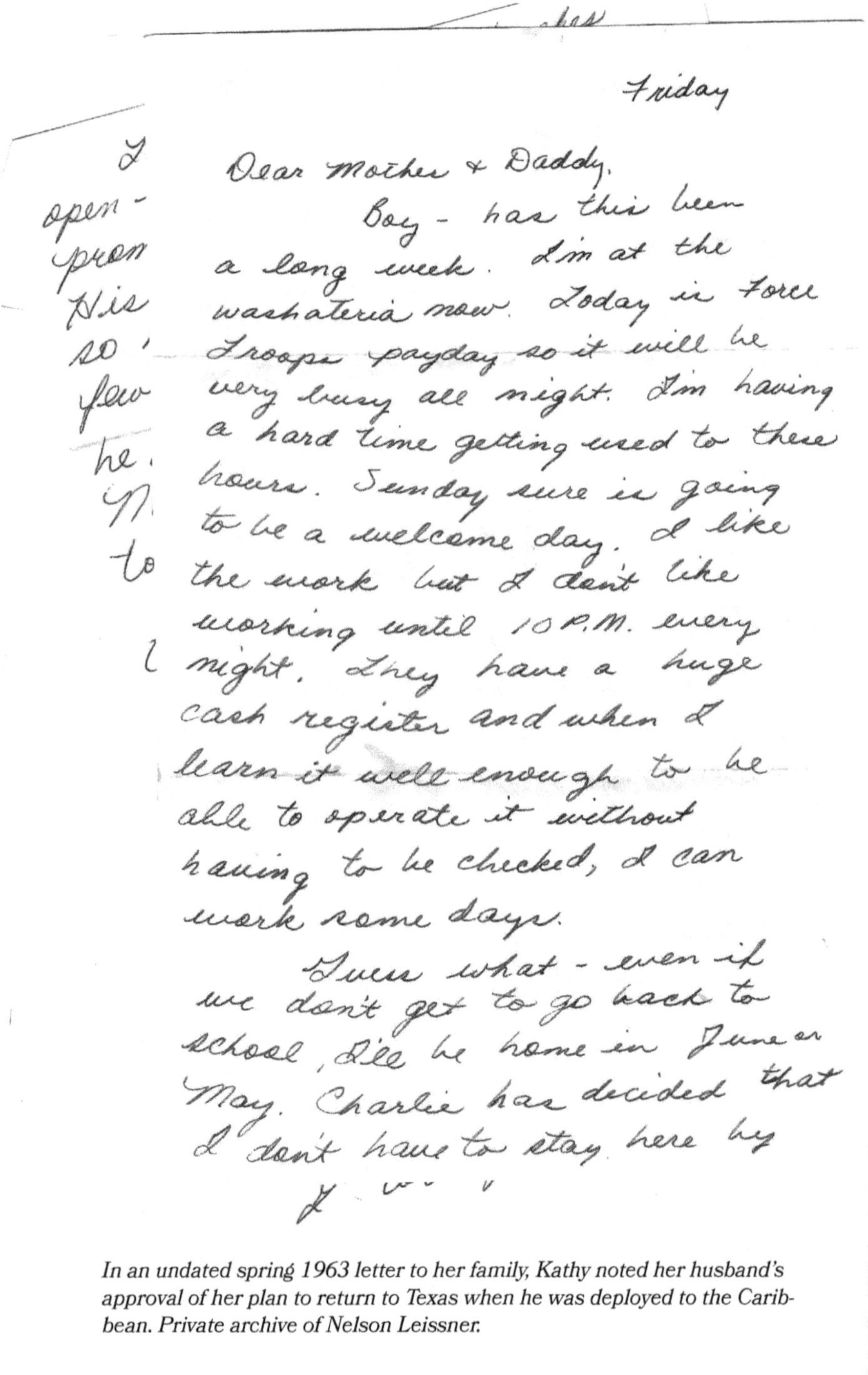

Friday

Dear Mother & Daddy,

Boy - has this been a long week. I'm at the washateria now. Today is Fort Troops payday so it will be very busy all night. I'm having a hard time getting used to these hours. Sunday sure is going to be a welcome day. I like the work but I don't like working until 10 P.M. every night. They have a huge cash register and when I learn it well enough to be able to operate it without having to be checked, I can work some days.

Guess what - even if we don't get to go back to school, I'll be home in June or May. Charlie has decided that I don't have to stay here by

[margin notes, partially legible:] I open- prow His so' few he. n. to l

In an undated spring 1963 letter to her family, Kathy noted her husband's approval of her plan to return to Texas when he was deployed to the Caribbean. Private archive of Nelson Leissner.

spoke to her. She also admitted a personality conflict with a coworker. "I don't get along at all with one of the girls, and when we work at night by ourselves it is lovely," she wrote sarcastically. In mid-May, Kathy gave notice, but this choice gave her a rude awakening about how workers were treated if they dared to seek better opportunities. "[T]hey have a very poor business policy of firing any girl who gave notice," she wrote. "I had heard this from several girls in the office, but I decided I would be considerate and give notice instead of just walking out on them. . . . That's what I get for being fair with them!"[29]

What happened to other women had happened to Kathy, too, and it is compelling that she acknowledged their warnings. Just as the application process had taught her something about hiring discrimination, here she had learned how women could be "taught a lesson" for moving on. Even a good worker at a low-wage job was disposable—and could be punished—if she dared to seek a better opportunity. The analogy to marriage should not be lost. How could she change her pathway with Charlie without drawing his retribution?

As she established a more confident routine, new friendships (or at least alliances) allowed her to feel socially valuable. Fairly regular, if scheduled, phone calls were now interspersed among reciprocal letters, and Kathy calculated the logistics of a return to Texas. She hatched the plan in a letter to Frances, even allowing room for deception as part of the necessary strategy. "First of all," Kathy wrote, "I can complete the 6 weeks training period at the telephone company [here] and then tell them you're sick or something so when I come back they will still give me a job." Kathy brainstormed options for living at home and taking classes affordably at Wharton, adding that she could return to Jacksonville in September when Charlie's anticipated deployment would end—clearly an inducement to head off his objections.[30]

There is no written record of Frances's response to this message. In fact, Frances's last letters that spring are dated at the end of March, including one message where she repeated her offer to "foot the bill" for a phone.[31] None of her letters survived from the next four months—from April through early July. This gap matters not simply because it was Kathy's habit to save them, but because returning to Texas was her heightened focus. Kathy acknowledged a steady stream of letters as well as packages from her mother and other family members, referring to family pictures, a package of books and candy, even an Easter basket. It is perhaps telling that the record of Frances's voice is muffled at this moment.

As her job took her into Jacksonville for stretches of time starting in April, Kathy likely carried letters in her purse to enjoy during breaks. Like her mother, she frequently started and finished letters in locations other than home, whether at the washateria or the Chevy repair shop or the office. "It seems as though I carry a box of stationery with me everywhere I go," she said. "I end up writing you in the most out-of-the-way places."[32] It would make sense for the occasional letter to be lost due to her increased mobility and divided concentration. Kathy may have kept these letters closer to herself due to any controversy their content might stir with her husband. But also, for several days a week, Charlie was home alone when Kathy was working. It would not have been out of character for him to take these letters as his own—"carelessly" misplacing them to sow confusion and disorient Kathy—a textbook maneuver that could have been lifted directly from the film *Gaslight*.[33]

Regardless of how Frances's letters went missing, the record demonstrates that as the spring wore on, Charlie intruded very deliberately upon Kathy's communication with her family. On multiple occasions starting in May, he would triangulate messages inside letters and through phone calls, not in acts of collaboration or coauthorship, but in deliberate attempts to manipulate Kathy. Despite his intrusions, Kathy's social intelligence, her bond with Frances, and new training as a phone operator enabled her to identify interruptions and reconnect the proper circuits.

CARIBBEAN TURMOIL—A BRUTAL MASSACRE OF Haitian civilians in late April and ongoing conflict between Haiti's then-dictator Francois "Papa Doc" Duvalier and the Dominican Republic—amplified Kathy's stress as a military spouse. Her twentieth birthday had not yet arrived, but the previous six months had taken a heavy toll. Reflecting on her mother's news about a friend entering business college, Kathy wrote, "Golly, I sure do feel old. It just seems like yesterday that we were graduating."[34] In early May, just days before she started as a phone operator, she was on heightened alert. In two long letters—one to Frances, another to both her parents—she did her best to capture her impressions.

The first letter included segments written on two different days. The Thursday segment, the longer of the two, included the most frantic details:

> Tues. night about 12 o'clock I was dead to the world
> and the MP's came banging on my door with an
> emergency message for me to call Charlie's exten-
> sion on the base. I was so scared I just threw on a
> housecoat, grabbed the car keys + took out for the
> corner phone booth only to get there + realize I'd for-
> gotten a dime. When I finally got to the base, Charlie
> was on the phone + said for me to come pick ~~me~~ him
> up + he wouldn't tell me what was wrong. I almost
> killed myself getting to the base + was a nervous

wreck when I did get there. I imagined everything in the world that could have happened to you + Daddy + the boys. Well, when I got to the barracks I knew what was wrong before I even saw Charlie. His whole battalion had been called out of the field off a regimental problem. They are on air alert for Haiti and were being shipped out. I had to bring Charlie home to pack his seabag and he had to be back at 6 o'clock Thursday morning and didn't know when exactly they were leaving.

Kathy's narration captured how she was jolted between locations—and sources of information—within the space of several hours, her stress compounded by lack of access to a phone. She added the infuriating contrast of Charlie blithely "popp[ing] in" to her workplace after this harrowing night with a casual update that the ship-out had been delayed. By the end of the letter, Kathy had absolutely determined to return to Texas "in June." Even a curse word crept in: "If Charlie is gone do you think Nelson could come down here and help me. I would have to pull a damn trailer and take everything back to Texas + I sure don't want to take that trip alone."[35]

Two days later Kathy found herself on alert outside the barracks again. This time she wrote with her stationery box propped on the steering wheel, watching in real time as Charlie's company piled into a convoy of trucks braced for possible deployment to Haiti. Her "on the spot account" recognized the predicament she shared with other waiting wives, and her voice in this letter is fascinating. She interjected several sentences about preparing for work the following week with Carolina Telephone & Telegraph (CT&T). Then she cut right back to resume her report, inserting even more commentary: "The trucks just started up and I zoomed out to get behind them and all they did was drive around right back into the same parking places they have been in all day: *Only* in the Marine Corp could things like this happen. . . . Don't you think this letter would make a good novel?" Kathy's clarity about the zig-zaggy events here contrasts sharply with her frantic account the previous night, including even an awareness of her authorial impulses. Her postscript emphasized the agency she was claiming: "I stayed out here until about 11:00 and then decided to go home + then I came back again this morning." Here, as elsewhere, she tried to insert choice into chaos.[36]

WITHIN DAYS, AS VARIABLES CONTINUED TO shift—among them, Charlie's likely deployment date and his possible (though unlikely) reinstatement into the UT scholarship program—Kathy began training for CT&T, which at the time served most of eastern North Carolina. Direct dialing in households was steadily becoming the norm in larger cities, but operators remained responsible for aiding with person-to-person calls, collect calls, calls from pay phones or calls using credit cards, calls from areas where direct dialing was not yet in place, and even emergency dispatch. In a field where and at a time when nearly all operators industry-wide were young white women, Kathy learned how to operate a switchboard with grace, calm, and a thick skin.[37]

The work was challenging. Customers could be confused, impatient, distressed, or even angry. Occasionally, callers treated the women on the line as a captive audience to flirt with, harass, or insult. In Jacksonville the Marines drove heavy phone traffic when men lined up at pay phones to call their sweethearts, wives, and parents on paydays. Operators learned quickly to distinguish the sound of a quarter from that of a dime or a nickel in coin slots.[38] Starting with simple

In Jacksonville, North Carolina, Kathy received her initial training as an operator to work at a switchboard much like this one. Steve Schapiro/Corbis Premium Historical via Getty Images.

tests of hearing and pronunciation, the training progressed to switchboard simulations—all the systems of lights, cords, plugs, and keys—and concluded with one's own closely monitored first shifts at the board. Kathy would later write about how easy it was to break nails on key pulsing machines.[39]

Not surprisingly, the instructor approved of Kathy's performance. By mid-June, as her training concluded, she updated her parents. "They have decided to break me in right away with the 9 o'clock rates after 9 o'clock until 12 o'clock," she said, as late evenings with slower traffic made it easier for new operators to learn. As intended, however, she wrote two weeks later from the washateria that she had stuck with her plan: "I told my boss today that I was quitting work at the telephone co. and [she] was none too happy about the whole deal as the telephone co. did spend a pretty penny on me in training." She added, "I work every night until the 4th of July."[40]

Kathy's calculated Independence Day departure understandably annoyed her new boss, but she was not fired as she had been at Liberal Credit. Leaving the phone company would be more straightforward than her imminent separation from Charlie, who was outwardly supportive of Kathy's return to Texas but had been running interference since she started her job at CT&T.

KATHY'S MOOD LIFTED CONSIDERABLY DURING HER work as an operator. Responding to her mother's latest batch of photographs, she began one letter with a series of exclamations: "O-o-oo-oo! I'm so proud of you! Those pictures are just beautiful of everybody! I just want to show the whole world my wonderful beautiful family! I love your hair! Wait until you see mine!" A renewed sense of meaning and energy infused her descriptions. The usual frustrations (a storm raining on Charlie's utilities that she had hung out on a line to dry) paled when compared to a picnic she had enjoyed with other families on the base. Sewing felt pleasurable again, and Kathy had made an entire "button-up-and-down shift" in two and a half hours one Saturday night. She was especially pleased that the new dress would go nicely with her latest hair color, Lady Clairol's "champagne toast." She found inspiration in new fabrics and planned new outfits: "red denim + pink + white striped oxford cloth to make a wraparound shirt + blouse." She even seemed relaxed about whether Charlie would be reinstated in the NESEP program at UT. ("[E]verything in the service takes so long to get done because of all the red tape! All we can do is wait!") Kathy had adapted well to the challenges at CT&T: "I like my new job—it's confusing at first but I'll get used to it."[41]

But it was not just the new workplace lifting Kathy's spirits. Going home to Texas had evolved from a hope to a plan, now an open subject with her parents as well as Charlie. With the increasing likelihood that his battalion would be sent to Haiti, Cuba, or possibly the Mediterranean, Kathy did not want to remain behind. The same military system that had justified her husband's pressure to join him in Jacksonville six months earlier now provided her with rhetorical ammunition to resume her education at home, which meant that she could separate safely from her husband without divorcing him. Encouragement from social allies increased the pressure on Charlie to agree. "Everyone we talked to thought it was ridiculous for me to stay," Kathy wrote. "Most wives even with 2 + 3 children go home when their husbands ship out." Among these supporters were wives of the Baptist chaplain and Charlie's captain, who were both returning to Houston temporarily and who invited Kathy to travel with them.[42]

It was certainly uncomplicated logic: if Kathy were going to be living alone anyway, she might as well do so in Texas where she would be closer to family and could resume school. Although on the surface Charlie appeared to accept this reasoning, he simultaneously sought to undermine her confidence as well as her representations of marital consensus. His separate and competing message threads attempted blatant manipulation of Kathy as well as her family. Ultimately, however, his efforts—for now—would fail.

CHARLIE'S TRIANGULATION APPEARS IN THE VISIBLE record during the most serious discussions of Kathy's return. With explicit or assumed consent, Charlie completed three of Kathy's letters dated May 25, June 3, and June 10. Importantly, he addressed the envelopes for the first and the third letters in this batch, suggesting that he easily could add his message, seal the envelope, and mail it without sharing his portion with Kathy. During this period he also arranged at least one phone call to her parents that she did not discover until afterwards. Kathy's last three letters dated in the days leading up to her departure—June 16, June 20, and July 1— together demonstrate that she resisted his interference.

On May 25 Kathy started a letter at home before work. First, she indicated difficulty concentrating. "I've started no less than three letters to you this week," she began. She then informed her parents of the bad news: the commandant of the Marine Corps denied Charlie's request for reinstatement at UT. Kathy did not belabor this development, however, and moved on quickly. "We have decided that I will come home on July 5," she wrote, but her next sentence began with just one word: "Charlie—" The name stood at the beginning of a breakage, an unresolved subject, as if Kathy had been inter-rupted or was offering him an opening.

In this space, Charlie continued the letter, explaining that Kathy had to go to work, then announcing rather redundantly that he was going to finish the letter. He began in a straight-forward manner, explaining his failure to be reinstated (not maintaining a C average for three out of four semesters at UT). He recommended a movie titled *The Ugly American*. He asked his father-in-law about a "claim race" for horses. But then he attempted to pull Kathy's mother into a private confidence, stating that he was trying to "talk his wife into having a baby" because "it sure would be good to be a Daddy," and he asked Frances to discuss it with Kathy. Before fold-ing the letter and addressing the envelope, he also corrected Kathy's heading, adding in the month and date above her day of the week (something he later nagged her about).[43]

The June 3 letter began similarly, starting in Kathy's voice and Charlie adding an addendum. Kathy opened with

a description of how the couple's beach plans were inter-
rupted by rain and how they enjoyed a canasta game with
friends on Friday night. But then Kathy cut to the chase. "I
didn't know Charlie was going to call you the other day," she
wrote. "He told me about it when I got off work." None too
happy that she might be sidelined about travel details, Kathy
offered her own questions and implied that she did not fully
trust her husband as go-between: "Is Nelson going to come
down here on the bus or what? You do understand that I am
not bringing all our stuff home? We can store it here for $.50
a 100 lbs. per month so I'm first bringing my clothes + stuff. I
hate for Nelson to have to come but Charlie doesn't want me
driving by myself and he said you didn't either." Kathy had
already indicated that she was not keen on making the drive
alone, so the function of the last sentence seemed mostly
to underscore that she was fully aware of a conversation in
which she had not participated. She added, "Call or write +
we'll call you to get last minute details on when [Nelson] will
get here." She closed with her usual litany of inquiries about
family and friends and promised to write again the next day.

Charlie still managed to insert a few sentences on the back
of her last page, first gratuitously explaining that he "had" to
tell Kathy about calling them. Rather than apologizing for
not including her, he attempted to sideline her again—as if
she herself was the intruder. Charlie also referred cryptically
to Frances's negative response about his pregnancy-related
message, his pose of self-awareness forced and insincere.
"[A]bout our secret," he wrote, "you are right, but I imagine that I am soft-headed sometimes. We'll just have to wait
until we get out of the corp." Where Kathy had abruptly
cut short her previous letter, this letter she concluded and
signed herself. She also addressed the envelope, suggesting
that she was privy to this stage of communication—likely
with her mother's help—seeking to nip Charlie's approach in
the bud.[44]

Six months earlier, Frances had implored her son-in-law directly, by phone as well as by letter, to treat Kathy as a logically thinking young woman. Frances also remembered well Kathy's pregnancy scare in March and her daughter's relief at a negative result. Charlie continued to underestimate Kathy's intelligence and the bond of mutual respect she had with her family, especially her mother, as he simply retread the same patterns—now with pregnancy as an explicit pressure point.

June 10 brought another letter started by Kathy and completed by her husband, this one much longer. Written on another hot day in the cinderblock apartment with no air conditioning, Kathy's content made up most of the letter, and she somewhat reprised her intercessor role. But in this document she sought to keep the central message clear even as she blurred "I" into "we": "We could not make up our minds about whether to write or call you and then decided that it would be too hard to explain over the phone," she said, as if aware that by telephone her voice would be more easily crowded out of the planning. She proceeded to list all their considerations for her return to Texas, including their timeline of educational goals, finances, Kathy's potential employment, and starting a family. "We have thought it all out," she wrote, "and we're trying to figure every angle as to the good and bad points of the deal." The central question, as Kathy reported it, was not whether she should leave Jacksonville but whether she should go to the University of Houston for summer classes and then whether she would return once Charlie's tour ended. She concluded, "Charlie said to leave him a place to drop you a note," indicating that she was fully aware that he would participate in the message—but also recording that he had demanded it.

In his portion Charlie first focused on the logistics of separation: the cost to store their possessions for eighteen months (a subject she had already explained) and an explicit appeal for the Leissners to pay for her tuition and books. Towards the end of his message, Charlie cast doubt on Kathy's ability to manage on her own, and he suggested that she did not grasp the realities. Again, he invited her parents—through a direct appeal to Frances—to aid him: "I know she can do it scholastically, but I don't know if she is fully aware of the everyday difficulties she will have. Would you and Daddy please write us a sober letter as soon as possible mentioning all the stumbling blocks you can think of and giving us your opinion of the deal." His request for "stumbling blocks" was punctuated as a declaration rather than a question, and he continued with reminders that money would be tight until he got a raise in October, when he expected his rank to increase. Perhaps most galling: in his examples of ongoing bills, he not only referred to their car payment but also to the cost of the sewing machine—his present to Kathy the previous Christmas.[45]

Whether she saw the full content of the June 10 letter or not (Charlie addressed the envelope), Kathy recentered her perspective in all correspondence from that point forward. On June 16 Charlie started rather than finished the letter, composing a single paragraph referring to the latest family phone call and thanking Kathy's father for a letter that had included advice. (This document did not survive.) Charlie's expressions of confidence had a mechanical and patronizing edge. "I am quite sure that Kathy will handle herself and everything so as to make me proud of her," he wrote. "It'll be a hard row to hoe but anything worth having is high priced."

As Kathy's voice took over in the letter, she too referenced the phone call, though her emphasis was much different: "Hello, everybody. It sure was good to talk to you last night, even though I didn't get to say much." She told them she hoped to secure a phone operator job in Texas for the remaining summer months and assured her parents that she would manage money carefully when she reenrolled at UT. Kathy emphasized that she would locate a cheap room with kitchen privileges and would shop for discounted food and toiletries at Bergstrom. There was an undertone of frustration with Charlie again, as she referenced another subject he had preemptively shared by phone: his application to Officer Candidate School (OCS). "We hadn't planned on telling you about the OCS program until something definite happened," she wrote, understandably cautious that Charlie overplayed his hand. Managing her own expectations was one thing, but it was exhausting being married to a man who always pushed the proverbial envelope. "We should know pretty soon about what is happening on that deal," she wrote. "I didn't know Charlie was going to tell you last night."[46]

Kathy composed her final two letters alone, resuming her original pattern of writing outside the apartment, beyond Charlie's supervision. From the beauty parlor at the base for a six-week update of her hair color, Kathy started off a note to Frances, "I'm going through misery to be beautiful again. . . . Right now I have the bleach on, the toner is what hurts." She lamented her inability to get a bathrobe finished in time for Charlie's upcoming birthday and described how they had shopped for his presents—a pair of new tennis shoes and a wallet—the previous weekend. "He had them all picked out before he even told me what he wanted. . . . He's going to be 22 and to hear him talk he's an old man already." Continuing, Kathy spoke frankly about her father-in-law. "We got a telegram from Daddy Whitman yesterday, asking us to call tonight," she wrote. "I'd give anything if I didn't have to talk to them. I know it's going to be one big argument." Trying to make light of her dread, Kathy added, "I have to hold my tounge (how do you sp. tongue!) Ha! Wish me luck!" Kathy focused on the wrinkles she could control, asking Nelson to pack a travel iron.[47]

Charlie did not add any message here, nor in Kathy's final letter on July 1, composed just before she escaped Jacksonville. That same week storefronts and shop windows began to blossom with red, white, and blue advertisements, flags, streamers, and bunting, all in preparation for the Fourth of July festivities downtown, along the New River, and at the base. In the midst of packing up the apartment—preparing for her fifth move in ten months—Kathy reflected on the process from the washateria when Charlie was on shift as duty NCO at Lejeune.

This letter documents the final instance of Kathy's regular ritual in Jacksonville, writing as her clothes spun clean and dry. She started at 9:30 p.m. Friday night, her envelope not postmarked until Monday. "This is the most difficult move we have made yet," Kathy began. "We have to get the things packed that we are going to store, pack things for Charlie to take to Cuba (which knowing Charlie will be half the house), and then the things I'm bringing to Texas. . . . To top it all off, we have to mark all, and I mean all, of Charlie's gear, because he will be using a base laundry now." As she had predicted, the phone conversation with Charlie's family had gone poorly. "Just as I told you the Whitmans spent 45 minutes trying to talk us out of doing this. Their whole point was that they didn't think our marriage would hold up to being apart so much." On this point, however, Kathy stood firm. "That is really the least of our worries because we know it can be done. I'm anxious to start back to school." She thanked Frances for sending university course information, a brochure, and application. Just before she wrapped up ("better put the clothes in the dryer"), Kathy ended with an important request: she needed to know exactly when Nelson would arrive to take her home. Kathy could not find the message where her mother had spelled out all the details. "I lost the letter," she said.[48]

Kathy's last day at the telephone company was Thursday, the Fourth of July. Her coworkers would have been sharing potato salad recipes and gossiping about planned cookouts, dates, or day-trips. Kids around the Morton Avenue apartments would have played with Black Cat firecrackers, smoke bombs, and sparklers along the walkways and in the parking lot. Kathy's new friends would have milled in and out, offering goodbyes and good lucks. Perhaps someone with a batch of brownies wrapped tightly in foil. Or someone saying, "Are you coming back in September?" Likely a wordless embrace from a woman who had seen Kathy blink away tears or reflexively cover her mouth with a hand. Perhaps Kathy bent at the knees to get on eye level, one last smile and hug for two little boys, one with his own scarred lip.

After Kathy's final shift at CT&T, perhaps she and Charlie took time away from the stacked boxes and packed bags for a picnic with their canasta partners. Perhaps they drove alone one last time to the riverfront to watch fireworks from the hood of the car. The annual ritual was eerie: giant sparks filled the sky and fell from far above the glittering water, a beautiful simulation of terrifying bombs no one truly wanted to explode.

Separated and Almost Safe

UNLIKE AFTER HER HONEYMOON, THERE WAS no race to get home. Kathy and Nelson could take turns at the wheel of the Corvair, twisting radio dials for good music across state lines until repeated tunes of summer 1963—Leslie Gore's "It's My Party," the Essex's "Easier Said Than Done"—grew tiresome. The siblings could stop at Stuckey's for a burger, a Coke, or a cigarette and stretch when they felt like it, and they planned an overnight break. Even when they faced a fender bender in Augusta and a flat in rainy Baton Rouge, they didn't have to worry about Charlie's temper at the wheel. "[N]aturally I had to supervise + got my hair soaked," Kathy reported to her husband, framing the latter event in terms of her desire for a new, less expensive hair color treatment. "I was a lovely sight when I got home."[1]

She and Nelson pulled into the Leissners' gravel driveway at 2:30 a.m. Tuesday, July 9. Kathy slept in her bedroom on the south side of the house, the room where she stored her scrapbook and formal gowns from high school, the room where a year ago she had dreamed of a happy marriage. She woke after a few hours to find the kitchen filled with friends. Her mother was babysitting one of the neighbor's children, yet another sweet diversion. ("He looks 5 years old + talks like he's 20! He can tell you the make of every car in the neighborhood.")[2] The familiarly warm and loving environment was a relief, and she spoke to her husband by phone two days after arrival. From that point forward, Kathy's detailed correspondence to Charlie began: seventeen letters in twenty days.

Kathy admitted that she fought back tears "sometime in broad daylight in the oddest places," but she wasted no time feeling sorry for herself. She had doubts from afar about pleasing her husband, even as she underscored that she would trust her own good judgment: "I'm trying so hard to do everything just the way you would want me to. Now that you aren't here to remind me I have got to think for myself."[3]

Kathy enrolled in two summer classes at Wharton Junior College and arranged a carpool with friends. She also secured a new job within two days. When prospects of working for a cotton buyer faded, Kathy applied with the telephone company in nearby Rosenberg. Capitalizing on her recent training, she secured thirty-three hours a week. The chief operator informed her that the switchboard was transitioning to a new electrographic card method for operators to input billing codes for calls, a Scantron-like system known as "mark sense." Kathy was delighted by her good luck. She would start the following week with shifts on weekday evenings from five to ten p.m., all day Saturday, and a "split shift" Sunday. Kathy's wages were only slightly higher than in Jacksonville (starting at $52.50 per week, before taxes), but she was not discouraged. "Because I'm working past 9 o'clock every night I get $.40 per day extra," she wrote, adding, "I'm dying to hear what you think of it all."[4]

As busy as she was, delays in marital communication this first month of separation stoked insecurities. She wondered whether her letters arrived in order, or at all, and she did not understand the pace of Charlie's correspondence. "I sure wish mail service were faster," she wrote. "When do you get my letters? Or have you the same problem?" Here, as later, Kathy often masked her unmistakable anxiety with cheerfulness: "I have an idea—let's set up a pony express between you and I personally! . . . Ha! I'll probably get a whole pile all at once."[5] While Charlie was in transit from Lejeune to Cuba, Kathy composed multiple letters without receiving any. Such conditions afforded room in these diary-like pages for clearer self-expression, even as her confidence ebbed and flowed.

The weekend of her twentieth birthday, she went camping with her family and longtime friends in New Braunfels, on the banks of the Comal River. It was a welcome excursion before her new schedule began, and Kathy brought notepaper with her, delighting in a melancholy letter, her mind's eye envisioning a trip she and Charlie could take later "on a shoestring," assuring him that it would be "just as much fun or more than staying in a motel and eating out. I know you will love this country." She set the scene:

> I'm writing [this letter] on top of my purse by torchlight. . . . We are camped under big trees and right on the bank. The river is as clear as Barton Springs and we are right between two sets of rapids. We have 2 torches set up, one next to the river | one under the trees. Ray + ——— are out in the river under torchlight and I'm fixing to join them.
>
> Honey, I wish you were here so bad. It's so

romantic and I miss you so much. The only thing is that we are sleeping on cots out in the open and I wouldn't be able to hold my sweetheart.

Sunday evening Kathy pampered herself with evening rituals after nearly three whole days in her bathing suit: "I've had my bath and washed and rolled my hair so I'll look nice for my first day at school and work. My skin felt so dry and pulled from so much sun, I rubbed down with lotion, so now I'm all good-smellin' and smooth."[6]

Kathy's weekdays from this point forward were long. She rose early for her carpool to Wharton, thirty minutes southwest of Needville, for history and government courses from 7:15 a.m. to eleven a.m. Then she had a "study break" at home before driving north to Rosenberg for her five p.m. shift at the switchboard. On the second day of this routine, she reported candidly about what surprised her and what she disliked:

I hate to say it but I like the Carolina office much better. Mabe it will be alright when I become familiar with the [switch]board. This office is much more inefficient than N.C. The girls talk, and do not keep their position neat and cross their legs at the board. All three were taboo in N.C. Also, remember how I had trouble understanding the Yankee accent, well, now I can't understand this dumb Bohemian + German lingo! I can't seem to win. Also the phrases used here are different, these girls aren't near as polite as N.C.

I have history 1st period and government 2nd. My profs can't even compare with Dr. Soukeep and Dr. Morgan, but then, I didn't really expect them to. They are terribly fact-conscious and dull. I have to have a term paper in gov't. But it's very simple and short!

She concluded by telling Charlie to "keep his chin up" and documented exactly how the letter fit into her packed schedule. "I have 3 long chapters of history to consume before 4:00 so I'd better close," she wrote, signaling that she would soon take her post at the switchboard.[7]

As July ended, she found it challenging to live again at home. "I have to try so hard to stay in a good humor," Kathy wrote. "Mother is being so good about my ridiculous hours." One Friday afternoon she helped in the fields with Nelson and her father, rounding up cattle, cutting out calves and a sick cow, and spraying them in preparation for market. Afterwards, she wrote, "Nelson and I had to ride the horses into town to the house. . . . I got so hot I thought I would faint. By the time I got home it was 3:45 so I had to take a bath + get to work."[8] At the switchboard Kathy maintained composure in response to other people's emergencies. She dispatched an ambulance when a motorcycle rider—a person she recognized—was thrown into a car windshield. "I remember thinking about how I hoped it wasn't anyone I knew!" she wrote, noting that he needed forty-two stitches. "I sure hope he'll be alright."[9]

Her first exam scores were excellent. "I made 94 in history (highest grade was 97), and 97 in govt," she reported. "I was so proud and happy. That should boost your confidence in me!"[10] She also wanted Charlie to approve of her goal to lose fifteen pounds. She exercised when she could and at work she drank Sego, a diet beverage. In her few moments of downtime, Kathy visited with cousins as well as former classmates, catching up on gossip about the latest engagements and wedding showers, new babies and college plans. She played tennis with Ray or with Nelson when the temperature was not too forbidding.

Charlie's letters trickled in at first, more precious and intense due to their scarcity, later arriving swiftly or in batches. At first, Kathy replied that she was "on cloud nine" and relieved that he had landed safely at a base en route to Guantanamo. Kathy poured her heart into communications, pressing for fundamental improvements in her marriage and stating outright, "There are just so many ways we could get along much better." This coded language—about "getting along" and "the way we fight over little things"—would be among the signal phrases Kathy used when referencing his abusive behavior. She framed her desires cautiously, stating that she was unsure of how to express them in a letter or in person, even as she assured Charlie that she did not want any "drastic change" in him. She also detailed her own self-improvement efforts, showing how deeply she had internalized his pressures. "I'm doing lots of little things to try to be completely in the 'habit of' by the time we get back together," she wrote. "I'm taking vitamins every day + I feel fine. I'm not nervous anymore and I don't get tired near as easily. I think it was just Jacksonville + the way we had to live with never knowing what's happening next."[11] In these hasty explanations, especially about "nervousness" and fatigue, Kathy could not yet admit to herself that separation from Charlie was the most likely reason for her calmer state. Meanwhile, he tracked scores for poker games on the backs of her envelopes.[12]

Kathy worried about pleasing her husband not only as a wife but also in the role he expected her to fulfill—as a mother—but she wanted the time to be right. She suffered unusually intense cramps at the end of July. ("[P]robably the effect of being off Enovid," she wrote.) With Frances, she paid a visit to a recently married friend who already had a child. The father was blond and handsome like Charlie, she wrote, emphasizing, "Honey, I can't wait to have a baby and make you proud. They are about as old as we will be so that made me feel better." She also wanted a couple's "favorite song," suggesting "Moon River," which had been popular when their courtship began. "It is almost a classic," she wrote. "What do you think?"[13]

On July 30 Kathy looked forward to picking up registration materials in Austin and investigating new housing options, but she also addressed the bigger picture of her needs and her husband's mood swings, specifically his temper:

> [A] letter from you more than once every 8 days would sure help. I hope you are keeping your chin up and not being too impatient with everyone. I know you are quite capable of getting down in the dumps and becoming short-tempered with the men. . . . I'm proud of myself for being able to stay above water by thinking about what we're doing. I guess I'm talking pretty big considering I've only been at it for 23 days, but if I don't start out with high hopes I certainly can't finish with them.

Common wisdom had taught Kathy that a man's ego could strike when threatened, and her husband's volatile tendencies were easier to name from a distance. But she knew well what she was accomplishing "above water" even as she recognized the long stretches of time, labor, and loneliness that lay ahead. Upon receipt of this letter, Charlie listed ideas on the back of the envelope, later crossing off words as he addressed topics himself, as if cues for a script.[14]

Meanwhile, he wrote a long letter on medical forms taken from a sick bay where he had a cast removed for a hand injury. He detailed his own self-improvement plans mostly in terms of what he would stop, citing an article in *Readers' Digest* about not "sweating the small stuff." He pledged "to try and not cuss" in her presence and to stop "being so quick temper[ed] and harsh" when she did not fulfill a precise demand. He also alluded broadly to his previous use of physical force, committing "never to lay a hand on you unless it is in a moment of passion or gentleness."[15]

The conditional nature of his promise recorded a disturbing loophole. But his letter had arrived quickly, and in her response Kathy was eager to move forward. Using her signal phrase about "fighting," she responded, "Honey, there is not one thing I want to change except the way we fight over little things. And we can't do anything about them, together anyway, until Jan. 65." She added that she herself had not cussed in a very long time.[16]

AUGUST BROUGHT MORE REPORTS FROM CHARLIE. He bragged about his loan-sharking and his poker wins. He shot rather than captured a seven-foot rock python with a .25 caliber pistol ("was going to tease the colored boys with it"), sent Kathy a money order for $72, and complained about the "animals" in the barracks and despicable "mannerisms" the military had shaped in him. Responding to new photos she sent, he disapproved of her makeup, emphasizing the next day how he wanted her to be "the suavest honey on campus."[17]

August 17 marked Kathy's first wedding anniversary, a milestone she celebrated alone. "It's going to be a terrible day without you," she wrote to Charlie after receiving his early card, sorry that she had not yet been able to pick up his present in Houston. Thanking him for the new perfume and razor, Kathy wrote, "Darling, you certainly know how to make a girl feel like a woman. You have such good taste." A few days later, she admitted to sadness: "I feel half empty every minute of the day. I can't sleep at night either." Rather than visit the local doctor for pills, Kathy wanted to see if the insomnia subsided after summer school.[18]

Charlie apparently asked Kathy to contact Father Gil when she visited Houston ("I called," she wrote, "but he wasn't home"), yet welcome support and validation came from other sources. She received her first paycheck, clearing $83.93 ("pretty good for two weeks part time!"). Despite her worry about underpreparation, she breezed through a history exam. A test for government was a different story when the professor added a question from an outside reading assignment: "[He] knew he was going to catch most of the class off guard, so when I turned my paper in he immediately wanted to see what his 'A' student had answered. I felt horrible!" But Kathy was encouraged later when they spoke in the parking lot. "[H]e said I had the 1st part completely right but missed some points down the line . . . so I don't feel so bad, as far as I know, that's all I missed," she wrote.[19] Within days, Kathy presented "2 A's under her belt" as tangible assets itemized alongside a detailed accounting of her latest bank deposits and expenses. She also met with a family friend who helped her think ahead about strategies for navigating the saturated teacher job market in Austin.[20]

Kathy and her mother visited UT to finalize housing arrangements and meet with an advisor. About the trip, she wrote, "I'd forgotten how pretty Austin really is. The whole thing made me terribly lonesome for you though because I kept thinking about how terrible it's all going to be without you." She effused about local changes and campus improvements. The route to Bergstrom Air Force Base now had a new bridge that eliminated a traffic bottleneck. The university had constructed new women's residence halls. Best of all, according to Kathy, was the completion of the modern undergraduate library on campus, commonly referred to as "Harry's Place," after UT Chancellor Harry H. Ransom. "It's absolutely beautiful," she wrote.[21]

After consulting with the dean of women, Kathy visited

La Fontainebleau, a university-approved apartment within walking distance of campus. After comparing costs and amenities, Kathy was convinced about the wisdom of this location. "I talked to some of the girls + they said their food cost them $15 a month because all 4 girls usually bought food + ate together," she said. "I fell in love with the place." She was relieved that the manager understood her unique circumstances as a married resident. Interactions during this visit reminded Kathy of social connections at UT. She ran into a friend with whom she and Charlie had lost touch—the man and his wife were expecting their first child. "He was real concerned about your being in Cuba," Kathy wrote. "He said to be sure and call them when I got to school + I think I'm going to do just that. They could prove to be a lot of help to me while you are away." After meeting with an academic counselor to map out an educational plan, Kathy emphasized how she finally felt heard. "This was the first time I've felt like the man really cared what I was saying," she wrote. "I even had the head of the science ed. depart. calling the registrar's office to see how soon I could get a full copy of my transcript."[22] If academic bureaucracy could finally work smoothly, certainly there was hope for her marriage.

Wishful thinking did not alter the reality. Coming off the high of her visit to Austin and her anniversary presents, Kathy received "two great big letters" and a phone call from Charlie that deeply rattled her. In one letter he scolded her to "give [her] husband a little bit of credit" regarding letters and phone calls, and he advised her to establish a calendar "reference system" to track their communications. He expressed his envy of another couple having a baby, told her to send the UT schedule (because he might "surprise" her—"plan ahead so if I pop in, you have a clear conscience"), and admonished her about cigarettes: "Will you please write back to me a solemn *promise* not to smoke *at all* while you are at school." In the other letter he referenced their first days married: "You thought I didn't need you except sexually—it isn't true, it has just taken time for me to let go and reveal myself to you." Recalling when Kathy confronted him in January 1963 about how he "wasn't doing [his] job" in the marriage, he recanted his angry reaction at the time, urging her to always tell him what no one else would. He described himself as a man who was "so sexually active" yet had not "touched himself" or thought about other women since they separated. He praised her grades but expressed disappointment that she had not yet seen the dentist.[23]

Kathy's exhaustive response—a single letter of more than sixteen hundred words—provides wrenching insight about how deeply his reactions affected her and how much responsibility she accepted to appease him. "First of all," she began, "I want to apologize for complaining about not hearing from you. I hope you will forgive me. You sounded mad in your letter and I just cried. Please, don't be mad at me. I love you so much and I'm so sorry if I made you mad at me." This sad and submissive stance continued as she answered a series of questions Charlie had sent on many subjects, including a doctor's visit about her period and birth control pills, her maintenance on the car, and her clothing for school. Kathy assured him that the razor he sent was working well and that she kept it clean "with the little brush that came with it." She promised that she was conserving her perfume, a bottle of Joy he sent: "I wouldn't think of using it on my letters so don't worry." Kathy also found herself repeating that she was capable of managing money. "I've already told you what I'm going to do about my budget," she wrote, adding reflections that proved she was already thinking well ahead to the next year.[24]

Among her husband's more nitpicking questions, there had been deeper demands. Kathy agreed not to "nag"

about his gambling. "I've decided I've had the wrong attitude toward the whole business," she wrote. "I'm really
very lucky to have such a wonderful sweet husband with no
vices such as drinking or smoking (or chasing women). . . .
I'm not going to stop you from doing something you enjoy."
She did not, however, allow the same permission for herself
about smoking cigarettes—apparently a worse "vice" than
gambling. "I figured you would ask me about it and you
certainly have a right to," she wrote. "That is the least I can
do for the man I love." Kathy continued to express dismay
that he was "cutting [him]self down," writing, "I think you're
the best person in the world and I don't like to hear you
calling yourself all those awful names." Most of all, Kathy
tried to reassure her husband about his romantic abilities.
In this most intimate area, she expressed her vulnerabilities
even as she centered Charlie's feelings and echoed phrases
from his letter:

> I do need you as much as you need me. Please, don't
> think that I still have that dumb notion of your only
> desiring me for sexual release. Darling, I do realize
> how you feel. I promise I will never mention any
> woman you have had before me. It's funny how that
> never bothered me before we were married and then
> when you were all mine, I resented the idea of any-
> one else ever touching you. I hope I've been enough
> of a woman to make you forget they ever happened
> and I think I have.[25]

Surely her relationship to him was different. Surely being
married changed everything, even at a distance. Despite all
her hopes, Kathy seemed convinced to take the blame: "I
have got a lot of making up to do, and I'm not talking about
these nights we are apart. I am referring to the many times

I was such a pain to you when you wanted to make love. I hope I can make it up to you."[26]

YET ANOTHER VEHICLE ACCIDENT THREW MORTALITY into stark perspective when Kathy's younger cousin, Cheryl, was killed in a car crash along a new freeway in Huntsville on August 27. Devastated, Kathy wrote to her husband at midnight. "Charlie," she wrote, "this is the first time that someone this close to me has died and I haven't been able to justify it by age, illness, or something like that." Kathy described the shock and grief of her aunt and uncle, and she admitted dreading the funeral: "[It] will probably be massive because Cheryl had so many friends + everyone loved her so. . . . Remember I love you and pray for your safety." She included a thought about prevention: "The first thing I thought about was 'If she had had seat belts!'" The next day, she discovered that her cousin had lived until she reached the hospital. "I just can't seem to fit this into God's plans," she wrote. "Cheryl was so young and beautiful."[27]

Charlie's letters crossed Kathy's mournful accounts in the mail, his content and tone incongruous. He described nude sunbathing on top of the barracks and how he had enjoyed a recent mail call, which had produced "6 or 7 letters" from Kathy. He lectured her about resting, vitamins, resuming her contraceptive pills, and checking on her fingernails and her teeth before she returned to UT. ("I want you to look so good while you are at school and that is so important to me," he wrote.) He said that he was imagining ways to improve their relationship "for your benefit," assuring her that his new name as a romantic partner would be "Mr. Gentle," and that he promised "to be a good boy." He added that he decided he "liked [his] wife better with dark hair" and offered to send her a book he was reading, *A Marriage Doctor Speaks Her*

Mind about Sex. His letter acknowledging Cheryl's death arrived more than a week later, its compassion stilted and stiff, more worried about how expressing belated condolences might look "awkward" to her family than about how Kathy was personally absorbing the loss.[28]

As summer classes ended she extended her hours at the phone company, planning to work straight through until registration, and she finally saw the dentist for a cleaning and a filling replacement. She played a few more tennis games with Nelson, went to see the movie *Beach Party* with family, and helped her mother around the house, giving the dog a bath, packing for school, and prepping the Corvair with a final polish. Kathy was incredulous about Charlie's exhibitionist sunbathing. "You nut," she wrote, "what are you trying to do, get court-martialed + stuck under the brig?" She was also relieved that his brother Patrick would resume school after abruptly attempting to join the Navy. Although anxious to start again at UT, she felt wary after falling a semester behind. "I'm going to have to make some powerful good grades," she wrote, "to bring up my very poor average." Charlie had recommended she add pushups to her workouts and sent hairstyle photos clipped from women's magazines—with some heads crossed off to indicate his displeasure. Although Kathy wondered what it would feel like living again in Austin without her husband, she did not want him to show up unannounced: "Please don't surprise me this 1st time," she wrote, seeming apprehensive of his scrutiny, "cause I may not be ready like I want to be."[29]

ON SUNDAY, SEPTEMBER 15, KATHY UNLOCKED the door of apartment no. 106 at 803 W. 28th Street before an evening of spotty thunderstorms and heavy rain in Austin. Frances and Nelson accompanied her, and they had hit

heavy traffic along the Drag—a mixture of "moving-in traffic" and "church traffic," Kathy wrote to Charlie. To celebrate
Nelson's birthday, the three family members ate dinner at
Hill's Steakhouse. She was excited to be assigned a room of
her own in the shared apartment. "[T]he little bit I've been
around the girls today, I think I would find it hard to live
with one," she wrote, admitting self-consciousness about the
change in her status—from single coed to married woman. "I
seem sort of out-of-it when they start laughing + giggling just
like I *used* to!" Kathy also shared photos of her husband with
the roommates. ("They were all very impressed," she wrote.)
She made an appointment at Mr. Pat's to have her hair done,
just as she had as a freshman in fall 1961. She was starting
over. Almost.[30]

That same day in Birmingham, Alabama, a Ku Klux Klan
bomb exploded at the Sixteenth Street Baptist Church, killing four African American girls in a Sunday school classroom. It was a sadistic strike following civil rights victories
for integration the previous spring—a graphic reminder that
some men would always claim the prerogative to dominate
and terrorize. Two days later Austin activists organized quiet
solidarity protests at local churches, schools, and on the UT
main mall.[31]

Charlie's long letters dated on the cusp of this moment
reminded Kathy of his own violence. On tiny address book
papers, he wrote, "Baby, I am so sorry that I ever hit you particularly the time in the car in Jax when I hurt your mouth."
Instead of "punching on my honey" and "picking on her in
the kitchen," he said he would "overwhelm you with kisses
and hugs next time I see you," adding oddly, "You're going to
be a loser." He also wanted to bathe her and recommended
she consider electrolysis for hair removal. ("[I]f you'll have it
done, I have the cash.") He annotated an article Kathy had
sent him about the fidelity of American wives and closed by

asking her to recall the intimate Polaroids he had taken in Jacksonville. A vague threat in his rationale belied the assurance that he burned them all: "I wouldn't want anyone to see them and through some accident they might." His wishes were few, he said, just some hunting rifles, specifically a Weatherby Magnum.[32]

Kathy did not receive his letters for a week. Frances meanwhile was attuned to her daughter's new "aloneness" and wrote to her immediately. "My, that ole' bed looked awfully empty this morning!" she said. "Funny what a difference just a few miles can make—We miss you." A second letter opened with questions about Kathy's registration ("Have you gotten your schedule straightened out now? Did you get in the college of Ed?") and her hopes for Charlie's safety. Frances included an update about Hurricane Cindy ("didn't bring us anything but wind—and not much of that") as well as family details. Cousin Cheryl's parents were still grieving. ("They sounded pretty good, but you know how it is," Frances wrote.) She tried to communicate the hole Kathy had left behind: "I asked your dear old daddy if he had anything to say and he just looked silly and said to tell you to ~~Buk~~ 'Buckle down!' It's funny how lonesome it is around here— even tho' you were gone a lot of the time you were here."[33] In both letters Frances reminded her to send the new phone number.

Not yet at home at school, Kathy returned to Needville for one last, long weekend before classes. After the challenges of winter, spring, and summer, she was resolved to put her "best foot forward" in a fresh chapter at UT. Charlie would soon joke about her "magical" impact on a new policy restricting gambling in his company and tell her he passed his E-5 test for sergeant status, anticipating promotion in December. Kathy looked ahead to his first leave, dreaming of dancing and dining with him at Club Caravan ("supposed to be the best spot this year!"). But when she returned to Austin the night before fall semester commenced, she found Charlie's letters waiting, the ones containing apologies for physically hurting her. She identified the document precisely without mentioning any details. "Your little letter on the address paper was wonderful," she wrote with relief, adding hopefully, "I'm looking forward to all the things you have in store for me."[34]

Kathy did not want to name the ugliness—she wanted a new beginning. Yet despite all his promises to be "a good boy," Charlie was headed for trouble. The coming months would prove traumatic for Kathy personally, just as violence in the country came to another terrible head.

THE FIRST WEEK OF CLASSES KATHY sent her family a full report of her promising reentry to university life. Her apartment had hosted a house party to go over rules, and she was settling in nicely with her roommates. She enrolled in more upper-division science courses alongside her final general education requirements, and she was "real pleased" with her professors and courses, a heavy load: geology, botany, and zoology, on top of logic and a class she referred to as "Bible 301." Despite all her years at summer Bible camps, it was the religion course that concerned her the most. "Dr. Fletcher has just about lost me in his terminology," she wrote. After spending a whopping $50 on books, she requested that her parents send her the New Testament and a geology workbook from an old closet to help cut down on expenses.[35]

Thankfully, Bible 301 was a small class—just ten students, Kathy told her parents, "so I'm not really too worried about getting lost." At the other end of the spectrum, the geology survey was her "massive class," a lecture section of three

Kathy poses happily in the bright kitchen of her new apartment near UT in September 1963—a far cry from the cinder-block rooms of Jacksonville. Private archive of Nelson Leissner.

Kathy relaxes with Frances in the off-campus apartment living room during move-in day, September 1963. Private archive of Nelson Leissner.

hundred. "It's my easiest course," she wrote. Zoology and botany were another story: "They are both advanced courses and I'm going to have to really study. They both have about 60 people in them." She was not quite sure what to make of her unnamed logic professor. "I already have misgivings about his sanity," Kathy wrote. "[W]hen he walked into class Monday, most people thought he was the janitor until he got behind the podium! He is really something else."[36]

Kathy passed along Charlie's requests and news. He wanted a large tan suitcase he had left in Needville to be sent to him at Lejeune. "Write and let me know how much it is [to mail it]," Kathy told her parents, as if to offset any impression of taking advantage, "so I can reimburse you." He had neglected to renew their auto authorization sticker for base access, and Kathy had been pulled over and cited on a visit to Bergstrom. "We still have our '62 sticker and it's time to be getting our '64!" she wrote. "The cop pulled up beside me and tapped on the window and almost scared me to death!"[37] Charlie had a more serious scrape of his own, which Kathy rendered for her parents in detail based on his account:

> You'll die when you hear about what happened to my accident prone husband! He drove a Jeep off a 60 ft. cliff and it flipped 2 times and landed right side up, thank goodness. He was in the hospital for 4 days for observation, but he didn't even get a scratch. He was just terribly sore from being bounced around. . . . The other guy wasn't quite so lucky. He got a broken spleen, and split his liver! . . . I don't know how you can "break" your spleen, cause that's an organ, but that's what he said![38]

This time her husband's driving had caused drastic injury, but at least his passenger had not been killed.

Charlie seemed grateful that the investigation determined no misconduct in the accident, but he asked Kathy to thank God on his behalf because he felt "guilty" for praying. Only a few days later, he described feeling enraged when his captain ordered him to quit playing casino in the sergeants' quarters after taps and go to bed. "For two cents and I swear this," he wrote, "I would have told him to shove the Marine Corps and knocked the devil out of him." It was thinking of Kathy, he assured her, that kept him from crossing over the line.[39]

HARRY'S PLACE BECAME THE CAMPUS SYMBOL of Kathy's new aspirations. "I'm dying to take you through it," she wrote to her parents in advance of their late September visit to Austin. "I'm not even going to try to explain it. It's located between the Union and the tower or main library!" She enjoyed the steady pace of her first days, adding an intermediate tennis class to her schedule, collecting a sample of "dirty water" from a nearby stream for her zoology lab, and picking up her copy of the bright orange 1963 annual, *The Cactus*. She noted to Charlie a minor extension for girls' housing curfews and encouraged his latest thoughts on OCS. One mellow evening she listened to Johnny Mathis and sipped a beer she found surprisingly "not bitter," though her mood was low. She had started the day with terrible cramps and her thoughts turned to their coming reunion: "[I]t will be like walking out of hell into heaven," she wrote, then adding, "I'm so sorry for all the things I've done that made you mad and disgusted at me. I must have been an awful pain sometimes."[40]

Mail delivery lag times made it difficult to track Charlie's maneuvers. "Tonight I am sitting on the phone praying that [he] will call," she wrote to her parents. She had received a letter from Cuba, and he described packing for the return. She calculated that his timing could put a crimp in her plans to visit Needville. "I have to wait and talk to Charlie," she said. "Can't ever tell what he may be doing. I will call if I can come home." Kathy watched her academic calendar carefully. "So far I have one exam scheduled for Oct. 16," she wrote, "just watch Charlie be home right when I have a crop of exams!" The Whitmans had sent a letter pressuring about the upcoming holidays, and Kathy passed on the information to her parents without replicating any guilt. "Daddy W. said to try to talk you into coming . . . to spend Christmas [in Florida]," she wrote. "If you want to, fine. If not, that's fine too!"[41]

As it turned out, Kathy's instincts were correct: Charlie visited for ten days in mid-October, just as her first wave of exams and due-dates hit. In advance of his visit, she worried that he would not like the color of her hair. "I don't want you to be too shocked," she wrote. "I wish there were some way I could be normal by the time you get here, but there is no way." She was terribly anxious about how she measured up. "I don't know why you ever took a second look at me," she said. "There are so many precious girls up here, and you could have had your pick. . . . I should just be thankful and not question why!"[42] Despite these doubts, Kathy appears relieved and happy in photographs from the couple's visit to Needville on Saturday, October 12, a warm Texas day.

When her husband returned to Lejeune, Kathy scrambled to complete a paper for her Bible class, relieved that Charlie was back stateside for good. She wore the shower shoes he left under her bed. Overall, she took heart that the leave demonstrated how they might be able to start over. "We proved Sat. that we can have so much fun doing things together," she said, apparently referencing an easy day playing pool. "We must do things like that more often when we get back together." She would later recall his affections one morning during the visit. Still, she worried about Charlie's happiness and encouraged him to consider OCS, assuring him that they could both still get their degrees. "I know you and I know the prestige would do you good," she wrote.

Kathy and Charlie on the back patio of her parents' home in Needville on October 12, 1963. Private archive of Nelson Leissner.

"Honey, we are still so young and have so much time. . . . It's not going to be 'instant anything' when you get your degree, so why rush, at the most it will be a 2 yr. delay (if that long)."[43]

Phone calls in the coming days would cause Kathy to doubt the OCS idea because Charlie suggested it might require an additional year of separation. But meanwhile she completed zoology drawings, talked with the registrar about her educational plan, watched *The Lieutenant* on Saturday nights, and attended campus events with friends—a German film about the Third Reich, a controversial speech by Madam Nhu. She wondered how Charlie was spending his time. "I'm glad you promised not to go into Jax too much," she wrote, "to Jazzland and those places, because I don't like the idea of you looking at those women even though I know you don't have any desire for them." She also needed treatment for a painful infection following his visit: a doctor at Bradfield diagnosed cystitis and prescribed antibiotics.[44]

WEATHER AT THE END OF OCTOBER was wonderfully mild, and on Halloween Kathy started a letter to her parents that she finished and mailed the next day. She recounted a party in the apartment lounge, where the house mother served hot apple cider and donuts. "It certainly was sweet of her to do all that," she wrote. When Kathy opened her door to leave for class, "the girls next door had covered the entire opening with newspaper as a Halloween prank." Kathy had also gotten back a score of 90 on a pop test in Bible 301, boosting her confidence in the subject. Even so, she was overwhelmed. Charlie's visit, while enjoyable, had indeed disrupted her study schedule during a term that she expected to be challenging. In contrast with August, she now felt like she was "drowning." "I've been trying to finish this letter and I just can't seem to get anything done," Kathy told her parents. She went on to list the unrelenting schedule—exams, papers, and lab practicals—from November 4 through 18: "I have had so many tests assigned for the next 2 weeks I can't see straight. . . . By then, the whole mess should start all over again."[45]

The mess she anticipated, of course, was the usual cycle of struggle for undergraduates navigating the peaks and valleys of an academic term. Kathy was grateful that friends took her to the circus, and she looked forward to roommates leaving for a few days, allowing more quiet time to "spread out on the dining room table" and study. "Thanksgiving should be a welcome relief," she wrote. Even so, she was having trouble sleeping, in part because Charlie was unreachable again: he had not returned her latest phone call.[46]

Meanwhile, Charlie was composing a letter very early Halloween morning, just after midnight, not to Kathy but to her parents. Referring to the "catastrophe" of his separation from Kathy, he referenced their "wonderful 10 days together" and thanked his in-laws for their latest hospitality. He looked forward to Christmas, joking that he would rather go hunting with Raymond than comply with "Mother Marine Corps." He observed that the barracks had quieted down since he took his post as the Duty NCO that night, and he signed off with his usual stilted valediction, "May God Bless You All."[47] It was the choir boy's perfect, calming alibi: all is well. But the very next day Charlie was arrested and detained by the military police at Camp Lejeune. In a matter of weeks Kathy would be torn again from school and catching a flight back to North Carolina, where she would witness her husband's special military court-martial.

KATHY'S SLEEPLESSNESS AND WORRY ABOUT HER unreturned phone call overlapped directly with Charlie's arrest at 9:45 p.m. on November 1. For two weeks he was held in the military brig under "minimum custody" in Dorm No. 5. During this period he began keeping short diary entries in a Memoranda notebook. His own notes recorded the charges: carrying a concealed weapon, threatening another serviceman, loaning money at usurious rates, and gambling with subordinates.[48]

Kathy's first letter from Charlie was dated November 3 and written on an aerogramme, a single sheet of blue paper that folded into its own envelope. His handwriting was much smaller than usual, compressed tightly to fill every inch of the page. He intimated that Kathy had already received a phone call from his father regarding the charges, and overall the letter was incongruously breezy. Among his superficial references to the "fabulous time" he had on leave, how much he loved Kathy, and his encouragement of her studies, Charlie scrambled for excuses about why he had not returned her call the previous week. (Among them: "I had been awake for 26 hours and I had drunk 3 beers and I was completely out.") He barely addressed the subject of his arrest, expressing little responsibility. "I have done exactly nothing since I have been here, it is very boring," he wrote. "I try to keep my mind off all the things that could happen to me and as a result the effect that it could have on you and our plans for the future." Going on, he told Kathy to tell her family whatever she pleased about his situation since, after all, "the charges they have are all sussed up! none of them are right, but right now I have no say so about it." While in custody he knew his mail was being read, so he urged Kathy not to write anything that she would mind others seeing.[49]

On November 7 at eight p.m., Kathy received a phone call from Charlie—their first talk since his arrest—and in his diary he seemed mystified by her understandable change in mood. "She sounded so somber and unlike *my Kathy*," he wrote, underlining the possessive phrase. Her first letter arrived the next day, composed as she was knee-deep in her preparations for Bible, geology, and zoology exams. She even packaged and sent the watch he had left behind during leave. Written at the home of married friends who extended extra care as Kathy sorted through mixed messages and limited information, the letter recognized how Charlie's latest trouble had jeopardized his change of rank and potential for OCS. The fallout would increase the stakes of Kathy's degree, and she emphasized her need to remain "cold-blooded" in concentration on her studies. She advised him not to laugh off the idea of praying, and she rejected his narcissistic views: "If you'll look at people + friends around you + then look at yourself I think you'll change your mind about just who has a 'charmed life.' I'm tired of hearing about it because the whole idea is ridiculous. Most people don't need a charm to get through life in one piece." Implied here was the painful truth that Charlie could neither see nor imagine how uncharmed her survival continued to be.[50]

On her own, Kathy was numb ("I am so wound up I can't even cry!"), wavering between academic determination and personal uncertainty, wrestling with fear of the immediate and long-term implications, and turning blame inward. "Sometimes I think mabe you need me there more than we need my degree," she wrote, adding later, "It's this being in the dark that is so nerve wracking." Referring to the situation as a "bad dream" in a subsequent letter, she was thinking ahead to possible live-in babysitting jobs and assuring Charlie that she would stay by his side. She questioned how the charges would affect his sense of self as well as his long-term future in engineering: "I'm so worried about what this is doing to you as a man." Another letter written the same day doubted how well she knew him: "I have so many questions to ask that will have to wait until later. Mabe this is all my fault. I should have been stronger. I've always thought that you knew exactly what was right and I only questioned your judgment very seldom." With renewed clarity, she asserted, "I'll never stop lovin you no matter what, but if we are going to make anything out of our marriage, there are going to have to be some powerful changes as far as I can see. My only misgiving is that I don't know whether you will see the necessity for change or will be willing to make them. . . . [Y]ou can't raise children in conditions as unstable as ours."[51]

Charlie's response was telling, taking the opportunity to lay blame at Kathy's feet. "I am so very sorry you consider our 'conditions' unstable and feel that some 'powerful' changes are necessary," he wrote. "By not naming the changes, and telling me what it is you want to talk about, I am very worried and depressed." While he expected criticism from his mother, he turned Kathy's reasonable reactions back upon her: "It hurt very much for me to see you feel the way you do." Although he acknowledged breaking "MC regulations" by "playing cards and loaning money," he did not believe these actions were "morally wrong"—after all, he argued, they were inspired by Kathy's challenge to do "his share" in the marriage.[52]

After a week in the brig, Charlie was minimizing even further; he was "glad" to note that Kathy was "only" worried about the gambling as opposed to the other charges. She managed to reach him the Sunday before her deadline for a three-thousand-word paper. The conversation extended beyond the usual three-minute limit for prisoners because, according to Charlie, Kathy sounded "so pitiful when she cried." The next day he also recorded in his diary, taking time to relax outside, whistling "A Taste of Honey," and thinking ahead to when his wife would be "full of life with our baby."[53] He wrote to her again, a letter that had two segments, the opening segment now missing. It is likely that she destroyed rather than lost the first page because later in the letter, Charlie offered a backhanded apology for his opening, including a swipe at his own mother. "Please do not let the beginning of the letter make you feel bad," he said, continuing, "I was going to tear it up, but I thought I ought to let you know how I felt anyway." In contrast with the sentimental tone of his diary entry, this letter contained a mix of perfunctory contrition and impenitence: "I was sorry I have offended you and my unborn children by messing up my record and losing a wonderful opportunity, but it is past and I have no control over it." He contemplated "whether to take revenge" on the Marines he thought had turned on him. Regarding the Leissners, he pushed her to intercede: "[A]ssure them that I am not a criminal. I want them to respect me, very much."[54] This language was virtually identical to his plea for intercession in February 1963, when Kathy dropped out of UT because of his grades rather than her own.

It was a great deal for Kathy to absorb: her husband's arrest and pending trial, the way he was dependent and demanding all at once. Never mind that her exams and labs for botany and zoology would not wait. Charlie meanwhile composed another letter for her parents. Looking ahead to his court-martial date, he laid out the possible spectrum of consequences ahead (from dishonorable discharge to five years in Leavenworth Federal Penitentiary—"I suspect my punishment will be somewhere in between"). He continued to play down his actions as a business venture gone wrong. Humility was not on the menu.[55]

Just before his release from the brig, there was a prison riot, and Charlie was thinking about death: "When it overtakes me some day I must remember to observe it closely and see if it is as I thought it would be—" Kathy received a phone call from her husband on Thursday, November 14, just after he was released back to H Company, with barracks restriction, on full duty. They talked privately for the first time since his arrest. "I am definitely convinced that my wife and I have an everlasting love," he wrote. "I wonder when I will see her again."[56]

Kathy's letters indicate no intention or discussion of travel during this crisis before her Thanksgiving break. But with his special court-martial date finally set for November 26, Charlie pressed hard at the last minute. "I would really like to have you here," he wrote. "This is when I really need you for moral support." He sent a picture of an outfit—did she have time to make one in pink?—adding that he would

Kathy with her husband and in-laws, C. A. Whitman (far left) and Margaret Whitman, the day of Charles Whitman's court-martial at Camp Lejeune, November 26, 1963. Notice C. A.'s hand in the center of the photograph. Private archive of Nelson Leissner.

like to see her "all dressed up in heels, etc. Honey, your legs sure look fine when you are in high heels."[57]

How she afforded the ticket is unclear, but photographs record her visit to Lejeune, likely arriving the afternoon or evening of Saturday, November 23. For the court-martial the following Tuesday, Kathy posed for photos alongside her husband and his parents, with barracks and half-barren trees in the background. Her expression looked somber and wan, her shoulders wilted and eyes downcast, even closed. She appeared uncomfortable near Charlie's father, who in one photo reached behind Margaret, as if angling to goose Kathy's waist or grab her elbow. Despite the solemn circumstances, Charlie stood proudly in his uniform, chest

UT students gathered quietly on campus after news of Kennedy's assassination on November 22, 1963. UT Texas Student Publications Photographs, di_09039, Dolph Briscoe Center for American History, The University of Texas at Austin.

out and smiling broadly as if he were the star of a parade rather than a defendant in military court. Upon reviewing the photos later, he wrote to Kathy, "I don't like your smile." He reminded her how to position her chin.[58]

In his Memoranda notebook, Charlie recorded the date of his court-martial but made no mention of Kathy's arrival at the time. Only later—in January—did he reference a night of unprotected, "carefree" sex the night of November 23.[59] He was sentenced to thirty days of restriction and ninety days of hard labor without confinement, and his rank was demoted from corporal to private. (He conceded to himself,

"[T]he sentence was light.") Instead of the raise he had anticipated in a letter to the Leissners back in June, his pay would now be decreased.[60] Kathy had to rely on one of her husband's friends to drive her to the airport in Wilmington to catch her return flight to Texas.[61] She kept the corporal's patch snipped from Charlie's uniform—two chevrons above a pair of crossed rifles—among his letters.

But this was not all. As Kathy reeled from the latest turmoil of her marriage, the entire country had turned a terrible corner. Within hours of her sudden departure from Austin, an internationally important guest had not arrived in the capital city as planned. On Friday, November 22, President John F. Kennedy was shot and killed as his motorcade drove through Dealey Plaza in Dallas. Beside him in the backseat of the shiny black limousine, Jackie Kennedy had been splattered by her husband's brain matter and blood.

Stunned into silence and reflection, UT students gathered in common spaces on campus, sometimes around televisions. In the immediate wake of the horror, commercial programming was suspended on three national television networks: NBC, CBS, and ABC. Campus events sponsored by the university were also cancelled through the date of Kennedy's funeral.[62]

THERE IS NO RECORD OF KATHY'S reactions to Kennedy's assassination or the mad cascade of events that followed: Lyndon Johnson's oath of office, Kennedy's funeral, Oswald's arrest and assassination. Referring to a *TIME* article, Charlie seemed impressed by technical details about the crime: "Oswald shot 3 rounds in less than 5 seconds at over 200 yds, he shot Kennedy in the neck, then he shot Connelly, then he shot K. in the head again. I can't get over the cold-bloodiness of it." He added a perfunctory condolence:

"I didn't agree with K's politics but it was definitely a terrible shame that he was killed in such a manner." Kathy spent a somber Thanksgiving at home with her family, eating tuna fish sandwiches and watching a football game. She also reflected on Christmas shopping, circling back to suggest that guns were not what Charlie needed. "There is nothing that you really want right now other than that rifle and there are so many other things you will need," she wrote. "Why don't I think in terms of things I could get you now that you can use when we are back living together?"[63]

Kathy wanted to retreat from everything now. In a letter dashed off before exams, she longed for a different time. "I smell your Faberge all the time + I feel closer to you," she wrote. "It seems like so long since I felt really good. Oh Honey, why do things have to be this way?" Charlie pledged to take care of himself and never to "pull any irresponsible acts again."[64]

But when he wrote to her parents with his usual doses of ingratiation, he cast doubts on Kathy's mental state—repeating his patterns from earlier in the year. "Mother," he wrote, "would you all do your best to keep Kathy occupied so that she enjoys herself over the holidays. She really deserves the break from school and her worries over me, but I am afraid there is little I can do to stop her worrying." He went on to ask Frances if she liked how Kathy looked. "I really love her hair dark like it is now," he said, again centering his aesthetic preferences, as he was privately critical when Kathy experimented with lighteners. Even his postures of empathy sounded patronizing: "I wish I could help her emotionally, to calm down, but I don't know how to do that."[65] An obvious thought that likely crossed the minds of both Frances and Raymond: Charlie could start by treating their daughter with respect and living up to his marriage vows.

Back to classes after the long weekend, Kathy looked ahead to the holiday break: "Before Thanksgiving, I was just saying 'if I can just make it to Thanksgiving!' Now I'm saying 'if I can just make it 'till Christmas!' . . . Boy—I'll be glad when this semester is over! In fact, I'll be glad when this whole mess is over!"[66] Yet again, the "mess" Kathy described for her parents involved much more than school. She saw need for improvements everywhere. She wanted to fix up the car ("it was in poor shape and really needed some adjusting") and had another dreadful phone call with her in-laws. ("The Whitmans sound as usual. About all I can say.") Even holiday cheer seemed dim, as Kathy wrote out Christmas cards. Charlie had sent a comprehensive list of recipients, specifying not only how to address each individual or couple but in some cases how Kathy should sign their names in the closing ("certainly no fun, but a welcome break from studying"). Kathy offered a succinct assessment of Charlie to her parents: "He's worse off than I am, mentally"—her voice in this moment a distinct counterweight to his cloying doubts.[67]

When Kathy finally caught her breath, her message to Charlie in a Christmas card focused on an elusive future: "No matter what happens I'm still terribly proud and glad that I am your wife. . . . Just as you say, we have so many wonderful years ahead of us. . . . Sweetheart, please think of me always and all the things we have to live for." What else could she say, if she planned to stay married to him? A letter from her mother-in-law arrived with a $70 check, pledging that Charlie's father would continue to send Kathy money twice a month. The gift, however, felt burdensome. "By the time I get out of school we will owe them so much money I shudder to think!" she wrote. "[I]t obliges us in ways other than monetarily because of their generosity."[68]

Kathy's final letters of 1963 longed for a better reunion

than their most recent days at Lejeune. "I must admit I enjoyed our love-making more when you were home on leave," she wrote. "Things just weren't the same last week." On Christmas Eve, she reprised the subject. "I just want to lose myself in you but not like the last leave," she said, indicating she had not felt as "carefree" as he had about unprotected sex. "I wish we knew someone who had a cabin up in the mountains out in West Texas and we could go out there and forget about the rest of civilization for at least 2 weeks." Kathy seemed keenly aware that her vision was unrealistic. "I sure can dream up impossible, but nice, situations, can't I? I just love you so much and I'm so tired of being kicked around." Buried in the middle of this letter was her assurance that she was not expecting a baby. Her report sounded tentative and exhausted. "I have started, so you don't need to worry about becoming a father," she wrote. "A least not for a while. I guess I'm glad."[69]

But days later, following a phone call where Charlie was upset, Kathy seemed frustrated by his pressure to consult a doctor. It was too early for a definitive pregnancy test, she said, and the cost was expensive. So much weighed heavily. "I'm depressed and there doesn't seem to be anything to be happy about," she wrote. "Our whole life is so up in the air. . . . I don't know if we will ever be normal, sometimes." Charlie had also been talking of a new scheme that alarmed her: moving to Florida and working for his father.[70]

Barometer Dropping

THE SILVER BALL GLOWING ATOP ALLIED Chemical Tower in Times Square inched downward for forty seconds above the teeming crowd that packed 42nd to 46th Streets. Faces turned up as arms waved out to no one in particular. The NBC announcer observed that 1963 had wrought a year "laden heavy with history and tragedy": the church bombing in Alabama, the assassination of President Kennedy, the death of Pope John XXIII. As the ball dropped, the neon "1964" lit up the platform as if cutting a switch on the past. The masses let out a collective roar.[1]

In a different universe, as a single girl, Kathy could have been in a crowd among friends, laughing, blowing a cardboard kazoo, and passing a bottle of champagne in a paper bag. In a different universe, married to a different man, she would have closed her eyes for a passionate kiss on the couch as NBC cued up Glenn Miller's "Moonlight Serenade" and panned cameras across the crowd. But in real life, Kathy started the year with her family instead of her husband, simultaneously discouraged and daring to believe in renewal. She enjoyed the Cotton Bowl on New Year's Day with her brothers, witnessing the Texas Longhorns routing Navy with a score of 28 to 6, a glorious conclusion to UT's undefeated 1963 football season.[2]

Kathy had lost all patience with her in-laws, and she was deeply aware of how Charlie's family was impacting her marriage. At issue was an idea he had again proposed by phone: returning to Lake Worth after his discharge to work as an apprentice for his father. Her veto was unequivocal, consuming most of the letter. She zeroed in closely on the troubling behavior of her father-in-law and the dynamics of the entire Whitman household, still setting her husband apart within the family system that had shaped him:

> Honey . . . I've told you that I'm sure I could not
> be happy around him and I couldn't raise a family
> around him. Charlie, that's what I cannot understand
> about you. It seems like your childhood would prove
> everything I'm saying. Charlie, the only harmonious
> moments in your home is when Daddy is sleeping +
> then everyone else is at each other's throat. There is
> so little happiness + so many problems. Honey, I've
> never met people with so many problems that dom-
> inated the atmosphere constantly. . . . Charlie, does
> Daddy have any friends? other than business? Now
> I'm not saying that you are like that, I'm just showing
> you how I don't think I'm the only person who feels
> this way. Your family doesn't have any other familys
> for friends because Daddy is so obnoxious no one
> can get along with him especially on a family-to-
> family basis, because that's where he is worst of all.

Monday.

My Dearest Darling,

I love you so much, Sweetheart. I just finished talking with you. I wish we didn't have to talk about the things we do on the phone. Time is so precious and I had much rather spend that time telling you how much in love with you I am.

Charlie, maybe I shouldn't try to write this letter tonight because I'm really going to have to think to give you all the angles. Honey, you know how I feel about Daddy and his argueing and bickering. I've told you that I'm sure I could not be happy around him and I couldn't raise a family around him. Charlie, that's what I cannot understand about you. It seems like your childhood would prove everything I'm saying. Charlie, the only harmonious moments in your home is when Daddy is sleeping & then everyone else is at each others throat. There is so little happiness & so many problems. Honey, I've never met people with so many problems that dominated the atmosphere constantly. Honey, I just can't get alongwith him or Mother sometimes. Its not because I'm not trying either because every time I've seen them I start out with a clean slate & everytime it's the same thing all over again. I just can't be happy in fact I would go out of my mind around someone that handled himself like Daddy. Charlie, does Daddy have any friends? other than business? Now I'm not saying that you are like that, I'm just showing you how. I don't think I'm the only person

In January 1964 Kathy argued that living near her husband's family would not be good for their marriage. Private archive of Nelson Leissner.

> . . . I can't even be around Daddy for a day without
> being so disgusted and depressed I couldn't even *act*
> like I was enjoying myself.
>   . . . Honey, we have lived 1200 miles from Daddy +
> he has still managed to know every little thing about
> our lives, he has still got his fingers in your life up to
> his elbows! Charlie, my parents aren't like that! They
> don't know anything we don't absolutely volunteer to
> tell them. It's our business. Charlie we are in a posi-
> tion now that we have to depend on Daddy, but we
> let ourselves get that way + have ourselves to blame.
>   . . . Can you imagine what control he will have if you
> work for him + we live in the same town! Charlie
> I've seen how he treats his other relatives and I don't
> want any part of it. I had *much* rather struggle on our
> own than depend on or accept anything from him.
> Charlie, you're right, Daddy will do anything for me
> except turn loose of his son.[3]

After drawing this firm boundary, she tried to evoke a positive memory. On a previous visit to Needville, Charlie had sat
at a piano keyboard and played a duet with a visiting friend.
Kathy thus conjured a vision that he was not simply doomed
to repeat his father's behavior.

Kathy's clarity about her in-laws, however, was clouded
by ongoing and unrealistic discussion of pregnancy. Even
though she mentioned having a period around Christmas-
time, by early January she was still referring to the possibility that she had conceived. Kathy had not slept with Charlie
since the time of his court-martial in late November, yet his
diary reflects that he was still misty on the idea of a baby just
after New Year's Day. To complicate matters, he had already
rushed to inform his parents that Kathy was expecting. She

allowed herself to be swept up in the idea. "Well, so far there are still 3 of us," she wrote one day, starting off a subsequent letter in similar terms: "So far, we are still parents." Kathy reasonably imagined these reveries secured temporary peace with her husband, who continued to argue that she was "entirely unfair" in her objections to his father. She was well aware how stress could disrupt any woman's menstrual cycle but was often reminded that Charlie linked his motivations for self-improvement to their hypothetical children: "You are so delicate and intricate inside and you have to carry our children someday and I don't like to take the least chance with your health."[4]

There were no home pregnancy tests in 1964, so Kathy spent several days caught between her husband's fantasies, her knowledge about her own body, and the mixed impressions gathered from a preliminary—and highly unpleasant—doctor's visit: "I went to the health center Saturday + a woman doctor examined me. I thought she was going to punch a hole in me. She said she couldn't tell for sure but it didn't really feel like pregnancy. Then when she looked at my womb, she said it did look like I could be pregnant." To know for sure, Kathy needed an appointment for an animal-based chemical test ("a frog or rabbit test"), the method then used to evaluate pregnancy hormones in urine. Although she wanted conclusive information before final exams started, Kathy worried about the expense: $8.50 for a single test, not a small cost, particularly when, as she added, "I really deep down just think my period is late." Going on and off contraception during the previous twelve months had certainly made her body vulnerable to hormonal shifts, and Enovid caused many side effects not yet well understood. However, given Charlie's fixations about monitoring her body, Kathy knew well that he would not believe her unless validated by a medical authority, a view most problematic during a time when doctors were not known for listening carefully to women patients.[5]

The delay of any official negative test result created a momentary window of harmony. On the one hand, calling back to feelings from March 1963, Kathy admitted, "[Pregnancy] would be fun but I would rather wait until we are a little more secure." But she also seemed inspired by married friends—other university students and recent graduates—who were moving into this phase of life for the first time. One friend had just given birth ("her labor started at 5:30 Thurs. and the baby wasn't born until Friday at 12:00"), and another couple had spent $132 on baby furniture and was rearranging their nursery to prepare for the big day.[6]

After reporting a brief bout of nausea, Kathy told Charlie, "Enclosed is a little guide on all the things we have to look forward to if we are expecting a baby. . . . [I]t sure will be fun when we do have a baby if we aren't going to now. I think you will really get a lot of fun out of my pregnancy." She reminded her husband that there had been only one occasion—the weekend before his court-martial—when they had not used some form of birth control, so if she were pregnant, it was truly meant to be. Her anticipation had underlying doubts. Imagining a baby girl, she asked Charlie, "You wouldn't disown us would you?" She pictured a two-bedroom apartment where she could decorate. "I think it would be so much fun to make curtains and fix a real frilly bassinet and do some paintings for the room and make maternity clothes and everything." She had written before about pregnancy weight gain and stretch marks, desperate for affirmation that he would not physically reject her.[7]

In the meantime she delivered her husband a token of the pride she felt in the university: a clipping from the front page of the *Daily Texan* depicting the UT Tower with its windows lit up on each side to make a giant number 1. Kathy wrote her own annotation in the margin: "This orange tower is the prettiest one I have seen with the Big No. 1." The striking image made the cover of the university annual that year. Charlie responded eight days later by urging Kathy to hold off on registering for classes. "You still want to come here + live if you're pregnant and I don't get out of the Corp don't you," he wrote. Not asking but telling her yet again. Even more disturbing, Charlie wrote this message *after* Kathy had shared the final negative test results by phone and *after* he had acknowledged the results in yet another letter. His fixation on a phantom pregnancy at this point willfully disregarded her reality.[8]

Kathy untangled the disorientation. She admitted being caught up in the pregnancy idea "because everybody I know is having one and that's about all I hear anyone talk about. I'm already a regular pro about all the best brands of baby furniture, clothes, mattresses, and just about everything you need." One girlfriend who had given Kathy a book on pregnancy and birth seemed more disappointed than Kathy herself at the negative test. The atmosphere had been hypnotic, and she stepped back to put it in mature perspective: "I just didn't think about the reasons we didn't really need a baby right now." She emphasized that Charlie—not she—would need to break the reality to his parents, especially given his rush to celebrate prematurely. "Please hurry and tell mom and dad we aren't expecting," she wrote. "In a way I wish you hadn't given them a false alarm."[9]

AFTER WHAT SEEMED LIKE AN ETERNITY, the semester was finally ending. Kathy had an intense schedule of five final exams, her stress physical as well as academic. A large varicose vein suddenly appeared on one of her legs—likely another side effect of Enovid—requiring yet another visit to the doctor at Bergstrom. "I don't know whether it has burst or what," she wrote during an hour in the waiting room. "I've just about lost my patience. At this rate I won't get home until midnight."[10]

Her final marks did not reflect the promise of her grades earlier in the term. She ended up with two Bs (in geology and, notably, logic—a discipline Charlie saw as the purview of men) and three Cs (in botany, zoology, and Bible 301). The C grades especially discouraged her. "I'm so disgusted at this damn University I could die," she wrote. "I should have stayed home + gone to Wharton + then to Sam Houston + by now I would have my degree with good grades. Boy, after all I did this semester + come so close to B's and then make C's! Honey, I want to just give up! It's just not worth it!"[11] It was still easier to displace frustration onto the institution rather than onto her husband as a source of disruption.

Kathy struggled to give herself credit for what she had, in fact, accomplished under duress, and being disappointed by Cs was a far cry from failing. Kathy finally allowed herself a night to blow off steam with girlfriends, relieved to relax, talk, and drink. "I've never been that drunk + happy at the same time," she wrote. "We stayed at the apartment and drank. . . . [The girls] said I started crying about you twice + that that's all I talked about." She had much more on her mind than academics, and the listening ears of girlfriends helped. "I hope you are not too disgusted with me, but after all those finals, I had to do something," she said. "Boy did I have a hangover this morning."[12] Charlie would have been less judgmental about her drinking than threatened by Kathy's sharing confidences about her marriage with anyone, especially women.[13]

As she caught her breath during semester break, Kathy still wondered how Charlie spent his time. Even his assurances triggered worry and suggested pressure. He called one night after drinking beers to tell her that he "wasn't really drunk . . . just tight." He had seen *20,000 Leagues under the Sea* at the drive-in with two other Marines and urged Kathy not to "worry about me blowing up or something like that + getting myself in trouble. Darling, anytime I think something foolish or irresponsible I think of my Darling wife and everything comes back to me. I promise Baby, as long as I have you I'll be fine." It did not help that he bragged about being solicited for dates and rejecting them—because "you are the only woman I ever think or dream of."[14]

One romantic comedy Kathy saw with friends (*Move Over, Darling*, starring Doris Day and James Garner) gave her material to reprise the question of fidelity. The plot of the film involved a man taking a new wife after his first wife went missing in a plane crash. "Honey please don't ever even think about taking another woman," Kathy wrote. "I could never Make Love to you again as long as I live if I found out you had touched another woman," she went on, adding hastily, "Of course I don't worry about you because I trust you with any woman on earth." Kathy noted that her roommates thought any belief in Charlie's loyalty was misplaced and had teased her about it: "They don't seem to think there is a man alive who knows what the word faithful means."[15]

In similar vein, as Kathy still received the couple's subscription to *TIME*, she recommended that Charlie get a copy of the January 24 edition for its cover story on "Sex in the U.S.: Mores & Morality." Leading with a photograph of girlie magazines on a newsstand, an exhibit of what the authors called "Spectator Sex," the article provided an overview of research, literature, and pop culture for "The Second Sexual Revolution," as the authors dubbed it. The article concluded by calling for Americans not to retreat into so much sexual knowledge, rebelling against their Victorian forebears, that they forgot about love. "Let me know if you can't get a hold of it," she wrote, "and I'll send it to you." Knowing her audience, Kathy would continue to cite "expert" others as validation for her own insights or questions.[16]

She remained self-conscious, especially about her body. The varicose vein caused pain, but Kathy was more concerned about how Charlie would react to it. "You are going to have a fit when you see my leg," she wrote. "It looks horrible and there's nothing I can do about it." Knowing her husband's fixation on her legs and stomach, she was determined to maintain an exercise program, describing an article she clipped from *McCall's* magazine. Herein was a twist of independence—she chose not to use the exercise booklet Charlie had meticulously annotated and sent (suggesting she purchase an "Iso-Kit" for $5 or $6) along with a photo of himself among friends at Jazzland.[17]

Sensing the implied comparisons to other women, Kathy still tried to fit her husband's aesthetic expectations. Another of his bizarre fixations was her fingernails, about which Kathy repeatedly needed to assure him. "Sweetheart, my fingernails look better than they have since we got married," she wrote. "I'm real proud of them, you would really like them." But in his journal at this time, Charlie complained about the lack of reciprocity he perceived when asking her to conform to his tastes, his demanding nature steaming beneath the charming surface. "She doesn't seem to be impressed with doing something that I ask her, just for me as her husband who loves her very much," he wrote. "I put myself out of the way to do things for her, for just the reason that she is my wife and I love her very much. But it doesn't seem to be a 2-way process."[18] When and how had he ever truly "put himself out of the way" for Kathy? Despite his pledges the previous summer not to "sweat the small stuff," Charlie continued to move the proverbial goal posts according to arbitrary rules.

He seemed to hold his fidelity over her head, as if it were a great sacrifice for which she owed him total submission.

Meanwhile, flashes of women's resistance were raising the temperature in pop culture. By the end of January 1964, Leslie Gore's poignant single, "You Don't Own Me," peaked at number two on the Billboard charts, not quite smashing the vinyl ceiling.[19]

JUST AS KATHY REGISTERED FOR HER spring semester, there was more trouble on the Whitman family front. Charlie's brother Patrick ran away from home and ended up in Kissimmee, Florida, where he had a serious accident. Charlie borrowed a car from a friend to drive from Lejeune to Lake Worth, and Kathy was dismayed by the continued turmoil and by her husband's sketchy explanations. The reasons Patrick had run away remained unclear, as did the full extent of his injuries, which included a broken pelvis. Again, her husband's father seemed to be at the center of the conflict, which had taken an additional violent turn. "I wonder how Daddy got beat up," Kathy wrote, trying to make sense of it all. Repeating her theme from a few weeks earlier, she added, "Charlie, I've never seen people with as many problems."[20] Whatever muddy details he offered, her husband did not lay out one reasonable scenario: that Patrick had fought back this time against a beating or humiliation and driven away in a blind rage.

In a phone call to her parents for advice, Kathy had shared the latest Whitman family news as best she could. Her parents remained mystified. "They can't understand how one family can have so many problems," she wrote to Charlie. She was forcefully clear on one principle: "I didn't marry you to ruin our life together by tackling everyone else's problems in the family and I'm not going to do it. I don't think it's fair for you to expect me to. . . . Honey, you could waste your entire life trying to straighten out Pat and daddy and never succeed in doing anything but destroying our life and marriage."[21]

Kathy wrote two more letters a few days later, still trying to push through the Whitman haze. "I don't even know how [Pat] is doing," she wrote in the first message. "What or how was he hurt? Did he involve anyone else or was anyone else hurt? Where is he? I sure hope he is OK." Charlie called from Florida, and she remained troubled overall by her husband's lack of transparency: "You still wouldn't tell me what happened in the accident. In fact you sound so evasive every time I ask, you sound like you are hiding something." Charlie reported that he was standing up to his father ("I told Daddy to quit pushing me. I told him I was tired of playing the middle between Father + Wife") and worrying about his mother ("She is very dependent + feels that she is to blame for everything that happens"). He sympathized with Johnnie Mike, still recovering from a serious motorcycle accident ("He looks so pitiful the way he limps"), but he reserved a special disdain for Patrick: "He is completely out in the rain as far as I am concerned. . . . I don't even feel physically sorry for him." On top of everything, Charlie told Kathy he had fended off solicitations from a "little blonde nurse" at the hospital and exchanged sexual banter with girls near an archery booth at the Palm Beach County Fair.[22]

The mixed messages were draining. All Kathy could broadly infer about her brother-in-law was that his running away had to do with homosexuality, the secret that had surfaced the previous year. She had been warned by her husband not to let on that she knew about this when talking with his parents.[23] She took some comfort that, whatever had happened, the latest visit had soured her husband on joining the Whitman business. "You said that you had made the decision that you and daddy could never get along and that you weren't planning on going back to Florida to work with him. . . . I imagine you feel better and you know I do."[24]

Grateful for an antidote in her own family, Kathy spent one last weekend in Needville before spring semester. She and her mother went window shopping in Houston and visited the Sharpstown Mall. Frances bought some brown loafers that would not hurt her feet while teaching, and Kathy purchased some new makeup. She took care to justify the expense. "I think you will like it too," she wrote to Charlie. "It has a green base and takes the redness out of my face."[25]

CHARLIE WAS SUGGESTING THAT HE "MIGHT" make an early cut to end his USMC obligation, enabling him to return to Texas in time to register for spring classes with Kathy. She opted not to delay her own registration based on hope: "I don't think we should count on your getting out until you are officially notified," she wrote. Her parents validated this sound judgment to avoid disrupting her academic momentum again. "Mother and daddy think it would be worth taking the chance and spending the money rather than chance wasting a semester by waiting until June to start again."[26] Predictably, Charlie did not secure a spring release date, and Kathy's decision to enroll proved wise. She took on a heavy load of classes and labs, at first registering for organic chemistry, microbiology, botany, and anthropology.

After initial class meetings, however, Kathy adjusted her schedule. The organic chemistry professor disgusted her on the first day. "[H]e can't stand girls and bawled two out this morning in class," Kathy wrote to Charlie. "He even admitted he was hoping he could scare about 20 people into quitting or dropping the course after the first lecture." Kathy described the same professor unfavorably to her parents: "He's the one who can't stand women + segregates the classroom." After a private meeting with him—coincidentally, he was the same instructor who had taught Junior Ley, the Needville pharmacist who was a family friend and neighbor—she dropped his class and substituted a geology course. She also dropped anthropology and nabbed a zoology course in heredity instead. By the time she had her sciences sorted out, she had "some wonderful profs."[27]

Most interesting was Kathy's addition of a sociology course taught by Dr. Henry Bowman, titled "Marriage and Family Life"—a sixties precursor to contemporary courses in gender studies or human sexuality. After just a few class meetings, Kathy was enthralled. She not only wanted Charlie to attend a session with her when he came home on leave; she wanted him to enroll in the class himself when he returned: "You would have enjoyed the lecture today, I think, on male dominance in the household. I want you to take the course for an elective when you get back 'cause you'd do really well in it and really get something out of the course."[28] A week later, she cited a lecture she found particularly powerful:

> Dr Bowman was talking today about women being taught to protect and defend themselves against men from the time they are born, because of the advances and things men try to force upon them throughout life. This constant defensive attitude assumed by women often causes women to be unyielding and frigid in marriage. Therefore, when you think about it, men actually create the very thing they deplore in marriage. Pretty good hypothesis, huh?[29]

These lines were impressive in their use of a masculine authority figure to trace a logical premise for Charlie about

the problem of force in committed sexual relationships—
suggesting that blaming women for romantic dissatisfaction
or resistance made no sense under these circumstances.

Just as she felt the wind at her back, Kathy found herself on the receiving end of Charlie's depressed and angry
moods, guilt trips, and petulant demands, both by telephone and by letter. He said she was not writing enough. He
said she should date her letters. He said she should try yet
another exercise system. "I would like to see you exercise
also to improve your legs, and just to keep your tummy as
flat as it is. I see so many women with little paunches below
their belt line, you know what I call those, I think they look
terrible," he wrote, adding later, "I wish you'd give it an ear-
nest try *for me.*" He said he "worshipped" Kathy and had
grown incredibly dependent upon her, but also repeated that
he was "going nuts" or felt "berserk," like he would mentally
"snap" or "explode," and that he was "on the line of whatever
is on the other side of rationality." In this alarming equation,
he centered Kathy as the source of his salvation, and the
stakes were high. "All I will ever need is to know that you are
with me and love me very much," he wrote. "My love for you
is infinite."[30]

Austin weather in February was similarly extreme, veer-
ing from foggy mornings to sunny and clear days—even a
sudden and short-lived, if historic, snowstorm. "Yesterday
was summer almost, I didn't even wear a coat, and today it
snowed until 2 o'clock and Austin had more snow than it's
had since 1949," Kathy wrote her husband. "The campus
was one big snowfight, even in the classroom. I got caught in
5 bombardments walking across campus." Kathy resumed
her diet and exercised with roommates, also squeezing in
affordable entertainment before the heaviest work of the
semester became inevitable. She saw *Love with the Proper
Stranger*, a love story centered on an unplanned pregnancy

and possible abortion ("a real good but unusual movie. Steve McQueen is so cute and reminds me so much of you"), and a ten-cent old movie feature, *Three Coins in the Fountain*.[31]

Kathy was torn between exasperation with Charlie's self-pitying moments ("Why don't you start some project or something," she wrote. "Start designing us a dream home or something. Just anything") and trying to appease him. In a letter that began "solely to apologize" for not writing enough and for making him feel bad—a puzzling apology, as she had written twice in the previous six days—Kathy said, "I get so disgusted with myself for being a woman and making so many foolish troublesome demands upon my husband. . . . I have a horror that our ideal little perfect marriage is going to suddenly pop and become afflicted with all the horrible problems of most marriages." She went on, "We are so perfect in our relationship now, I pray to God that nothing ever changes any part of it."[32] The ironies remained painful as Kathy continued to express reasonable desires for change and, as harmony—never mind perfection—was most possible in the abstract, when she did not have to live with the man she married.

The couple debated when to plan Charlie's next leave, finally agreeing that late March would work best for Kathy's schedule. Based on her experience in fall 1963 with his ill-timed October visit and arrest and subsequent court-martial in November, Kathy was much more assertive about the plan. "It's so good to have something to look forward to," she wrote to Charlie. But she still worried about his social life. Reflecting on Jazzland, she wondered whether he had made "any decent new acquaintances," writing, "I don't like that place and I hate to think you go in there. . . . I really don't even like the picture of you in there because it reminds me of it all the time." Responding to his repeated demands for a perfect manicure, she assured him that her fingernails would suit his tastes, though she did not share his interest in pain: "Really I've never had my fingernails this long. You should have a pretty bloody back. . . . Ha! I'm only kidding. I don't like to hurt you, even when you like it."[33]

During this period Kathy considered other couples as points of comparison or self-reassurance. One couple they knew, for example, suffered from a mismatch of sexual desire. Kathy focused in on how frustrated the wife was no matter how she tried to entice her husband. "If she walked out into the room nude he'd probably look up from the book and tell her to go put some clothes on!" she wrote. "I sure hope you desire me as much as you used to when we get back together again." Newlyweds afforded a vivid proxy for her own dread. After one visit Kathy wrote, "I feel so sorry for [the wife]. . . . She keeps a perfect house and obviously worships the ground [he] walks on. . . . His old girlfriend has vowed to break up the marriage and is doing a pretty good job of confusing [him]. I hate people that do things like that." She continued, again raising the very insecurities she ostensibly dismissed. "You know I never once thought about you loving anyone else or ever wanting to back out of our marriage." Yet another couple embodied an elusive ideal routine: "He has an 8–5 job and gets at least two days a week off. . . . She just plays the normal housewife. . . . It must be nice to be able to do what you want and go to a show in the middle of the week."[34]

Kathy did all she could to please Charlie while studying for classes, getting tax forms together, paying bills, babysitting, and trying to maintain a social life. She moved into a new room at the same apartment complex, where she now had a roommate and two suitemates. A friend encouraged Kathy to consider a part-time job as a census-taker, going door-to-door in Austin with teams of students to complete questionnaires in people's homes. Upon inviting Charlie's approval and receiving no affirmation, she soon abandoned the prospect. Without his restrictions, her horizons would have expanded considerably.[35]

She took a quick weekend trip to Dallas to help with coat check for a friend's wedding reception at a swank country club. While she enjoyed meeting her friend's parents and seeing their home, she did not care for much else. "I've never seen so many mink stoles in one room in my life. I got so tired of smiling at rich old men!" she wrote to her parents, adding. "I liked the country around Dallas and Fort Worth but the people are snobs." She relished her geology class, especially for the field trips. On one excursion, she was the assigned note-taker for her three-person group. Kathy admired one of her classmates, a Mexican immigrant working on a master's degree: "He can't speak much English but is a brilliant geologist," she wrote to her parents. "The other boy, thank goodness, speaks Spanish fluently, so he will have to translate so I can take notes!"[36]

Kathy renewed her driver's license for the first time since being married, finally making her name-change official. Her Valentine card to Charlie included a separate paper where she hand-copied Sonnet 43 from Elizabeth Barrett Browning's *Sonnets from the Portuguese*, which concludes with the line, "I shall but love thee better after death." An additional letter the same day included a batch of three "naughty" elephant jokes and yet another apology—this time for forgetting their two-year anniversary of getting dropped, a date that still obsessed Charlie. She also reported jogging at night with a friend, emphasizing her reasons for concentrating so hard on exercise: "I think I'm doomed to fat legs. The only reason I want slim legs is because I know it would mean the world to you and I would be so much more appealing to you than I am now." Sadly, if she hoped with these vulnerable admissions to invite a reprieve from Charlie's pressures, she did not receive one.[37]

A week later, Kathy sent Charlie a long article clipped from *Modern Bride* magazine. In an essay titled "Sexual Communication," Eleanor Hamilton, PhD, emphasized the power of married partners to wound each other with criticism, discussing the case of a wife who said her husband would "needle" her about imperfections and then suddenly expect to have sex. Kathy wrote about the article, "It's the first I've read written from the angle that told me some new things I needed to think about. . . . [M]ost of these articles don't say much I don't already know firsthand."[38] Inspired by recent visits to Barton Springs as well as a field trip to Mansfield Dam, she recollected positive romantic memories, mostly from the days before they married.

Meanwhile, Charlie mentioned that he was again considering a job as a nightclub bouncer, just as he had the previous summer. Kathy did not like the reprise of this idea at all, not only because she worried that he would get drawn into the middle of fights with drunks but because there would be so many women. Kathy here redirected responsibility from her husband onto the "tramps" she imagined: "I know as sure as I'm sitting here, that they are going to use every trick they can muster to get you to bed. And don't kid yourself, Charlie, you still have some things to learn about the female mind and its schemes!" Simultaneously, she tried to assuage Charlie's fears of sterility in the context of what she was learning in Marriage and Family Life. "Sometime when a man's sperm count is low even though he's not sterile, he can't make his wife pregnant," she wrote. "In some cases a doctor can use artificial insemination to correct it. I didn't know what you said about your sperm count. . . . Do you remember?"[39]

Kathy meticulously planned the countdown for her husband's leave, at first envisioning a carpool with one of her new suitemates to rendezvous with Charlie in Mobile, Alabama, at the end of March. But the couple finally agreed instead that Charlie would take a flight to Austin and catch a cab to campus. All signs pointed to a smooth visit with minimal disruption of Kathy's studies. She was making excellent grades, especially on her lab reports and exams, and she felt pride in her accomplishments again. She had four tests before Easter and looked forward to putting them behind her before Charlie arrived, although a severe bout of flu was not helping.[40]

Kathy sent Charlie a $75 money order to purchase his plane ticket, and the couple refined the details down to the minute. Kathy was deeply nervous about how their reunion would feel, especially after the circumstances of their last one. "It's hard to believe we've been married over a year and ½. I feel like we are still newlyweds sometime," she wrote. "Honey, it's going to seem stranger this time because we haven't seen each other in 4 mos." Several days later she expressed hypervigilance about physical contact. "I'm already imagining how it will be and I just get all confused. I try to imagine how it will feel to be in your arms again and what you will do," she wrote. She seemed desperate for reassurance that he would not push too hard for sex. "Please say we won't do much except talk and hold each other all four days and nights," she said.[41]

Kathy had been working on her tan and was also relieved to complete her midterms successfully. Since resuming her contraceptives, she had started her period—"so I will be all through," she wrote, "thank goodness." In the last letter Kathy mailed before her husband's visit, she indicated very precisely the time of his scheduled arrival: Charlie would get to Austin at 8:22 a.m. on Wednesday, March 25, while Kathy was in botany class, enabling him to change into civilian clothes at a hotel and meet her before Marriage and Family Life, the class she wanted him to attend with her. Kathy was excited, but she felt that a great deal of preparation remained necessary. "With only 6 days," she wrote, "I don't want to waste a minute."[42]

Unbeknownst to Kathy, however, Charlie made a last-minute decision to adjust his arrival time. He documented the change in his diary. "Kathy is going to just die when I arrive Tue. A.M. instead of Wed.," he wrote to himself. "Boy, I want to see how she acts with the surprise."[43] This surprise for Kathy was really a test, with Charlie positioning himself to judge her readiness and her response, poised to deem them lacking—a textbook illustration of what experts now understand as coercive control.

Between the Leaves

WHEN CHARLIE LEFT ON APRIL 2, 1964, the couple had spent a week in Austin, taking a few days to celebrate Easter with her family. After his departure, Kathy was in a reminiscent mood, writing about the fading love marks on her neck ("the only trace I have left"). During the visit Charlie had finally shared some good news: his release date from the Marine Corps was set for early December 1964. But he had also frightened her one night at a drive-in movie in Richmond when he talked obsessively about success.[1]

The December release date gave Kathy something concrete to hold on to, like an official "start date" of her future as she watched other students breezing across campus, drinking, and celebrating UT's annual spring festivities. Kathy remembered happier days. "I keep thinking about how much fun we had Freshman year at Round-Up," she wrote. Nostalgia was unsatisfying, however, and two days later

Kathy admitted questions about her husband's recent visit. "I hope I'm not asking for it + mabe this is just something that happens, but you didn't seem to enjoy our love-making as much as you use to," she wrote. "If you did, you didn't say so. I hope I haven't changed as a lover. I'd hate to be a disappointment to you. Please tell me the truth and don't just tell me what I want to hear." Kathy spoke to Charlie by phone and received one romantically assuring letter within two weeks—an envelope she annotated "Special Letter"—wherein, among other things, he pledged his "total devotion" and asked Kathy to promise "never to betray this sentiment I have for you," reminding her that "my Honey has to carry at least 4 little Whitmans someday." He also wrote a letter to Kathy's parents, thanking them for "the part y'all have had in her make-up." It would be two months before Charlie doubled back and responded directly, cruelly, to Kathy's worried question.[2]

Everyone around Kathy seemed to be moving forward: friends starting their families, one couple leaving Austin for good. Her parents were taking classes—Frances in "new math" and Raymond in real estate as well as "airplane wreck investigation." Even her in-laws were making progress: Johnnie Mike was having a kneecap replaced, Patrick was getting ready for prom, and her father-in-law was dieting to improve his health. Charlie, too, had started an eight-week history course towards his undergraduate degree.[3]

The biggest news of all, however, was that Frances was pregnant. Kathy saved and labeled the envelope that made it official: "Mother's letter about the baby!" Indeed, Frances sounded gleeful after she and Kathy's father visited a Rosenberg doctor. "I hope he's 'modern' enough (ha!) and I really got a surprise—Master or Miss Leissner is due October 1st," she reported. "I've been planning on the middle of November—No wonder I look so stuffed!" Just as Kathy had

Kathy poses with Nelson during her visit with Charlie to Needville for Easter 1964.

resorted to a doctor outside Needville to secure her first contraceptive pills, now Frances, too, went out of town to get the medical treatment she preferred. She reported how the doctor said she was "in very good shape" and provided vitamins and appetite-curbing pills as well as "some booklets on baby care. Tee hee!" Frances described breaking the news to Kathy's brothers: "[Nelson] seems quite pleased. . . . You should have heard [Ray] whoop! I was a little leery about his reaction, but I needn't have worried. I swore him to secrecy for a while, tho, and I think he'll keep it to himself—I heard him telling Princess [their dog] about it, tho'—That will always be one of my favorite memories!"[4]

Kathy's parents embraced the development, although her mother was certainly aware that pregnancy past the age of forty was unconventional, even when intended. "I doubt you ever expected to have any more brothers or sisters," Frances wrote in a letter to Charlie. "I'm sure all of our friends will consider us very foolish but I really don't care—I'm in a fog and Raymond is really proud of himself—Ha!" Kathy was delighted by the idea of being a big sister again.[5] She enjoyed the new excuse to bond with her mother. "I can't wait to go shopping, please don't buy everything before I get home," she wrote to Frances. "Let me know how the shower turns out. *Stop wearing those horrible girdles!*" For his part, Charlie admitted jealousy: "Heck y'all are starting a second family before Kathy and I even get to work on our first." He had recently bragged about "helping out a boy" by talking his girlfriend out of an abortion.[6]

Harry's Place continued to serve as Kathy's favored study retreat, and she applied for new jobs. She considered being the designated counselor of her apartment—which would reduce her monthly rent by $15 simply for locking and unlocking the gate—but, according to a dean, her course overload precluded approval for that role.[7] She investigated a desirable internship with a zoology professor, to no avail. She also applied for a promising position at the Austin Nature & Science Center, which offered a teaching post she had to decline due to a schedule conflict. ("The lady said to keep the idea in mind for next fall.")[8]

Eventually Kathy applied to and was quickly hired at Southwestern Bell in downtown Austin, a massive switchboard serving not only the city but the Texas State Capitol and university. The job would fit well into her schedule. She was excited to tell her family about the chief operator: "She is real nice and is really interested in hiring me for part time work this summer + all next year. . . . She said I could work as much as I wanted next year because of football season and then the legislature coming in for the Spring." Rather than miss a trip home because of a training period, Kathy squeezed in a quick visit before finals week instead. She was most nervous about one exam her professor subtitled, "how to live with the F bomb," referencing ads for the new film, *Dr. Strangelove.*[9]

Nuclear puns notwithstanding, Kathy managed her challenges well, just as she had during the summer of 1963.
When spring grades posted, Kathy framed the results for
Charlie with self-diminishment: "Can you believe your
dumb little wife has finally made some grades to be proud
of!" Determined to meet her goal of graduation within four
years, Kathy registered for two courses during the grueling
summer session: physics and educational psychology. The
former proved difficult immediately, and Kathy wasted no
time before getting a tutor. The new learning curve at Southwestern Bell was steep. "I like the work," she told Charlie,
"but the board here is so big and complicated. It will take
a while to become familiar with it." She described details
that made the Austin switchboard unique. "We have about
200 circuits that concern the president only. We handle all
Johnson City calls. It's going to be one ____ of a mess when
[Johnson] gets here for this weekend to speak at commencement." She added, "I'd give anything to go."[10]

As work on every front drew down Kathy's personal
reserves, her husband needled her vulnerabilities even as
he spoke of their reunion in drastic terms: "[W]e are never
going to be separated another day of our lives once I get out
of the Corps." He had taken on night shifts at Bernard's, a
men's clothing store in Jacksonville, where, as he told Kathy,
three women working as bookkeepers and cashiers "all have
their designs about me." His assurances were laced with
self-aggrandizement: "Honey, if it was just sex I was missing
that is easy to find. But I am lonesome, lost and very much in
love with my *wife*." In early May Kathy informed Charlie by
phone that she had received a strange letter from his female
coworkers, and he scrambled to explain, asking Kathy to
return it to him so he could "trace + trace it." His perspective was convoluted: "[O]ne day they mentioned writing you

a letter with a lot of crap in it and I made the grim mistake of showing concern and anger over it and they decided this is how they could get to me. . . . [D]amn that makes me mad."[11] The mysterious document did not survive.

Such gratuitous distractions contributed new stress Kathy did not need. Who were these women, and how much anger had her husband shown them? She knew Charlie did not trust alliances between women, and he often reminded Kathy that she had "more common sense" than other women he knew.[12] But was their message a taunt or a warning? And what exactly did he mean to do about the letter? Amidst these questions, Kathy cut herself little slack. One day en route to work, the car's engine light flashed, and she panicked. Dropping the car at a service station, she removed her shoes and raced twelve blocks to Southwestern Bell, arriving five minutes early. "I had time to catch my breath," she wrote.[13]

She found herself drawn again into the maelstrom of Charlie's manipulative and ominous moods ("[I]f I had not had you for my wife, I would have killed myself at least 6 times"), his brittle attitudes ("I like something that is definite, either right or wrong with no middle ground for disagreement between student and teacher"), and selfish demands (asking Kathy to write a research paper about Thaddeus Stevens for his history class—she refused and sent reference material instead). But Kathy continued to press her husband on their need to grow as a married couple, first crediting him with what she wanted to be true. "I have decided that you haven't really become any more dependent on me but now you are living for me as well as yourself," she said. "[T]hat's the way it should have been when you first thought you were in love with me." She went on, with mutuality as a premise for her desire to be heard. "I feel like our marriage has been strengthened but only because of the many trials we've been through, not because we've been together and talked about our ideas and plans. . . . We have both changed a lot I'm sure and we are both going to have to realize that when we get together and [we should] respect each other's new ideas."[14] Any evolution in Kathy's thinking, however, was exactly what Charlie would not tolerate.

During an enjoyable visit with her family, Kathy was "tickled" about her brothers' proposed names for the coming baby, and she described making dinner for her father and listening to a record he had recently acquired, *Judgment at Nuremberg.* ("I want to get that record, it's really good.")[15] She punctuated stories with the usual intimate banter she enjoyed, adding occasional naughty jokes for additional comic relief. But her reflective voice persisted:

> In your last letter you have been saying some awful
> nice things about me and sometimes it worries me.
> Honey, when you're not with someone you love, it's
> awful easy to build them up to something they aren't
> and I'm afraid this may be what you are doing. I even
> got this impression when you were home. . . . You
> seemed a little dissatisfied with me in some ways
> and I really am the same girl you married. I may be
> unjustified in my fear but it could happen. . . . [D]on't
> let me become over-special while we are separated
> and then find me not quite that special when we get
> back together. It won't be good for you or I.[16]

In straightforward language, Kathy expressed her knowledge that a pedestal was a dangerous place. Her husband's surprise arrival on the last visit provided only the most recent reminder of how he used standards as a cudgel.

In his response Charlie missed the point by proving her theorem, insisting that indeed he had a grasp of her "minor" faults, which he enumerated in offhand detail that threw back to the questions haunting Kathy after Easter: "When I was home on leave I was disappointed in your hair, legs, and I felt that in your engrossment in your studies you had let yourself go a little below your normal standards." He added that he wanted other men to admire Kathy and wonder who her husband was, rather than looking at her as an "old married hag" and feeling sorry for her "poor bastard" husband (though he would also emphasize just days later that sexy outfits were "only for [his] eyes"). He enumerated four expectations Kathy should consider as "little things" to "look suave" because "95% of the time you are a doll, but you happened to marry a guy who won't allow any slack for that other 5% of the time." He listed lipstick ("fresh" and not "faded out" or "eaten off") and makeup; nice looking nails ("either clear + not polished, or polished with no chips"); neat hair ("unless the occasion or surrounds allow otherwise"); and "shined shoes." Charlie also invited her to consider the many times she had let him down when he made requests, and he pledged "for the rest of my life by my actions I intend to show you how much I appreciate and worship you." When Kathy returned this letter to its envelope, she labelled "Important" on the back flap, as if recording it for reminders—or for evidence.[17]

Yet Kathy now had a clearer outlook on Charlie's character. She enjoyed a summer weekend at Lake McQueeney with her younger cousin, Nancy, who had visited Austin for Girls' State. When they returned to town, the two women went to see a movie, *The Carpetbaggers*, starring George Peppard, a film Charlie had recommended. "The way he desired women reminded me of you, *sometime*," she wrote, taking a deeper turn. "Don't get me wrong, but sometime, not every often + even less than at first, you did show an awful hunger that seemed sort of divorced of love. . . . There is nothing wrong with that, cause I think it's natural in men + women, + I feel that way too sometime." She drifted a bit, recalling the beautiful full moon on the lake and how she and her cousin had taken "a run" on the water with the lodge pro, a ski stunt man, who held "a couple of World Championships in skiing." The favorable and uncomplicated male attention had to feel good. She also described her new tan ("A good tan sure improves the look of the ole bods!"), her latest weight loss, and plans to meet a doctor "about helping me on a suitable diet." As Elvis Presley's voice came on the radio, "I Can't Help Falling in Love with You," Kathy circled back to her central thesis. "Honey, let's please try not to lose the romantic aspects of our relationship," she wrote. "I don't mean going to bed but just the opposite."[18]

Kathy reprised this theme in stronger terms the following week, questioning not only Charlie's sexual preoccupations but his general philosophy of life. Upon receipt of a letter that had contained some money, she sought to clarify a feeling her husband had distorted after latching on her use of the word, "hunger": "I am really sorry I ever mentioned it. . . . Honey, if we destroy all the subtle aspects of sex, we are doing to destroy ½ of sex." She went on, "I think it's good to be able to talk about our sex life out in the open in every detail when we meet an area of incompatibility, but I also think we can *talk* about it too much. Charlie—you and I are close enough to be able to perceive things in each other without verbalization."[19] At least she yearned for such closeness to be possible.

Within a few days, Kathy detailed her new diet ("can't eat much other than vegetables + meat + no bread which cuts out sandwiches") and said she wanted him to be "very proud" of her, but then quickly delved into Charlie's obsession with material success. On this point she doubted his ability to hear what she was saying. "I realize we live in essentially 2 different worlds when it comes to interpreting life's goals," she wrote. "If you were sure of yourself + your motives you wouldn't have to constantly be aggressive + hurried." She again connected to the main character of *The Carpetbaggers* as a cautionary example:

> Honey—I hope this doesn't upset you but being very honest with you—there are very few times that I can recall us doing things for pleasure without your being hurried, anxious, and aggressive about some factor of what we are doing, and I can't recall any business type task you have done without exhibiting all the things I mentioned. There is no sense in it—it doesn't make you any better because you're anxious— you could accomplish the same thing without it and add 10 years to our lives. You see it affects me even worse than you.[20]

The last two lines included a measure of foresight as well as a direct articulation of how his attitudes and actions harmed her. She added, "Precious, please don't talk about success being an obsession with you because then there won't be any room for me. I want to be the only obsession you indulge in." Concluding, she conceded that her new job was causing too much stress and that she had quit. Here, as elsewhere, Kathy found it easier to eliminate stressors other than Charlie, even as concerns about his behavior came into vivid focus from afar.[21]

As the summer session wound down, Kathy's confidence grew. She had enjoyed her first education class, even though she anticipated that the final test was going to be tough. The reward was right in front of her. "[After that exam] I will then be a Senior at the University of Texas," she wrote to Charlie. "Honey, I never really thought I'd make it."[22] Studying at a friend's house, she jotted a short letter and did something reminiscent of her carefree scrapbooking days, affixing two whimsy stickers to both stationery and the envelope: red lips and a UT pennant. The next day she celebrated her twenty-first birthday at a party Frances organized. ("We are going to BBQ and mother had a cake made + everything.") Kathy mused how empowered she felt with the success of her new diet, adding that "married or not, I still get a thrill out of turning a few heads now + then. You don't mind do you."[23]

KATHY ANTICIPATED ANOTHER REUNION WITH Charlie's leave in August, shortly following their second wedding anniversary. She was thrilled that this visit would be much longer—nearly a full month—and that, barring unforeseen problems, it would be their last visit before her husband's final release from the Marine Corps. As initial plans took shape, she looked forward to a more independent adventure on the first leg of the trip, when she would carpool with a friend's sister to Jacksonville. Charlie and Kathy would take the car to Lake Worth to spend time with the Whitmans, then would return to Austin together before Charlie flew back to Camp Lejeune. Even if all went smoothly, this leave would mean a great deal of time on the road.

During all the anticipation, Kathy suffered several panic attacks. In physics class she "broke down in front of my prof because the grader didn't grade one of my problems + my lab inst. said it was right." The experience derailed Kathy's attention before the final, which she only half completed ("I really thought I must be the stupidest person in the whole world to study as hard and know as little on the test"), but she was relieved to survive with a C on the class curve. She also experienced a physical breakdown after an afternoon outing with three friends. They started for a day-drive in a hot car when it was already 103 degrees and had "2 flats in the middle of nowhere." Kathy described her condition upon returning: "I started getting this pain in my chest so bad I couldn't breathe. The Dr. said I was just exhausted + the pain was caused from nervous tension. He gave me some pills to relax and told me to stay in bed for 3 days. (be sure)."[24]

Deeply aware that Charlie's affection was always conditional, Kathy felt an increase in the stakes of their coming reunion. Although happy with her weight loss, Kathy observed how her clothes didn't fit well anymore, and sexual anxiety remained at the top of her mind. "I really feel like a vegetable now," she wrote. "I don't think I am going to be a very good lover for a love starved man." In a subsequent letter she was apprehensive about his scrutiny. "[M]y clothes look awful on me," she wrote. "I'm so happy about the way I look and I hope you will like me like this." She added, "I might be a little boney in bed right now. I have a feeling I will enjoy sex much more now. I always enjoy it more when I know I look nice and that you think I'm sexy and attractive." Kathy also felt the wear of her marriage, using humor as a buffer. "When you think about all that hasn't happened that we planned on, it seems short," she wrote. "But considering all that has happened, I feel like a Granny!"[25] In his responses he compared her to a piece of furniture that can be polished to be "the finest piece of furniture in all the land." Although he praised her new weight of 117 pounds, he withheld final approval until he saw her in person. "I might not like it or I might think it's fabulous," he wrote. "In my mind I think you should look fabulous at about 112–115 pounds, but I'll have to wait and see."[26]

Charlie was completing the second of two correspondence courses for the summer, and in early August he complained about his mental stamina. Considering all that she had managed on top of her own coursework, Kathy was incensed by his self-absorption. "[Y]ou made me so dis-gusted I was really mad," she wrote. "I know the next 20 days could not be any worse than the last year. All you have to do is *tolerate* your surrounding, no one will ask you to make any other effort."[27]

The contrast in their circumstances could not have been starker, and Charlie still failed to demonstrate the capacity for true self-reflection. Two days later Kathy addressed these discrepancies in more depth, first showering his ego with compliments about his "character + brains" as well as the "courage and confidence" she "loved to watch" when she compared him to other men. This premise, however, laid her foundation for a significant critique:

> I think the Marine Corp has taught you the most
> important lesson you have ever received and that's
> a lesson in honesty and straight-forwardness. You
> needed it! If I ever had any doubts about your char-
> acter, that is what it was: honesty and integrity. After
> we were married for a while and I really got to know
> you better, it seemed to me that you were a young
> ambitious man who wanted to set the world on fire,
> but by *your own rules*. That doesn't work in any facet
> of life and I think, at least I pray, that you know better
> now.[28]

Whatever drew Kathy to her initial browse of the popular and controversial *Atlas Shrugged* (1957), whose author she identified as "Ann" not Ayn Rand ("over a thousand pages long and worth every page"), Kathy decisively rejected Char-lie's brand of entitled individualism—and she hoped he "[knew] better now."[29]

Such moments revealed the conflict between Kathy's growing confidence in asserting her own perspective and her strategic use of appeasement. Positive interactions with classmates and professors helped her to stay grounded, as during a weekend field trip to the Marine Institute near Corpus Christi Bay. When a friend that spring disclosed that she had been "taken by force" by a man she had been dating for some time, Kathy reported with unequivocal outrage: "[She] hasn't had any sleep all weekend and looks terrible. Charlie, some men are the biggest bastards. She said she felt like she'd been hit over the head it happened so fast she was almost in shock. I can't believe some men will stoop so low." In a phone call soon afterwards, Charlie cast doubts on her friend's credibility. Even worse, his subsequent letter expressed minimal sympathy and deep adherence to myths about rape—views Kathy supposedly knew he held: "[Y]ou know that I feel a woman can't be raped unless she puts herself into position," Charlie wrote. "The guy was definitely a no-good SOB to take her against her will, but she should have known him and realized what she was doing before she put herself into a compromising position."[30] By his definition, an assaulted woman was always to blame.

Kathy later minimized the event to Charlie on two occasions, but she brought the friend home to Needville for a weekend visit with her parents. Her real-life interactions in this crisis thus did not entirely conform to her husband's rhetoric, regardless of what she told him after he reminded her of his philosophy. Even after transferring to another college, the friend maintained an attachment to Kathy and her family.[31]

In the most ordinary terms, Kathy was tired of the sexual double standard. When Charlie gleefully recounted how his youngest brother was carrying around a condom in his pocket, she rejected her husband's attitude. "I hope you are not proud of him for it!" she responded. "I don't mean John Mike is so bad, for all I know he may be carrying it around to show off to his friends . . . but I'm talking about a boy 15 years old who does think he's the ladies' favorite stud!" She connected this sexual bravado to her view of a broader social dynamic, referencing an article titled "Sex and the College Girl":

> [A]ccording to interviews with boys, it's no longer the "thing" to make everything in a skirt before you are married. In fact, most college caliber men would like to be virgins when they marry. It makes pretty good sense to me and I'll be damned if I die and have an irresponsible punk for a son! . . . I don't know why I get so heated up over that. I guess I've always hated anyone who excused men + boys "just because they're males." Mabe women ought to start having 2 dozen affairs before they are married + see how the man who wants to marry a virgin likes it.[32]

In her critique Kathy fundamentally challenged her husband's fixation on her "naiveté" before their marriage and his pride at "being [her] first and only lover."[33]

Indeed, despite continued expressions about how much she trusted Charlie, Kathy remained wary of his interactions in Jacksonville, and especially on Court Street. Conversation about her youngest brother-in-law again afforded an opportunity to raise the subject. Johnnie Mike traveled to Lejeune to help Charlie transport many of the couple's belongings to Lake Worth in preparation for their final move back to Texas. But Kathy did not like the idea that Charlie had offered to fix his brother up "with one of those little cuties" on Court Street. She continued, "You said he asked you to, and you didn't say whether you did or not. I wish you didn't even know those women." She likely imagined dancers or prostitutes, but with Charlie it could have been anyone. He referred to unnamed local women in his diary as the "whores" in town, and he had shared entries with Kathy on their last visit and apparently left it with her.[34]

Money remained an area where Charlie retained a great deal of psychological control, especially since Kathy had quit her job. The couple had a lingering bill for what she referred to as "those dumb no good encyclopedias," an expense dating back to a purchase Charlie made before they married. Kathy repeatedly argued that they should sell the books off to make room for other expenses, but Charlie dragged his feet, at one point even sending her a two-party check for $40 and writing, "I was going to buy you something real nice for your birthday, but with our getting short I figured you wouldn't mind if we put it toward the Encyclopedia bill instead." It would be mid-October before he even considered the idea. He also seemed to have lost his position at Bernard's.[35]

LETTERS FROM THE END OF JULY through mid-August document Kathy's concerns about her coming trip to Lejeune, especially since she planned to drive this time. As usual, she managed details about which her husband was withholding. "Will our base sticker get me in the base?" she asked, referring to the special military tag on their car. "I think you said it would, but what about the little white sticker that expired in July? . . . Please check to be sure?" She also inquired about facilities at the Lejeune hostess house for military guests and family members: she did not know if she needed to bring sheets for the bed.[36]

News arrived not long before Kathy left Austin. For weeks Charlie had talked up an even earlier "cut" in September—at one point in June either totally deluded or plainly lying, he wrote, "[M]y cut came through, we get out Mon. AM Sept 4"—but predictably, this was not granted. Kathy had grown accustomed, if not inured, to the pattern of redirection and letdowns. "I don't guess it should have surprised me," she admitted. "I just hope this is the last disappointment for a little while at least." Anticipating their second anniversary, she alluded to future celebrations as if they were not to be counted upon: "Maybe, just maybe, if we're real extra lucky, we will be able to celebrate our 3rd anniversary together. Far-fetched as it may seem." In his anniversary card, Charlie stated how Kathy herself was the possession he would most like to give her. "[M]aybe some day the intensity of my love for you will strike you," he wrote.[37]

Kathy's letters stopped abruptly on August 12, as she prepared for summer exams and experienced a reprise of an unidentified illness. Charlie urged her to get to the doctor to "straighten out" her period: "We couldn't stand to have my Honey's system messed up, she has to carry 4 little Whitmans for us sometime in the future." Roughly four days before her scheduled departure, he continued that he was "sure worried," adding, "I won't feel relaxed until you are examined in Fla. and are much better." He had already made an appointment for Kathy with a Lake Worth physician, and he offered to abstain from sex until after she was examined because, in his words, "I'd never forgive myself if I harmed you in any way." Kathy found another urgent note in her husband's postscript: "*Please, for me*, ask the Dr. in Austin to write out his diagnosis + medication so that the Dr. [in Lake Worth] will know what's been done. Sorta like a health record. *Please.*" The last word was underlined twice. He had predetermined an emergency, and no record preserved Kathy's feelings. The plan for a relaxing excursion had shifted, with Charlie assuming control of what needed to be done, and how.[38]

Meanwhile, Hurricane Cleo brewed in the Caribbean and South Atlantic, demolishing Haiti and pounding across

Cuba. Just as meteorologists predicted the storm to calm down, Cleo reactivated and plowed directly into the area in and around Miami, causing more damage than anticipated.[39] Kathy found herself in Lake Worth, smack in the middle of it all—staying with the Whitman family and preparing for a procedure that would permanently alter her fertility.

KATHY HAD GYNECOLOGICAL SURGERY ON SEPTEMBER 4 to remedy symptoms that, as drawn from characterization in later letters, seem to have included uniquely painful menstrual periods. Full medical records do not survive. Diagnosed with a cyst, one of her ovaries was reportedly removed, likely via oophorectomy: at the time, along with hysterectomy, a commonly aggressive treatment among male surgeons for women's "complaints." Her previous experience of being taken to the Whitman family doctor, her husband's constant pressure for medical solutions and postures of expertise, and physicians' attitudes of the time altogether would have complicated Kathy's straightforward desires for diagnosis and relief. Her compliance should not be interpreted as fully informed consent to such a drastic procedure, especially within the well-established pattern of Charlie's control and aggression.[40]

Such surgery at the time necessitated general anesthesia, a large abdominal incision, many stitches, and a significant recovery period for even the healthiest woman at such a young age. Beyond its long-term impact on her fertility, Kathy would experience complications in her overall health—perhaps inhibiting any imaginings she dared about a future beyond Charlie. Given his deep fear of sterility following a genital injury in a motorcycle accident at a young age, this procedure also evened the physical score, binding her to him more completely. Kathy's thoughts about

Goldwater supporters pose with black eyes in the "rather fight than switch" campaign before the 1964 Republican convention. Bettmann/Bettman Collection via Getty Images.

motherhood had been long bound up in his expectations, as she had echoed poignantly during her pregnancy scare in December: "I mean after all, I am a woman and that's what I'm for!"[41] Among other manipulations, he could easily now make her feel like damaged goods.

Recovery time with the Whitmans was not ideal. One family physician, who had treated Kathy's mother-in-law for menopausal complaints as well as bruises after beatings, later reported that her father-in-law crudely questioned the couple's sex life around the time of the operation.[42] Again, she was caught in the cycle: the controlling impulses of her husband, the humiliations of her father-in-law, and the complicity of male enablers. She would not have known that the gynecologist who wrote her painkiller prescription had been sued for leaving a needle in a woman more than a decade earlier.[43]

As she recuperated in Lake Worth, a shocking political advertisement aired during the NBC Monday Movie, *David and Bathsheba*, on September 7. Criticized for being hysterical, even defamatory, in its attack on presidential candidate Barry Goldwater, the ad was pulled immediately by Lyndon Johnson's campaign. Even so, the infamous "Daisy Spot" was rebroadcast in full during programs that debated its impact. The sixty-second ad depicted a blonde, freckle-faced little girl picking petals from a wildflower in a country field. As the girl stopped counting and looked up from the bare pistil, the camera froze and zoomed towards her face. A man's voice cut in, counting down as the shot zeroed in closer and closer to the pupil of her right eye, eventually melting into the darkness. A mushroom cloud exploded and filled the frame as the voice spoke a warning across the bursts of fire and smoke. A final line was adapted from W. H. Auden: "We must either love each other, or we must die."[44]

Goldwater supporters meanwhile had battled fiercely at rallies and inside their national convention to ensure his place as the Republican candidate. Some fans showed solidarity in the "rather fight than switch" campaign, which riffed on ads for Tareyton brand cigarettes. Photographers gravitated to images of young, fresh-faced white women, their eyes smudged to simulate injury, smiling in triumph. One photo appeared in *TIME*.[45]

Disturbed Horizons

AFTER TWENTY-SEVEN DAYS WITH CHARLIE, KATHY'S letters resumed September 21, 1964. On top of everything, she had relocated to a new off-campus duplex apartment at 1001 Shelley Avenue on Austin's west side. The hot, humid summer days lingered, and Central Texas had been invaded again by crickets—an annual plague and harbinger of autumn. The insects were thick on exterior walls, on driveways and sidewalks, and they swarmed in the halos of streetlights. Dead crickets slicked the streets under car tires and in gutters. The smell was terrible.[1]

The new location isolated Kathy once again. A social creature by nature, she felt the solitude deeply. "It's awful to be so lonesome for one person and to be alone on top of it all," she wrote to her husband. "The TV is my only savior." She added her strategy: "I'm about to go mad! I'm going to spend most of my time at school just to be around people."

Charlie had done the barest minimum to help Kathy settle in before he returned to Lejeune for his final stretch. The furniture was sparse, there was no air conditioning, and the gas line for the stove still needed repair. Kathy did not have a proper desk for her schoolwork or a dresser for her clothes, but Charlie had bought a new car, a larger one, that Kathy found more difficult to park around campus. He left a bottle of a sexual desensitization medication in the bathroom cabinet and a stash of firearms in the attic.[2]

On top of it all, Kathy again had no phone, an outrageous reprise of the pattern in Jacksonville, even more senseless following Kathy's surgery. She needed to see a local doctor for follow-up visits, and she was wary of some tasks Charlie assigned to her in the mess he left behind. "I can't get your guns down to oil them," she said. "I'm afraid to climb up around there for a couple of weeks." She added later, "I'm sure that if I felt better physically and could do all the things I would like to and need to, it wouldn't be so bad. I have the kitchen looking better, I straightened up that mess of tools + stuff and put it all in one corner. This place really needs a man!"[3]

She wrote to Charlie from the washateria, where she managed to haul loads of dirty clothes, including "all those sets of your underwear that were piled on the floor for a week." She included her report from the doctor's visit, which had generally gone well (aside from the fact that "he sounded a bit disgusted because I didn't give him my business!"). Perhaps he questioned the drastic and sudden nature of the surgery. After giving her a "complete post-operative exam," Kathy wrote, "He said everything was fine and I didn't have to worry about what I could do or not do because I wouldn't over-do it. . . . He said I could tell because it would start hurting + I would tire real easy to protect my body." At least part of his message was that Kathy should trust herself. The doctor prescribed a new birth control medication but held off on additional hormone supplements "for balance" until after her first period. She slipped one day on campus, badly pulling her side: "It's sore now but I don't guess I did any real damage." Charlie said he "winched [sic] himself" when he read about that slip. But his sympathy proved shallow as he went on to lecture about his new dietary expectations and complain that he had been "hurt" that Kathy did not wear red shoes when she got off the plane: "God I feel bad, when I ask you to do something and you completely disregard it. Before I come home would you think about it and please try and do some things for me, because you love me and because I am your husband."[4]

Frances was in the final weeks of pregnancy, yet another reason for a reliable phone line. Kathy waited almost a week to broach the subject with Charlie, and even with the distance between them again, she had to tread carefully. Her delicate framing for such a straightforward need—and the fact that even now she asked permission—suggested that his domineering treatment had left a renewed physical and psychological impression during their month together. Her language illustrated how Charlie still nickle-and-dimed their budget, especially where Kathy's needs were concerned. "Honey, I hate to say this," she wrote, "but I can put up with no air conditioning + many other things, but I must have a phone. If I can get Mother + Daddy to sign so we won't have to put up a deposit + I promise not to make any long-distance calls, can I do it? I will be making $24 a month + I'll pay for it out of that. Just $7.00 a month and I really need one." After a few more days, she raised the subject with her mother, asking her parents to sign. She did not mention Charlie at all.[5]

A UT senior at last, Kathy was on track to graduate as if she had never dropped out. Even with a mixture of science lectures and labs as well as education courses, she now carried only twelve units instead of twenty, leaving her more time for paid work. The job at the Nature & Science Center was available again, and she accepted a Saturday course to teach about living things to third and fourth graders. Kathy recognized the benefits to her future career even though the hours and wages were limited. "The experience will be invaluable," she wrote. She was grateful for the opportunity to study with the same professor who taught her summer educational psychology course—"the man I made an A under in EdP"—and she experienced a poignant affirmation on the first day of class. "He remembered me," Kathy wrote, "and even called me by my first name."[6]

A "terrific rain" one Saturday night in late September offered a break in the heat, signaling a welcome change of seasons. Kathy had friends over for dinner and television that evening. "Fall has finally hit Texas," Kathy reflected the next day. "It feels so good. It sure was nice sleeping weather last night and this morning." But some things were not changing. Charlie's responsiveness was not ideal. "I wish your letters were a tinge bit longer," Kathy wrote. "So far I feel like I'm getting a note." As if to inspire his protectiveness, Kathy recorded an unpleasant experience during the standard fingerprinting process for her new job. "It was real weird," she said, referring to how she was treated at the police station. "The men in the dept. teased me all the way through. I had to go right into the jail to have the picture taken. I could see the men in the cells + everything." She added how one officer took her on a detour that included a prank with a denigrating connotation: "When I was leaving one Lt. said he had saved a special padded cell for me—he showed me the padded cell!"[7]

Weird messages normalizing men's strange behavior, and much worse, came from authoritative sources. In its final issue for September, *TIME* published an article under the heading "Psychiatry" on the subject of "The Wife Beater and His Wife." The experts cited in the story suggested that men's drunken violence against their partners often provided a helpful outlet to release anxiety about his bossy wife, who herself received "masochistic gratification" from the attacks. Kathy must have seen this article, but she did not point it out to Charlie. Its rationale blaming women would have felt grimly familiar.[8]

KATHY HAD A PHONE INSTALLED IN the apartment the first week of October, and just in time: her mother was preparing to leave for the hospital, cooking "things like meat loaf and roast and freezing them so that Nelson can heat them up for the family while I'm not here." Frances was glad to be able to talk with her daughter. "It surely was good to hear your voice—and I am really relieved that you have a telephone," she said. "Maybe I can even call you from the hospital!" In a letter composed shortly afterwards under a message (*"THINK PINK!"*) printed at the top of the page, Kathy wrote, "I really can't wait till Saturday so I can come home and see you both. Please take it easy! . . . Wait till you see the outfit I'm going to get 'her' if she's a 'her.'"[9]

Meanwhile, Kathy's letters to her husband were consumed by intensifying stretches of reflection on their relationship. When Charlie reported that he was not picking up any more hours in the clothing shop, she worried again about him taking shifts as a bouncer. ("You had best be a sweet boy. . . . [B]e careful and don't let any cutie pull you off to her bedroom. Ha!") Her physical recovery was much on her mind, even as her body healed. "I don't feel raw anymore," she wrote, "but the scar is still a little touchy. I can do almost anything now, but by the end of the day I'm bushed and my stomach is sore." Her husband's pledge "not to hurt her" before surgery had apparently not applied to her recovery time. Kathy recalled uncomfortable sex ("pampering an incision") even as she longed for him to "always hold [her] close."[10]

Kathy now reminisced about a past that seemed more and more distant, perhaps because it contained the thrill of so much potential. Arriving to campus early for lab and finding a spot to write in the Exercise Science building, Kathy painted a moving scene: "[A] couple just wandered through the swinging doors at the end of the hall. When I looked up, I could see him kissing her through the windows in the doors—I miss you so much." These longings mingled with realism as she revisited Charlie's mood swings, including his use of emotional blackmail. "Precious," Kathy replied, "I want to be a very large part of your life but not all of it. That's why I don't like to hear you talk about not wanting to live for anything but me and killing yourself if I died. . . . If you really live for me and not for yourself at all, then I don't have a man to love anymore." She went on to address a subject that had bothered her in his recent letters. He had lately repeated that she completely "rejected" him by not complying with a "request" that sounded more like an order—likely a reference again to her choice of shoes. "You keep reminding me not to take advantage of your need for me," she wrote. "Honey, I rarely see or realize your need and have no idea how to capitalize or take advantage of it." She continued with lines that read, in hindsight, as wishful thinking about his character: "No one could go through life thinking as highly of himself as you did without getting knocked down a peg or two. . . . [Y]ou now realize that there are other people in this world and they weren't born to let you step on them on your way up, Honey—I may be a lost idealist, but I'm happy this way and I suspect I shall remain one." Balancing on eggshells, she concluded by enumerating Charlie's externally positive qualities, including his "mannerisms (except when you shake with anger)."[11]

By October 8 Frances had safely delivered a son, and Kathy wrote immediately about her new brother, Adam. "I can't wait to see him," she said. "I'm so glad it's over with and Mother is OK. Daddy sounded like a little boy on the phone." She added details about her baby brother: "6# 12 oz . . . Daddy said he wasn't wrinkled or anything—he's all filled out." That same night Kathy had an emotional phone call with Charlie. "I sure did enjoy talking or shall I say crying to you tonight," she wrote. She had started her period right after they hung up. "An emotional jolt I guess. . . . I think time will go by quicker now that school is really in full swing. I've noticed that I don't get quite so tired anymore. I'm going to start on my birth control pills as soon as the 5th day gets here. Then we won't have anything to worry about." She listed activities to enjoy when Charlie returned for good—not only tennis at the courts nearby but also shooting practice at one of the local gun ranges. "I sure would like to learn to shoot well," she wrote.[12] One strategy for neutralizing a tool of intimidation might be to appropriate it.

Adam's birth boosted Kathy's morale. She had finished new curtains "in our 'lovin' room" and purchased material to cover windows in the living room. She seemed to trust her financial judgment and creativity again. ("[I]t just cost too much to buy them and I can make prettier ones.") In advance of her first Saturday class hike at the science center, she visited to scout the trail and break in a new pair of boots. Regarding her health, she happily reported "good normal cramps." An overall appeal to Charlie tied everything together: "I hope you have enough confidence in me to know I can do just fine on my own until Dec. 4 or longer if I had to."[13] The sentence betrayed a serious truth: Kathy did well—if not better—without him.

Kathy (front, holding Adam) with Mama Leissner (front left), and her parents, Raymond and Frances, on the back patio in Needville, early 1965. Private archive of Nelson Leissner.

Her first visit home to meet baby Adam was the brightest spot of the fall semester. Writing to her family midweek after returning to Austin, Kathy wrote, "How's the newest member of our family? Eating like the rest of us I hope. How is he doing with his formula now?" Already looking ahead to stretches of babysitting, she added, "I hope you will let us keep him when and if you do vacation. I will never forgive you, if you let someone else." She said her mood had been brightened by three new letters from Charlie. Reprising her intercessory role, she included a carbon copy of a typed recommendation her husband had forwarded, a document he had requested from a commanding officer: "I thought you might want to see what the MC thinks of him," Kathy said. "Really, I'm just proud and want to show off!"[14] Her husband was certainly adept at getting other men to vouch for him.

CRADLING IN HER ARMS THE NEW brother whose life had just begun, Kathy longed for the day when she would not be "marking time for the future."[15] Despite her positive spin on Charlie's most recent letters, the reality in the envelopes was much less sunny. Her responses to him from mid-October until the end of November 1964 record an urgent awareness that the terms and conditions of their marriage needed to improve. The discussion would become increasingly fraught as the weeks melted into days before her husband returned to Austin permanently.

Kathy's first response to these three letters is one of her longest in the entire archive: nearly three thousand words. Addressing his messages that week, including one that "was quite angry as best I can tell," Kathy first apologized at length for recent phone conversations as well as for unspecified behavior at the end of the summer. It is unbearable to read how she accepted the brunt of blame for "disheartening" Charlie during the most recent leave when she had surgery. "Can you ever forgive me for being such a self-pitying, selfish, self-centered, and inconsiderate person?" she wrote. "I have no right to be anything but lonely for you, and I shouldn't have let that affect my morale and purpose as it did." She documented the circular and nebulous nature of his complaints, even as she went on to beg his forgiveness further: "[H]ow do you apologize for something you can't name. It's something I didn't do and should have, and then again it is something I did. I tend to attribute it to my general health and the way I felt at the time. But anyway, I want to apologize for the horrible, horrible, horrible way I acted or something our last two weeks together. You were so sweet to put up with me." This section concluded with a glaring reversal. "You know," she wrote, "it's a good thing we got married when we did, because if you had known me any better you may have decided you didn't want to put up with all the terrible things you have learned about me since we were married!"[16]

Self-diminishment, however, did not consume this document. For one thing, Kathy referred to weight loss as a matter of her own self-satisfaction: "I'm so glad you like the weight loss, because as you well know I'm extremely proud of myself. I feel better mentally even more so than physically when I am confident that I look as good as my 'natural resources' will allow." She also encouraged Charlie not to obsess about his own weight, thus not replicating the exacting physical standards he imposed. "Why don't you wait and see if you really have a problem losing weight?" she asked him. "I'm not worried about your weight. You don't either."[17]

More deeply into the letter, Kathy pushed back vehemently against a criticism he had made about her crying. "What do you call a *genuine* reason for tears?" she asked. "I cry when I need to, not to gain sympathy, my way, or your attention. As long as you understand that, we should have no trouble." Charlie had also accused her of deceiving him ("thought lying") during discussions of the type—and price—of a kitchen stove. Here also, Kathy rejected his reasoning, although she addressed the exhausting tangle of his argument:

> I'm sorry—but to be honest with you right now I must say I think you have blown the stove business way out of proportion. I was not "thought lying" when you asked me if I wanted a large range if you could get it for less than $30, I said no! Because—at the time the mental picture of a large stove was not a pretty one—I considered the prospect of one and I did not like the idea. A neat little apartment stove appealed to me more. Then—We started looking and I saw that there really wasn't that much difference and after reconsidering or shall I say giving it as much consideration as I should have in the 1st place, I decided it wasn't such a bad idea. . . . I am sorry but I really can't justify the extent to which you have taken this

very simple incident of my changing my mind about the size of a stove. Please think about this because it worries me.[18]

The tortured lengths Kathy went to in reasoning with her husband on this seemingly innocuous point demonstrate, in painful miniature, the incessant patterns long in place.

The most excruciating topics of the letter concern Charlie's romantic and sexual behavior. He had been angry that Kathy did not enjoy his last night in Austin. When a nightspot called the Peanut had been closed, he suggested getting a six-pack of beer to go park and drink somewhere. Kathy did not like the beer, something he clearly recalled, yet Charlie now scolded her for expressing dissatisfaction afterwards. "You should have brought it up then," he wrote.[19] Kathy's cool, robotic response sounded well-accustomed to these exchanges. "I will try to remember to tell you at the time when I feel something like the disgust I felt in you that night," she answered. "I'm sorry. I understand." Clearly, more than beer had disgusted her.

The truth was that Charlie usually refused to take no for an answer about anything. He had often demanded that Kathy rake her fingernails down his back, an act she did not enjoy, and her demurrals angered him. On this point she believed that he was not attuned to her expressions, capturing the fundamental problem she had raised before: that he seemed to ignore her communications, especially when it came to sex. "Honey," she wrote, "I didn't ever stand up and lecture on how I hated to scratch your back but I know that not a time passed that I didn't say I didn't like it." Even more telling, Kathy had asked Charlie to perform one sexual activity less often, and he had been insistent and defensive. "Sugar," she responded. "I didn't mean that we were 'abnormal.' I couldn't think of another word and I was sure you knew me in our opinion of our relationship well enough to understand what I meant. . . . [A]ll I wanted to say was that *I*"—here Kathy underlined the first-person pronoun—"want to make a special effort."[20]

At the wounded heart of the conflict was Kathy's desire to be fully present, seen, and heard during intimacy: she was resisting the role of passive witness to her partner's mechanical directions in experiences she did not enjoy. But Charlie informed Kathy that her body—as if entirely separated from her awareness—showed him how it was "controlled" by "subconscious + conscious desires for intercourse." Underneath his mandate that Kathy "must make him understand what, where, when + how [she] like[d] her loving," lay the powerful and contradictory myth that her consent as a woman, and as his wife, was already assumed. When she resisted or disliked something, he simply blamed her for not obeying her body, fulfilling her role, following desires "*deep down inside of [her]self*," or enjoying his performance.[21] These ideas overlapped with his belief that it was a "constant fight" for him to channel his sexual drives "down the right paths"—the implication being that it was a wife's role, Kathy's role, to relieve all sexual agony.[22]

In her closing, as she often did, Kathy focused on a vivid, nonsexual memory. Agreeing that, yes, she would purchase a record Charlie had requested (the Four Tops' song, "I Need Your Loving"), Kathy wrote, "You may think this is silly . . . [b]ut you have no idea how thrilled I was the time you sang part of that song to me when you were home. . . . [Y]ou were looking at me, so I assumed you were singing to me. I like the record too and I think of you long after I hear it." She also gave herself more credit in their intimate life than she had ever written before, although the sad subtext of her cheerful words grasped for an elusive validation. Referring to herself in the third person and reflecting on their limited time together, Kathy said, "[Y]our wife who has been your lover for approximately one year in the true sense, has had such a fabulous experience in lovemaking, that she thinks she's an authority on the subject already!" Her final affirmation underscored a painful reality: "I am sure that I have experienced in one short year what most women never find in an entire lifetime!" It was 5:30 p.m., the late middle of her day, allowing only enough time after this long letter for a quick dinner "before lab at 7:00," a detail she took the time to record.[23]

School pressed forward with assignments and dead-lines—at one point Kathy prepared a report on "the particle theory of light"—and welcome field trips. Kathy now tracked football games on television. One friend had a hilarious experience at a game when she sat near Rock Hudson, an incident Kathy described both to her family and to Charlie: "Needless to say she didn't watch the game! She was so excited I almost died laughing!" When she found time, Kathy pampered herself with oil in the bath and painted her toenails pink.[24]

Student teaching was on her horizon, as was the prospect of teaching in Austin after certification. A classmate already working in the district helped her calculate starting salary, benefits, and retirement, and Kathy considered how all these elements would fit into her plans for a family. Her picture of the future included an idea about how to mark the milestone of Charlie's graduation: "How would you like to go to the Olympics in Mexico City in 1968!" she wrote. "Wouldn't that be great?"[25]

As her reunion with Charlie loomed, Kathy anticipated that the history she had endured could be wiped clean. "We have so much time ahead of us and I feel like we are all new to each other again." She added, "I want to know your every whim all over again and I'm afraid I've forgotten some of them. Will you help me learn to be a good lover?" Around this time, he wrote that he regretted his recent anger but found it necessary. "I can't wait to make you pregnant—very very much pregnant," he said. "I got your letter and it sure made me feel all my angry [*sic*] was worthwhile."[26]

As THE 1964 PRESIDENTIAL ELECTION APPROACHED, Kathy noted the political rallies in Austin for the candidates, Republican Barry Goldwater and Democrat Lyndon Johnson. Now twenty-one, she would be eligible to vote for the very first time. Her letters up to this point included no mention of any US politician other than a passing mention of Johnson, whose UT commencement address she had wished to attend in May. In early October she joked to Charlie about her likely presidential vote, using the context of a visit with another couple: "All they talk about is politics and how we should help the poor and am I still voting for Goldwater! Ha!"[27] Absent philosophical details, Kathy seemed to gloss the subject to shore up a certain if temporary area of noncontroversy with her husband.

It was still a common belief at the time that married women should take direction from their husbands about voting.[28] Charlie advised Kathy about forms for the poll tax and exemption slip, asking her if she would be able to vote, and he referenced his own registration, absentee ballot, and candidate preference. ("Sure hope Goldwater makes it.") The summer of Kathy's surgery, when she was recuperating in Lake Worth, Charlie's father was reportedly reproducing political materials against Johnson in an outbuilding behind the Whitman home—enlisting even Patrick to help distribute pamphlets—suggesting Kathy would have had more than an earful during her last visit.[29] Kathy's father was simply a life-long Republican.

As typical within her age group and expected marital role, Kathy played to her audiences.[30] To the Leissners she reported that John Wayne would be "the star attraction" at a Goldwater rally in a city park. To Charlie, she emphasized the anticipated scope of spectacle: two hundred thousand projected to attend Goldwater's speech in the Municipal Auditorium, and the Young Republicans put up "ten thousand" posters across Travis County. "Ole Johnson's hurting in his home state!" she said to her husband—unaware of, or ignoring, projections of his anticipated landslide. "I wish [Goldwater]'d carry Texas so bad—" she wrote.[31]

Considered altogether, within the context of her thoughts on other matters, Kathy's short-lived political expressions appeared to serve mostly a performative function. Notably, although Kathy said she "wanted" to attend Goldwater's rally, she rationalized her absence due to Saturday at the science center. Despite telling Charlie that she planned to listen to Goldwater on television, she went instead with a friend to the Johnson rally. "I just had to see the excitement," she wrote, overemphasizing her disinterest. "We didn't even stay to hear Johnson because we were so far away and couldn't see him + I didn't want to hear him."[32]

Kathy never wrote of casting an actual ballot, and most intriguing: historical voting records from Travis County suggest that Kathy did not register. Although she did not contradict her husband or other family members about politics, neither did she appear to care enough for Goldwater to endorse him with a vote. The political meaning of such a discrepancy should not be assumed, but within her specific circumstances it would be reasonable to view lack of registration as a private and meaningful instance of passive resistance to Charlie's expectations.[33]

Kathy also tested her independence in more visible ways at this time. In the days before observing the Johnson rally, she recorded going out to a movie and a bar, the Split Rail on Lamar Street, where she "drank 2 glasses of Lone Star." It was rare for Kathy to omit a movie title or the names of friends who accompanied her on outings. But the evening activities and the beer put her in a "relaxed" as well as introspective mood, and her narrative omissions dared to conjure a picture for Charlie—just once—in public without a group or chaperone, even though it was unlikely that Kathy went out by herself. Back in June Charlie had written that she was a "very lucky woman to have a husband with such standards and self-discipline" when it came to fidelity. What kind of husband bragged this way? His words still bothered her now, a source of unfairness she felt deeply. "Did you ever think real seriously about how you would feel about it—if I ever made love to someone before we were married?" she asked. Charlie's judgments of other women were so harsh, even as he said he "would die professing [Kathy's] wonders and virtues" as his "Angel" of "Perfection." Through all these months back at the university, Kathy found herself identifying more with other "girls in skirts," even as Charlie's denigrating comments had intensified about women he assumed to be promiscuous—most recently military wives and "BAMs" (broad-assed Marines).[34]

THE NOVEMBER 1964 ISSUE OF *READER'S DIGEST* contained an article titled, "The Power Women Have over Men: A Symposium," a sampling of quotes from more than fifteen hundred responses the editors received in response to a previous article about male domination. In a letter he began with extensive self-loathing about the erections that continued to plague him at night, Charlie told Kathy the symposium captured his view of dynamics in marriage.[35]

Kathy purchased a copy or found one at the library, and in her response to Charlie, she said that the article was agreeable. She took exception with a crucial point, how-ever—essentially the premise of the entire symposium. "I hope I can learn how to use my 'supposed' power over you," she wrote. "I sure don't like to think of it as power though." She again stressed her desire for mutually satisfying inti-macy, a negotiation of pleasure rather than control or force. "Do you realize how long it's been since we have really had intercourse like we both prefer it!" she wrote. "A long long time. We had to be careful for so long for one reason or another—But from now on anything goes (*almost*)."[36] Her use of the pronoun "we" and emphasis of "almost," under-lined and smuggled into parenthesis at the end, hinted at some caution and pleaded for empathy.

As heavy as these realities weighed, Kathy sent snap-shots of baby Adam to show how much she enjoyed doting on him, even when he was cranky. "In one of them he's not very happy with his big sister!" she wrote. "I'm cleaning his face after he ate." She kept grounded, as had become her habit, by studying at Harry's Place and fixing up the apart-ment. She prepared for student teaching, finally purchasing a filing cabinet to organize all her materials. Exceeding min-imal expectations for her Saturday living things class at the science center, Kathy phoned parents to check on absent children. Later, she visited Texas Memorial Museum to meet with a professor, Dr. Jerry Round, who allowed her to check out preserved specimens to show her class. "He was very nice . . . and we wandered thru 1 million snakes, frogs + turtles looking for the ones I needed," she wrote. "Anyway, there are now about 8 snakes, 2 frogs, 6 lizards, and 2 tur-tles on the back seat (excuse me—on the floor) of our car!" Her contributions clearly appreciated, Kathy was invited to appear in a skit with her students on a beloved KTBC tele-vision program, *The Uncle Jay Show*, to explain about an animal.[37]

Charlie's scripts meanwhile played out like a broken record: he worried about her "casual attitude" towards her period, sulked that she did not spend evenings by the phone, and envied the new babies of friends as well as his in-laws. "I will be so glad when you are full of life with our baby," he wrote, repeating language almost verbatim from his diary a year earlier. Although he bragged about the "many excellent compliments" he received from other men about Kathy since returning to base, the fact that she was already "full of life" seemed to escape him.[38]

ELECTION DAY FELL ON TUESDAY, NOVEMBER 3, setting records at the time for in-person as well as absentee voting in Travis County.[39] Johnson soundly defeated Goldwater, not only in Texas but across the country, carrying all but six states: South Carolina, Georgia, Mississippi, Alabama, Louisiana, and Goldwater's home state of Arizona.

The election returns overlapped with newly disturbing letters Kathy received from Charlie, including one extra enclosure of a "vivid note" so sexually distasteful that she recorded destroying it. Despite Kathy's latest reassurances that she no longer thought he "made love to [her] without love in the picture," the note enacted yet another awful test of Kathy's boundaries. He also reminded her of incidents that still "haunted" him from the apartment when Kathy had been repulsed during sex, including once on the bathroom floor. Aware that she had endured rather than enjoyed the experiences, he admitted his failure "to recognize the grossness of the relations . . . and how you felt about it." Nevertheless, he continued to shift responsibility to Kathy for not communicating in a timely manner, just as he previously emphasized how "privileged" she was that he took her to bed.[40]

Kathy wrote two letters in response right after the election. In the first, she "[blew] off steam" about Johnson's win. "Your sweet little wife who worries about the principles of our leaders is no longer worried," she wrote. "I've decided that if the way to get rich and not suffer is crooked in my books + not the country's then to hell with my ideals!" She went on, "I hope it rains all day in Johnson City like it is here, so it will spoil his stupid BarBQ!"[41] The second was much longer, written as Kathy nursed a skinned arm from her latest field trip. After a few preliminaries, she got to the heart of the matter, referencing the note she had destroyed:

I guess you are waiting for a comment from me about your letter. . . . I really needed to hear from you. The note on our sex kinda upset me. . . . I didn't like reading parts of it. It ruins things for me. I'm not going to keep it. . . . I don't know if I will ever be able to accept some of your terminology. I just don't like those words! Why do you want to use them—I mean is it just easier for you or does it give you an extra sensation to use them. Don't get me wrong—some of it I don't mind but I sure would hate to have a lover or husband rather who never used any of the good old fashioned sweet-talk. And never refers to our relationship as making love! . . . If you [had] been here to go through all the things you wrote, I'm sure I would have enjoyed it beyond words, but on paper it was a little rough on this end.

Her conclusion stretched hard to avoid sexual rejection or shame, also offering him an excuse: "Please don't be sorry you wrote it and feel bad because you had no way of knowing because I can see where men + women see things like this very differently." She concluded with a definitive refusal of his plan to establish a daily schedule for her, starting with exercise at 5:30 a.m. The implication that she needed to account for her own time remained strong even as she grasped for boundaries in advance.[42]

The very next day a drunken phone call from Charlie unsettled Kathy further. "I wish you wouldn't drink when you are at Lejeune," she wrote afterwards. "Why don't you wait until you get home." She tried to be playful as she referenced some of his comments: "Your teasing was so cute tonight, but I really would have slapped you for some of those cocky remarks." But as in the letter she had already mailed, she remained deeply bothered by her husband's fixations, and again she asserted what she needed. "You rarely express a desire for anything romantic lately," she wrote. "Do you ever think of sex as not being hot and passionate and urgent? I mean while we are separated? You don't ever mention it if you do." She concluded with a list of ordinary honey-do's at the house, then begged him to take it easy on the alcohol. "I hope you aren't too rough when you get home!" she wrote. "Please, please don't drink. I will be so disgusted I think I'd sleep on the couch. We can celebrate by getting drunk on each other." Kathy clearly dreaded that alcohol might well lead to his forceful claiming of "marital rights," and she was trying to avert it ahead of time.[43]

CHARLIE'S POSTELECTION LETTER OPENED BY addressing Kathy as his favorite "split tail," crude military slang for women, and closed with amazement that Goldwater "carried the Deep South States." The next day he recanted an insulting comment he had made to a friend of Kathy's, who had been present during his drunken phone call, and he apologized again for his "little note," asking her to throw it away, offering an empty replay of self-recrimination and excuses. "I was the typical Marine animal," he wrote.[44]

In letters that followed, he added that he was terribly insecure and needed Kathy's "applause, compliments, and prodding" in order to behave more calmly. Regarding his use of sexual pressure, Charlie included a chilling rationale: "I think that is why I am so rough and fierce in our relations," he said. "I have to see with my own eyes that you *must* be enjoying me." He continued that he wished he could "cut the desire completely out of my body, as if it were a disease; where my lust causes me to offend the woman I love more than life itself, and scare her so that she has to ask me to be gentle." He begged her to reprimand him, jumbling his words slightly, if he did not "henceforth be a gentleman and very gentle + kind and romantic as I am capable of being in all our relations." He also infused objectification with compliments, writing of her skin, "[Y]ou couldn't buy anything that smooth or sweet smelling for $1 million/per inch."[45]

Charlie also included one bizarre P.S. that nitpicked a misspelling of "to" and "too" in Kathy's letter, expressing hope that he would not be "to[o] rough." On the surface, such a critique could be interpreted as clearly obsessive. But in the precise context, it suggested something even more horrifying: a false equivalency between his violence and her occasional spelling mistakes. The underlying premise—that Kathy was easily confused and needed his correction—sought to undermine her voice at a vulnerable moment, and the distorted perspective would resurface in her own letters, with this exact word, during the last month of her life.[46]

By mid-November Kathy was wary that something bad would disrupt the normalcy for which she longed. Her unease was rational based on all she had endured. "I have a horror of something unknown now coming up + keeping you in the Marine Corp," she wrote to Charlie. A few days later, plagued by itchy arms and face because of a run-in with poison oak or ivy on a field trip, she added, "Please be careful of what you sign from now until December 4th! OK?" If only doubts could be treated with pink daubs of calamine lotion. He had been reminding her to collect his writings "about death" in a folder for safekeeping.[47]

As if on cue, her husband landed in more strange trouble, and yet again Kathy heard about it afterwards. Charlie and another Marine had been "jumped" one night returning to the base by bus from Court Street. Charlie was vague about details, and Kathy was done with surprises and evasions—particularly from a man so obsessively detail-oriented when it came to her. "I have a feeling you are beginning to apply the same psychology to me that you do to [your] mother," she wrote. "I don't like being in the dark. I guess I'll soon take the stand most women do—if he tells me about what he's doing OK—if he doesn't, I don't guess I'm worth the effort. Please tell me when you have a run in like that business about the fight or shall I say mugging?"[48]

Two letters, both dated November 12, captured the highs and lows of Kathy's moods awaiting Charlie's return. The new couch in the "early American" style had arrived, and she was working to finish cushion coverings and plan color schemes for the rest of the rooms in the apartment. She enclosed the results of a psychological assessment she had taken the previous summer in preparation for student teaching. Her inclusion of the results at this time hearkened back to the early days of their marriage, when Charlie had questioned Kathy's mental health and marital adjustment. "All in all I'm normal!" Kathy wrote, following an appointment with the department psychologist to review the results. "He said he could tell that my actions had been my own responsibility since I was little and that's what makes me what I am character-wise. . . . He said I liked to think of myself as on the ball, but at the same time I feel like I'm not doing my best! He hit the nail on the head, didn't he!"[49]

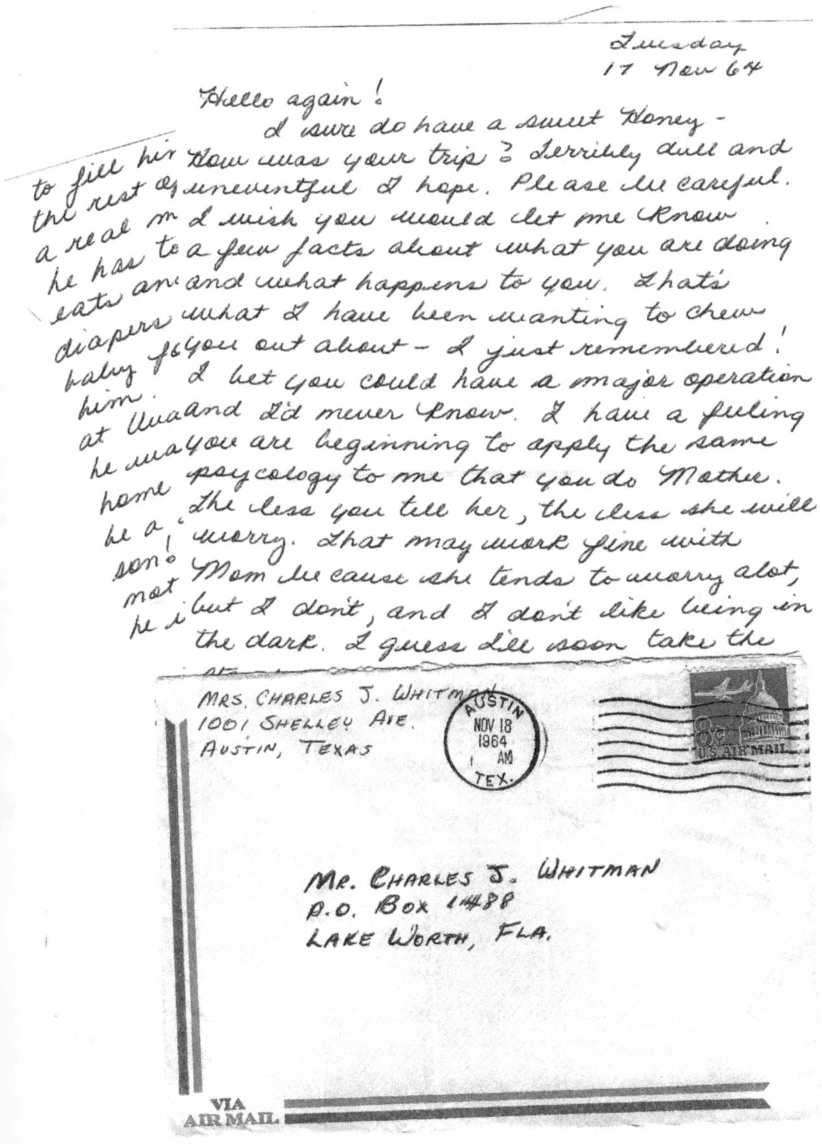

Tuesday
17 Nov 64

Hello again !
I sure do have a sweet Honey -
How was your trip ? Terribly dull and
uneventful I hope. Please be careful.
I wish you would let me know
a few facts about what you are doing
and what happens to you. That's
what I have been wanting to chew
you out about - I just remembered !
I bet you could have a major operation
and I'd never know. I have a feeling
you are beginning to apply the same
psycology to me that you do Mother.
The less you tell her, the less she will
worry. That may work fine with
Mom because she tends to worry a lot,
but I don't, and I don't like being in
the dark. I guess I'll soon take the

(margin notes, written sideways)
to fill her
the rest of
a real m
he has
eats an
diapers
baby f
him
at Uva and
he wa
home
be a
son
mat
he i

MRS. CHARLES J. WHITMAN
1001 SHELLEY AVE.
AUSTIN, TEXAS

AUSTIN
NOV 18
1964
AM
TEX.

MR. CHARLES J. WHITMAN
P.O. BOX 1488
LAKE WORTH, FLA.

VIA
AIR MAIL

In November 1964, shortly before Charlie's permanent return to Austin,
Kathy wrote that she did not like the way he withheld information from
her—this time about a "mugging" he experienced near Camp Lejeune.
Private archive of Nelson Leissner.

The confidence of this letter—employing a male authority figure and an external scientific instrument to validate the quality of her psychological health, character, and family history—was followed by an intensely despondent letter penned later the same day. Kathy had been agitated by something new Charlie expressed by phone or by an underlying awareness, perhaps from rereading his latest letters or reviewing the diary he had left behind. "I can't seem to console you at all and you somehow don't feel like we have any unspoken means of communication," she started. A Johnny Mathis song was playing on the radio, "My Love for You," and Kathy continued, writing, "You aren't the man I married—you have changed and so have I. I don't feel like I know you as well as I want to." The truth was much harder to say: that she knew Charlie better than ever. But how dangerous was he? She rested her attention on tender details: how he fell asleep when his head hit the pillow, her pink nightie on the end of the bed. Even so, she remained insecure about something as simple as how to wear her hair when he returned: "You must not like to feel my hair when we make love, or you wouldn't want it up? I will have it up that Friday night."[50]

Looking ahead to his arrival in Austin, Kathy sent her husband want ads from the paper ("You can see what the prospects are like"), cleaned and changed the sheets, worked on ironing. She also found time to reflect on Charlie's feelings about leaving the Marine Corps. After all, he had just twenty days of service left. "I'll bet you feel really funny about closing the door on the corp," she wrote. "Within a few years you will forget most of the bad things and remember only the good you received from it. After all—you gained a wife?"[51]

Knowing that Charlie would visit his family before coming home, Kathy sent her best wishes. "Please say hello to mother and dad and Pat and John for me," she wrote. "How's Pat's love life coming along? Is he still enthused about junior college?" By the hour she seemed to grow prouder of touches made to their nest. "When my man comes home it will be a real home," she wrote. "It's looking better with everything I do to it." Her mood was noted by friends as the clock ticked down before Charlie's return. "I think I must be beaming the fact because '5' people have asked me how many days we have left and it's only eleven o'clock." Her grades as a senior were holding steady—As and Bs—and her favorite professor was encouraging her to think past graduation to a UT education fellowship. Charlie meanwhile prescribed a menu for his first day home: "Steak, spinach, 1 roll, ice tea, and some fine chilly wine."[52]

Stories of Adam, gleaned from Frances's letters and phone calls, brightened Kathy's days. "Mother said he has to have a bath every time he eats and he goes through four dozen diapers a day! He's eating cereal and baby food now. Wait til you see him." She added her impression that the new baby was bringing everyone together. "Daddy went deer hunting up at Uvalde last Thursday. Mother said he was already planning to come home before he left. I think he must be a little attached to his brand new son!" Kathy tried to imagine the exact moment her husband stepped off the plane. "I don't care if you have had your uniform on for a week and haven't had a bath in three weeks—I can't wait to put my arms around you and hold you, just to make sure you're really there."[53]

"Making sure" with Charlie was always the trouble, especially as Kathy learned to trust her own eyes. Before he came home, Kathy worried about the lack of heat in the apartment. She worried about whether he would like her hair in a flip. She worried that he did not understand how attractive he was to other women. Ever-present sexual insecurity reared its head, this time through humor: "I hope you don't ever have to have a secretary work very close to you 'cause she'll be terribly frustrated! No kidding!" She ended with a question that allowed the ambiguity of double-reading—both as a compliment and as an echo of her most intimate doubts. "Where did you develop your technique anyway?"[54]

After a special Thanksgiving with her family, baby Adam's first, Kathy noted how the brothers she missed so much were maturing quickly. "Nelson is going steady now and lives on the phone. Ray and Nelson both have let their hair grow out, you won't recognize Nelson!" Adam remained the apple of her eye. "I hadn't seen him in a month, and I really wouldn't have recognized him. He is getting so big and now he smiles and coos and is a lot of fun for everyone. She added, "Everyone asks about you and all want to see you." The extended family had drawn names for Christmas presents, and Kathy and Charlie got one of her aunts and uncles.[55]

She had come so far and achieved so much as a married woman alone. Kathy could almost release a breath as she dared to imagine that life could be better, that the re-set she desired since the first days of their separation might come true. "Well, Darling," she said. "I'll write again Monday and then no more letters to my Marine—you know, I kinda hate to see him go." In another letter, she added, "I just can't believe we are so close to the end." Her husband's letters had become more contentious and exacting even as he indulged in extreme self-pity, calling himself "a poor specimen . . . an egotistical procrastinating weakling." It was Kathy, he insisted, who made him feel "like a King."[56]

Soon, Kathy would no longer struggle to diffuse Charlie's moodiness and aggression on paper. Unless something drastically changed, she would face his controlling behavior in many forms, at unpredictable intervals, from now on. And unlike the summer of 1963, there would be no way to separate without confrontation over divorce.

"Back to Normal Soon"

FOR WEEKS KATHY CHEERFULLY PREPARED FOR Charlie's return, making thrifty improvements to the Shelley Avenue apartment. "[G]uess what your brilliant, smart, and ingenious wife did last night?" she asked, answering herself, "I made the bedroom curtains!" She enjoyed adding fringe to the kitchen curtains so much ("for the professional touch!") that she joked about adding some to his underwear. Resisting her husband's more expensive suggestions, Kathy emphasized the need for simplicity, especially after she paid $13 for a used table and two chairs, and then "scrounged around" for a used couch.[1]

The anticipation echoed the days leading up to her whirlwind wedding, a symmetry not lost on her friends: "Everyone asks me if I'm getting nervous about my approaching marriage!" A year earlier, Kathy was an exhausted and worried student wife, traveling to be with Charlie for his court-martial, just as the nation went haywire with Kennedy's assassination. "I want to hold you, love you, and be near you all the time," she wrote shortly afterwards, "not just 2 or 3 times a year."[2] At long last, that wish was coming true.

As the year wound down, Kathy wanted to believe her husband would finally move forward the way she had, re-enrolling at UT to complete his own degree. Yet as the high of reunion milestones passed and daily realities set in, patterns all too soon cast a long and familiar shadow. On the date of Charlie's return, December 4, 1964, the *Daily Texan* published a photograph that, in hindsight, telegraphed an ominous message. Taken from a low angle, the image depicted a solitary young woman in silhouette at the foot of the Tower. The caption read, "Tower Light Beckons." The couple would celebrate Christmas together for the first time since being newlyweds, and Charlie sent a private note in their card to her parents, casting doubt on Kathy's gratitude over the past two years: "What everyone has done either doesn't strike Kathy so strongly or she feels that y'all know we are grateful anyway. I want you to know that I feel I have some fine in-laws, in fact the best, I feel."[3]

NEARLY ALL OF KATHY'S LETTERS FROM January through November 1965 were addressed to her parents. She would compose only two letters to Charlie that year during an intermittent period of separation in late summer—the final surviving words Kathy ever wrote to her husband. Overall, her written record becomes much spottier. There are longer gaps between letters to her mother and family than during the first half of 1963, immediately after Kathy dropped out of university and lived with Charlie in Jacksonville, North Carolina. In 1965 Kathy wrote home roughly once per month compared to two to three times per week in 1963. The total volume of writing to her family was also significantly lower: just over six thousand words for the whole of 1965, compared to more than sixteen thousand from January through June 1963.

A reader must consider these differences in frequency and fluency in the context of multiple factors. During the transition of early 1963, Kathy was desperate to maintain connection to family when she moved away from Texas. Her departure followed a significant marital crisis known to her parents, and she seemed intensely aware of a need to reassure them that her choices were sound. The couple's trip to Jacksonville also had the flavor of adventure at first, and letters enabled Kathy to document her feelings and observations, from the fresh to the mundane, with a receptive and supportive audience. For much of the time Charlie was away on training maneuvers, leaving her without independent, reliable phone access.

In 1965, by contrast, Kathy was geographically closer to her family and friends, and she had a telephone. Under the best conditions, in a healthy marriage, it would be reasonable for the pace of written letters to slow. But it was not simply the tempo of Kathy's written communication that changed. As the months wore on, her style and content withered in Charlie's overbearing presence. Gaps in recorded conversation must be considered within the full understanding of interactions well-chronicled during the couple's nearly two years apart, and these patterns did not suddenly evaporate. It is also crucial to recognize that, in her husband's absence, Kathy—hardworking, cheerful, vibrant Kathy—had been the ambassador of the marriage, and of Charlie, to everyone she knew. The real-time incongruities would be more jarring for her now, her loneliness more confusing and even harder to express.

IN NOTES TO HER FAMILY FOLLOWING successful exams in January, Kathy reported her latest grades (all As and Bs), unabashedly proud of her academic achievements. She was also relieved to anticipate a lighter load. "Ed. history and philosophy is the only course I will be carrying along with student teaching. . . . What a great feeling—" she wrote. "[T]hose are the best grades I've ever made." The break between terms was more relaxing than ever. "I am having fun now—doing dozens of things I haven't had time to do these last few weeks," she wrote.[4]

Kathy looked forward to student teaching and her second round of Saturday classes at the Nature & Science Center. She was anxious to plan family visits, especially because of Adam, who in January 1965 was barely three months old: "Has he done anything new? I can't wait to see how much he's changed," she wrote to Frances. Two weeks later, her worries were touching: "I have a feeling he won't like Charlie + I until he's old enough to know who we are. I sure hope he's not afraid of me."[5]

Meanwhile, Charlie kept himself busy before resuming his own studies. For one thing, he volunteered as scoutmaster in Austin. "[The troop] gave him a $20 money order or gift certificate to buy a complete scoutmaster outfit," Kathy wrote. "He looks so cute in it. We have a Boy Scouts Regional Banquet to attend Tuesday night. It should be fun." Charlie's new role demanded Kathy's sewing skills as well as her moral support. At one point she was assigned to make fifty scarves for Charlie's troop out of plaid material.[6]

The January 1965 letters documented a persisting economic reality: Charlie was still not a full contributor to the household, and the Leissners continued to pay for Kathy's studies. On the back flap of one envelope, Kathy wrote, "Need registration fees by Wednesday." She included a small paragraph explaining that her $65 fees were lower

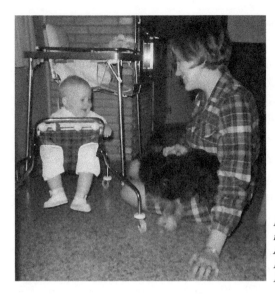

Kathy dotes on her new baby brother, Adam, in early 1965. Private archive of Nelson Leissner.

than usual because her course load was only nine hours. "Just think," she said. "This is the last time you will have to fork out money for my registration. I hope you don't mind."[7]

It did not take long for Kathy's hoped-for harmony to hit dissonant chords. By early February, noting how Charlie seemed to live on a parallel plane, she remarked that she felt she was keeping house for "a ghost." She tried to keep her chin up, describing how her husband made himself useful around the house, as when he built himself a desk for their apartment. ("The only problem is, it's 8' long!" Kathy joked to her mother.) He had no trouble chasing leads for part-time jobs, but he could not seem to maintain any position.[8]

As Kathy became consumed by student teaching that spring, her husband's inconsistency again began to wear. Charlie found a sponsor for a real estate license but then did not sell any property. He spent several weeks working at Scarbrough's department store before starting his own classes, then took on a job as a collection agent. That position was short-lived, too, and Kathy passed on this explanation to her family in March: "The finance company Charlie works for is cutting its entire staff because their delinquent accounts are below 15%, so he will only be there until the end of the month." Luckily, it seemed, he already had a new, unidentified job lined up, but Kathy went on to report a sadly familiar twist despite the wages of $1.75 per hour: "[T]he hours are from *2–7 AM*," she wrote, underlining the grave-yard shift. "I'll never see him now! I don't know how it's going to work out, but he wants to try."[9]

She shared no details of the position—though records indicate his employment with Central Freight Lines—but she was openly discouraged by how the schedule affected her husband. Following a weekend visit to Needville in early April, she wrote, "Charlie went to work this morning and came dragging in around 7:10. He wasn't too tired then, but by 12:00 and 4 hours of classes, he was dead. He came home around 1:00 and went to sleep. I woke him around 4 for supper + he said he felt great—I'll bet!"[10]

Kathy breathed easier at the end of the month when Charlie moved on to yet another position as a drive-in teller at the Austin National Bank, which offered much-improved hours, better working conditions, and security. "This will be easy clean work," Kathy wrote. "He will only make $1.25 an hour but in 90 days he will get a raise to $1.50. This won't make him near as tired. He works from 1:30 PM–6:30 PM." Her focus on the imagined ninety-day marker, which would land in July, was significant. Kathy was always thinking ahead, and she knew she would likely work at Southwest-ern Bell through the coming summer. She had also received encouragement about prospects for a full-time teaching job: "My cooperating teacher is so proud and impressed with my class, she told the Jr. High Principal about me. . . . [H]e said he's heard so many nice things about me, he's going to request that I be hired back to teach at Lanier next year. Of course that's nothing official but right now it's the best thing to a contract."[11] Presenting Charlie's prospects at the bank as similarly matter-of-fact, Kathy cast out a thread of reasonable hope for her family to see, as if saying that Charlie would keep the job might make it more likely he would do so.

She also celebrated her own achievements. She was a member of the Student Education Association in spring 1965, and, with excellent grades, she was initiated into Kappa Delta Pi International Honor Society in Education. During a quiet two-hour period at the telephone switchboard, she folded a copy of the ceremony program and enclosed it in a letter to her family. In the list of forty-seven spring initiates, only four of whom were men, Kathy circled her own name ("Kathy F. Whitman") along with a friend's. She had purchased material for a special new dress but did not have enough time to make one, wearing her "white silk Easter suit" instead. Even so, Kathy looked forward to new sewing projects for the warmer temperatures: "I bought a piece of black + white polka dot + some yellow for a jacket. I also got some pink for a little sheath. . . . I have got to get out some summer things." She went on, "It sure will be great to be able to relax a little this summer. I haven't had a break in 2 years."[12]

That last sentence was painfully true, not only in its obvious reference to the demands of her studies, but as it captured her struggle to survive with Charlie. At almost every turn since her wedding day, her efforts to foster stability and choice—never mind joy—had been chronically undermined. Kathy had learned over the course of two years that her husband's most predictable traits were his self-importance, volatility, and potential for violence.

No letters survived from May 1965, Kathy's final month at UT. Her graduation "on time" from the University of Texas was significantly muted, despite its massive testament to her perseverance and determination. Undated family photos

Kathy (center) with her mother-in-law, Margaret (left), and Frances (right) around the time of her graduation from UT Austin, spring 1965. Private archive of Nelson Leissner.

suggest a Leissner-Whitman celebration at an unidentified location around that time, but the only surviving image from the ceremony was one Kathy sent her parents weeks later: a poorly lit black-and-white photo snapped not by a proud husband who fancied himself a photographer but by Jack's Party Pictures.

WHEN KATHY ACCEPTED A FULL-TIME POSITION as a science teacher at Austin's Sidney Lanier High School, new summer challenges undermined her preparations. For three months, roughly June through September 1965, Charlie took on additional rent for an apartment in League City, southeast of Houston, as he enrolled in summer classes four days a week at Alvin Community College, only minutes away from Father Gil's bayou cabin in Liverpool. The couple maintained the Shelley Avenue apartment as well, and Kathy joined him temporarily, taking a job at Clear Lake Yacht Basin, where she worked alternate Saturdays and Sundays. Charlie also secured a brief and promising internship at NASA—an enviable opportunity at the height of the US space program. Kathy enthused about the prospect to her parents, but soon the promise faded.[13]

It was a good time to be away from Austin. Shirley Ann Stark and Susan Rigsby, two UT students and sorority sisters, were raped and murdered in August, their bodies discarded in a vacant field just north of the city limits. A twenty-two-year-old English major at the university, James C. Cross, was arrested and charged for the gruesome crimes. The same week a devastating fire erupted on the twentieth floor of the University Tower, smoke pouring from the northwest and east sides of the building, flames threatening special document collections. Firefighters extinguished the blaze, preventing deaths, but for a time sooty burn marks remained.[14]

Kathy's letters to her family were patchy that summer, her homesickness more intense than ever. Charlie's presence loomed at the margins—sometimes starting or finishing her letters, initiating or intercepting phone calls. Kathy's voice became more fragmented and abrupt, a bleak contrast to her writing during the previous two years. Even as the couple socialized with others—accompanying friends to church or movies such as *The Yellow Rolls-Royce* or *The Sons of Katie Elder*—Kathy sounded demoralized. After purchasing clothes for school, including "support stockings," she wrote, "They look sort of heavy on my legs but it's worth it for the comfort. They remind me of Granny every time I put them on."[15]

On her twenty-second birthday she wrote a short letter from the League City apartment expressing how she was sorry her parents had not been able to visit as planned. She thanked them for their cards and gift, presumably much-needed money for school supplies and clothes. She mentioned that Charlie bought her a two-piece suit but that their dinner plans were botched at Luigi's, which had been closed, suggesting thoughtless planning on his part—nothing like his promise to "make up for" lost celebrations in a birthday card the previous year. Kathy sounded resigned to this kind of treatment. "I didn't feel like I had a birthday," she wrote. "I guess it's only normal." Charlie's twenty-fourth birthday just two weeks earlier was a stark contrast, complete with a fancy dinner at Looks Sir-Loin House and the company of friends. "My steak was so tender I couldn't tell whether I was chewing the steak or potato! And the service! I don't know where they all come from," she had written, adding, "They served Charlie a birthday cake with a lit sparkler in the center." Her own birthday letter concluded, "I really haven't said much, but wanted you to know I've been thinking of you all." Her P.S. referenced her enclosure of the photo taken as she crossed the dais at graduation. Instead of expressing pride, Kathy emphasized the absurdity of the moment: "[M]e getting my 'envelope' saying I'll receive my diploma in 6 mo. Ha!"[16]

Charlie's presence at this time (even as a "ghost") crowded out room for the deepening clarity of mind Kathy had developed during 1964, and a new crisis seemed to be building. Triangulated interactions became visible again in June. Following a six-week gap in letters, Charlie started a brief message to Kathy's parents, then "let Kathy drop a line" at the end instead of telephoning them, as had been her first impulse. The result was barely half a page from Kathy, beginning abruptly, brightly (almost sadly), with "When are you going to come see us?"[17]

Kathy's voice continued in this vein, her letters shorter and flatter in tone as summer wore on. Her voice sounded more resigned, ill-at-ease, and self-interrupting. In the last letter to her family from July 1965, which uncharacteristically began with no names in the salutation, just "Hi—," she described waiting for a car headlight and taillight to be replaced. She admitted that she was tired of her temporary job, and she addressed an implied, lingering question about her well-being, likely due to suggestions Charlie had planted with her family: "I feel just fine. I'm going back to Dr. Riley in a few days just as he asked me to. I will feel a lot better if he can't find it to. That doesn't sound right—oh well. I haven't started taking the pills Dr. Williams gave me yet. They ought to do something. Nothing else to say. Not much happening."[18]

This was not the Kathy of May 1963, who could wriggle free from her husband without a direct contradiction of his coercive agenda. Her reference to "Dr. Riley"—likely Barton Riley, one of Charlie's architectural professors and an esteemed mentor to many at UT—stood out in the context of her apparent depression, the name of another doctor or psychiatrist, and an unidentified medication. Again Kathy found herself surrounded by men enlisted to "help" her without knowing details of her lived experience, likely reinforcing Charlie's perspective whatever their good intentions. The fourth sentence of self-annotation, however, like the scholar's "[sic]," indicated Kathy's editorial awareness of jumbled expression. All was not well, no matter her flat assertions that "nothing was happening." Self-silencing and subdued, she had internalized Charlie as an encroaching audience and intimate eavesdropper. A flash of conscious, if temporary, resistance was Kathy's delay in taking "the pills" for an unknown malady.[19] Her husband remained eager to pathologize—or tranquilize—any reasonable response to untenable conditions, just as he had in the earliest days of marriage.

The one spot of unambivalent happiness for Kathy was any time with baby Adam. She often mused about the extreme distance between Austin and Needville—not an easy trip for her mother with a new toddler, nor for Kathy as a brand-new teacher. It was clearer than ever that the confidence and open spirit she had known in the golden youth before her marriage would require more than language to recover, and circumstances were making it more and more challenging to shore up any allies independent of Charlie.

BY THE END OF AUGUST 1965, as the start date of her new job approached, Kathy made several trips alone between Austin and League City. Writing to her parents from Austin after one such drive, she described having "lots of energy until about 8 o'clock + then bang! I guess cause I go 90 miles an hour all day." As usual, she filled her time with domestic activities, even though "the heat is overwhelming up here and our apartment is like a furnace." She babysat for close friends, painted chairs for the kitchen, sanded down the couch frame, looked for new slipcovers, and tried to sell off discarded furniture, including an old bed: "I guess [$6] is better than nothing + just to get it out of the way would be great." Home improvement projects resumed a purgatorial feel, like Cinderella in reverse.

In the same letter, she reported her expected annual teacher's salary, "$4850 over a 12 mo. period." But her most significant news—and latest, last-minute stress—came from teacher orientation. The last Friday in August all new teachers in Austin (by Kathy's count, "375 new teachers") gathered at Reagan High auditorium ("one of the most unique and beautiful schools in the country"), then dispersed to their respective campuses for meetings. Once on the Sidney Lanier campus, Kathy found herself with fifteen other new faculty members waiting to be pinned with official nametags. But the vice principal presented additional, abrupt news for Kathy: he had been unable to contact her during the previous week, and her entire teaching assignment had been changed. "I almost fell out of my chair!" she wrote, proud but understandably overwhelmed. "I am the high school biology teacher, first year, using the new BSCS yellow version text, which until yesterday I have never really examined. I have started reading the text and all the guides! I only hope I can at least stay ahead of the kids," she wrote, adding, "I once thought my first year would be a small wall to scale. Now the wall has turned into a lot of work ahead of me."[20]

This administrator's offhand delivery about this major change illustrates how teachers' preparation time and expertise could be treated as a minor concern, but it also documents how Kathy had been outside the reach of her employer during the precious last days of summer. Yet again, accommodating Charlie had made her life much more difficult—this time, just as she began her career. The "wall" during this period (like the "mess" she referenced in previous letters) referred to much more than Kathy's professional challenges, as she mentioned to married friends the possibility of divorce.[21]

After traveling by herself for a family visit September 2, Kathy spent a long weekend with Charlie in League City, then made the three-hour return trip to Austin alone to start her new job. Almost exactly four years earlier, she had taken the same drive as a hopeful passenger in her high school sweetheart's car, in the wake of the worst catastrophe to strike her beloved Texas in her lifetime. The promise of an unknown future then, like the freeway now, had stretched out ahead of her. But this time she drove unescorted, her pretty hands on the steering wheel, her watch and wedding band catching the light, perhaps waiting for an attendant to refill the car with gasoline as she unwrapped a fresh stick of Doublemint. Alone again in Austin, hauling luggage and books from the trunk and the back seat, unlocking the apartment door, opening the windows to air out the stuffy apartment.

Some things were certain: She needed to complete final forms at the school district. She had to review lesson plans with the brand-new biology materials and stock up on teaching supplies, decorate bulletin boards in her classroom, and tidy the lab space. There would be roster grids to organize in her gradebook. She would plan her hairdo and dresses for the first days of teaching. But a sticky tension, like the summer humidity, lingered over it all. She had to wash it off, somehow, as she had written one year before: "I have made one big discovery. This apartment necessitates a morning shower."[22]

In a letter to Charlie shortly after settling into the apartment by herself, Kathy sounded wary of conflict, a woman who had learned to conserve her energy. Her first day at Lanier was another milestone that passed as an anticlimax. There was no partner at home waiting to ask questions, rub her back, or take her to Holiday House to mark the occasion. On the other hand, there was no one waiting to critique her hair or makeup, run his finger along a picture frame to criticize her housekeeping, or force himself upon her when she was too tired to resist.

Tellingly, Kathy chose to narrate her experiences to Charlie by letter instead of calling, suggesting either that the phone line was yet again disconnected or that she preferred not to interact. "My first day went real well," she wrote, "except that by 4:00 I was so exhausted and hoarse from talking, I just came home and collapsed. It wasn't so bad today + I'm not nearly as tired. My classes are all pretty good." Characteristically, she reflected on her process as well as her self-presentation: "I think I've made one mistake already. I've gone too fast and I think I've missed the lower students already. I'm going to slow down a little and review to see just how many I missed." As a young and attractive teacher, she seemed attuned to the dilemmas she faced as a woman in the classroom theater. "I was so strict and mean the first day," she wrote, "I have had few infractions of rules. Knock on wood. I have quite a few big boys that I need to get separated because sitting together they won't even learn to spell biology."[23]

Kathy also found herself alone with unfinished household details—improvements she had wanted complete when her husband returned nearly a year ago. How could she change what was happening to her life when time felt stuck in place yet passed so quickly? The edges of the domestic picture from any angle now looked chipped and frayed, embodied even in the packages that came by mail. "Your folks sent the dishes," she wrote. "Only 3 of the small bowls broke and now we have a real complete set. The covers I ordered did not fit so I am returning them." In closing, she employed her coded language about enduring problems, referencing her husband's anger and likely violence only days before she began her career. "Honey—I sure am sorry you were so disappointed in this weekend. That's all I can say," she wrote. "It will be back to normal soon + we can all get back to normal too. At least I hope we can. I love you, Charlie. There must be some way we can try harder to avoid little irritating arguments. Something to think about."[24] Dispirited and numb, Kathy knew that her husband's "disappointments" and "little" irritations were unrelenting.

Her last words recorded to Charlie were written September 11, 1965, four years to the day Hurricane Carla struck the Texas coast. Her first week had been a success. It had to be affirming that when she was at school, she had some authority to mitigate conflict. One of her supervisors affirmed her good judgment. A woman could get used to that—if it happened often enough:

I have been nipping it in the bud. I plan about 5
private conferences next week after class with some
boys in various classes. They say that usually helps

rather than continually calling them down in class. At least I haven't sent any to the office yet. . . . The Austin Dist. Science Supervisor came in on the 9th and sat through my 2nd period class, (one of my better classes thank goodness). He is real nice. I asked him if he could suggest any real improvement in my methods after one observation. He said, no, that everything was fine except he wanted to warn me about the rusty little minds of the students after summer and not to be too fast with them. He complimented my bulletin board + said he thought it was excellent for a beginning class in biology! I was glad, as after I put it up I was a little disappointed in the way it looked.

Anticipating the long drive to pick up Charlie in League City on Thursday and return to Austin the same night, Kathy arranged to administer a biology test the next day. She was already building fatigue into lesson plans.

She mentioned the season's first football game, noting that she declined an invitation to attend. "When you're not around I either have to be alone or working at school," she wrote. This was not the young girl who had been surrounded by friends at parties, serving cake and playing records and dancing in the den, the girl who clipped spirit ribbons from games and paper flowers from dates to remind her of happy times. Kathy focused her sympathies on the couple's small dog, Scocie (pronounced "sko-shee"), who had been recently hit by a car and now refused to walk or move, no matter what she tried. She improvised a treatment, the small animal serving as a proxy for unspoken suffering she could not cure:

[R]ight before I went to bed, I decided he wouldn't sleep all night at this rate cause he was whining real

often. So I decided to give half one of those pain
pills the Dr. gave me after surgery and force feed
him. This morning when I woke naturally the first
thing I did was call him + he came bouncing in out
of the living room all fine! He still limps + doesn't act
completely well but I think this is just something that
will be re-occurring after that accident. He must have
a pinched nerve or something, cause I could mash
almost anywhere with no response.[25]

That was the thing about "re-occurring" trauma: sometimes
creatures fought, sometimes they fled, sometimes they
fawned for attention, and sometimes they froze in place.

No letters from Kathy's mother survived 1965,
suggesting that the phone was more convenient during a
busy year for both women—and there was reason for caution
about letters being intercepted in Austin. Frances remained
concerned about her daughter's marriage, and Kathy
acknowledged this at the end of September in a rare letter
she dashed off without adequate postage. "We are both making a big effort," she said, answering the lingering question,
this time echoing a phrase Charlie often used when dismissing profound problems: "Enough on that."[26] Her discourage-
ment seemed at a breaking point.

Halloween fell on a Sunday in 1965, and on this date,
Kathy officially joined the First Methodist Church in Austin. It may have seemed a distant memory, but another
Protestant chaplain and his wife at Lejeune had been kind
to Kathy during the difficult days in Jacksonville and, most
importantly, had encouraged and supported her decision to
leave and resume her education. Now she attended services
alone most of the time, as Charlie made it clear that he was

not interested.[27] His absence would be a profound blessing in disguise: Kathy could connect with new people who had no charmed, preconceived impressions of him—or of them as a couple.

Trouble with the Whitmans reared its head shortly before Thanksgiving when Kathy's father-in-law arrived for a dreaded visit and hunting trip with Charlie. Johnnie Mike also came along this time. "I don't trust Mr. Whitman with a gun," Kathy admitted frankly to Frances, referring not to her husband but to her father-in-law. Reportedly, Charlie's father drew a gun on Johnnie Mike during this trip, prompting Charlie to draw on his father and threatening to kill him if he ever pointed a weapon at his brother again.[28]

Amid the stress, Kathy did something for herself. To prepare for her official teacher portrait, she lightened her hair to a sunny blonde and styled it into a flip. The yearbook picture preserved this unmistakable rebellion, contradicting Charlie's repeated insistence that she darken her hair. While publicly visible in the yearbook, no one but she and Charlie— or perhaps Frances—would have recognized this subtle but direct strike for bodily autonomy.[29]

As Christmas neared Charlie committed a physical attack in view of other students on the third floor of Taylor Hall, where he often studied. After bragging about his "brown belt in Karate," he put a classmate in a sleeper hold headlock, a maneuver of strangulation that caused the man to pass out. Charlie also threw him, and the resulting head injury was so severe it required stitches. Afterwards, he reportedly expressed no remorse.[30]

Kathy must have learned of this incident, though her response is not recorded. Did anyone ask, or even wonder, what it was like—really like—to live with a man who would strangle someone for fun? In the Jacksonville apartment almost two years earlier, Charlie had forced her to rehearse judo holds on a mattress he placed in the kitchen. Kathy may well have learned then, if not on other occasions, what it felt like to have Charlie's arm or hands around her throat. Domestic abuse advocates would come to understand decades later that men who use nonfatal strangulation as a show of force and strength are highly likely to murder their partners.[31]

Behind the Eyewall

THE HOUSTON ASTRODOME HOSTED A SERIES of bull-fights in February 1966. Unlike the Spanish version, in this "Modified Portuguese-Style New-American Bloodless Bullfighting," the toro was not killed in the arena, and the withholding of bloodshed was the whole show. The matador performed in his "suit of lights," a glittering and elaborately embroidered jacket and waistcoat with knee-length trousers of tight satin and silk. He swirled his cape to taunt the majestic bulls, whose shoulder muscles were padded to catch the skewering ends of the banderillas. The creatures seemed wary of inevitable doom, sometimes resting unamused in the center of the pen or else jolting suddenly towards the matador, as if to force an end to the torture. The Houston crowd, more than 107,000 spectators, applauded. But the Kay Packing Company had already made its bid, and after the bow of the matadors, each bull was quietly led away—to a different pen for slaughter, then to a truck.[1] The savvy producers counted on an American audience adept at denial and compartmentalization: if the kill was unseen, it need not concern them.

Kathy and Charlie attended the spectacle in Houston that month with tickets from her parents. She thanked them afterwards during a few precious free minutes at school. "Here I be in study hall, trying to keep my eyes on 30 little darlings trying their very best to keep from working," she said, adding, "Certainly enjoyed ourselves this weekend. . . . We are still telling everyone about it."[2]

Charlie had "already hibernated" for the spring semester, staying up to study mechanics with another classmate in the apartment kitchen after Kathy went to sleep, also bringing home study groups for other courses. Her service was expected, as she noted: "Tonight I play hostess to about four people (including some girl this time) who are coming over to study physics." Meanwhile, she worked on lesson plans for her five sections of biology and, naturally, graded the papers she brought home. ("I was an ole meanyie today + gave a pop quiz.") She continued to antique the furniture and worried that their couch still had no satisfactory covering. Charlie's classes through early evenings left her alone to take care of errands, and she watched for bargains on food. "Today is double stamp day," she wrote, "so that means grocery shopping." She attributed a recent malaise to a medication she had stopped taking: "I think it was those pills," she wrote. "I just don't understand their effect on me."[3]

Kathy's performance evaluation went well, although it unsettled her that the follow-up conference took place at the last minute. She received a strong rating in all categories but had difficulty accepting praise. "How [the principal] justifies his evaluation, I'll never know, as he's never been in my classroom!" she wrote to her parents. She breathed easier knowing that she would be rehired the next year, since in her principal's view, she "was way above average for a 1st year teacher."[4]

Like Frances, Kathy cobbled time to write during advisory periods. Twice in February she composed family letters using red ballpoint pen. She grew more invested in teaching even as everyday realities set in, from "long-winded" principals at faculty meetings, to endless dissections of earthworms in biology lab, to piles of quizzes and reports. Kathy's spousal social obligations did not relent, and she attended events to "rub elbows" in the Engineering Wives Club. After one evening she observed dryly, "They had a speaker on interior design and I learned a lot. Mainly, that it takes much more money than most students have to furnish your home so that it is a place of 'casual elegance,' as he calls it." She sometimes went out with other wives, as one evening when she attended a "fashion + wig show" benefit. But Kathy did not always socialize with her teacher colleagues. "Thurs. night there was a Faculty Party which we couldn't attend," Kathy recounted to her parents, "because Charlie just can't afford the time." It remained an enduring choice of Charlie's: not affording the time for Kathy. She seemed acclimated to routine isolation, telling her family that "a nice quiet evening by the TV" sounded better than a school event.[5] At least when she stayed home, she did not have to answer questions about her husband. The couple continued to host casual dinners, cookouts, and picnics with good friends, but Charlie's dominance now surfaced in front of others when he criticized Kathy's housekeeping, her weight, or her exercise routine—even oversharing about their sex life. He thought nothing of violating norms of marital privacy when it suited him, even as he pressured Kathy to maintain a spell of intimate secrecy.[6]

During the previous year Kathy had watched friends move into their futures with weddings, graduations, new houses, and, of course, babies. By 1966 she was intrigued by possibilities beyond the fairy tale. "Monday we found out that a couple we had made friends with last semester have separated," she said. "Surprises every time you turn around." She also did not fortify Charlie's storied legends of himself, noting to her family that one of his engineering professors told him he had "the highest GPA in the department" early in the spring term. From experience, she resisted premature celebration. "I know his grades will go down this semester, however, with 19 hours," she wrote. "He already has a project due Friday in one design course."[7]

Kathy's thoughts also included an acknowledgment of death—Charlie's, at least—and how he planned to provide for her if he died. Writing in February after the couple purchased life insurance from one of his old friends, Kathy told her family, "Charlie thought it would be a good way to save money and it's the kind that kind of acts like a savings account. If anything happens [to him] I'll be a rich widow—$25,700.00 as a matter of fact." She went on, "It has what they call 5 option dates up until Charlie is 40 at which times we can purchase $10,000.00 worth of additional insurance. . . . [W]e decided if we kept waiting, we would never start . . . and they say it's good to start young." She did not mention (or know yet) that the additional ten-thousand-dollar policy would be insurance on her own life, deemed less than half as valuable as her husband's, even though she was the primary breadwinner.[8]

Interestingly, despite her jokes to Charlie about government assistance after Johnson's 1964 election—practically a lifetime ago—Kathy now hoped a federal subsidy could help stabilize their finances. The Veterans' Readjustment Benefits Act of 1966, also called the Cold War GI Bill, passed unanimously in the House and Senate, sponsored by Texas senator Ralph Yarborough.[9] To her parents she wrote, "Charlie + I have decided that if Uncle Sam puts thru this GI Bill and starts paying us $125 a month for 36 months, next year will be my last year to teach for a while anyway. Just think we may have a family before I'm 30 after all!"[10] An additional benefit, the *Daily Texan* reported, was that the Veterans Administration would guarantee home loans up to $7,500 and direct loans up to $17,500 for those who could not secure private financing.[11] A viable alternative to monetary aid from her in-laws lay within reach, without the strange strings attached.

Kathy took comfort at the prospect of any financial relief in a marriage that had taxed her at every turn. Perhaps inspired by six months of salaried employment as a full-time educator, she opened a bank account in her own name in February 1966 at Austin Teachers Federal Credit Union, where she deposited $70.00.[12] This single step of independence offered a quiet yet profound juxtaposition to the brash lyrics that had saturated radio airwaves for weeks, as Nancy Sinatra's "These Boots Are Made for Walking" hit number one on the Billboard Hot 100 Chart. It is easy to picture Charlie strongly disliking this song and turning the dial when it came on the radio. Kathy might have taken care to do so herself. Regardless of profession or income, a woman could not walk very far unless she controlled her own money, and it was not wise to tip your hand with a violent man.[13]

MORE TURMOIL WITH THE WHITMAN FAMILY disrupted any thoughts Kathy had about new directions in her life. In early March the couple's Austin apartment buzzed with talk of an underwhelming police response to a reported altercation at her in-laws' home in Florida. Following the first anonymous call about two people "going to kill each other," officers reported that the house was quiet upon arrival and quiet when they left. The second call to police, placed by Charlie himself—yes, all the way from Texas—stated that he was preparing to retrieve his mother, Margaret, because his father "had threatened to do bodily harm" to her. A third call, two days later, apparently from Margaret herself, requested an officer to "stand by" at the Whitman home while she "removed her personal effects." The police, while technically responsive, did not perceive any credible danger; one officer dismissed the scene as "all nonsense."[14] Whatever details Kathy knew would have offered a cautionary tale about law enforcement's lack of training and sensitivity when responding to reports of violence in the home.

Within days, Charlie raced by car to Lake Worth, packed up his mother, and brought her to Austin. Once again, Kathy's needs were subsumed by extended family problems and her husband's performance as rescuer. No letters to her family survive for March or April, and notably Kathy withdrew $50 from her new bank account in March, then withdrew the remaining $20 in April, apparently closing it.[15]

Margaret soon rented an apartment in the Penthouse Condominiums on Guadalupe Street. Married at seventeen years old, she now had her own space for the first time in her life. The move relieved Kathy from duties as hostess to a mother-in-law planning for divorce, but relocation did not resolve every challenge. Even as Margaret secured a cashier position at Wyatt's Cafeteria, Charlie's father continued to send money. He also waged a campaign of aggressive phone calls at unpredictable hours of the day and night, arguing with Charlie that Margaret should return. Even the Whitman family physician, succumbing to pressure from Charlie's father, admitted to making similar calls. Once again, Charlie likely exploited the turmoil to extract sympathy from

Kathy and maintain a secondary tether to their marriage. How could she think of herself now, when her husband was making such a grandiose effort to help his own mother? The timing mirrored his "help" for Patrick in late 1962, coinciding with the first time Kathy dared to share her misery with her parents. This time, recognizing her husband's distress more than her own, Kathy urged Charlie to seek professional help. He had earlier refused a house visit from her Methodist minister but finally agreed to see a counselor at the university.[16]

Charlie made one appointment in late March at the UT Health Center, where a doctor prescribed Valium and referred him immediately to a psychiatrist. In notes from the single session the same day, Dr. Maurice Heatly had a clear impression, using the word "hostility" five times to describe Kathy's husband. Despite his outward appearance as a clean-cut, "All-American boy," Heatly observed that Charlie "retained hostility toward his father," admitted to "assault[ing] his wife physically," and recognized in himself "overwhelming periods of hostility with a very minimum provocation." Charlie wavered between tears and rage, whether about the abuse he had witnessed, suffered himself, or perpetrated. Heatly noted that Charlie admitted to one explicit fantasy: "Going up on the tower with a deer rifle [to] shoot people."[17] Buried under that now-notorious statement were Charlie's self-serving comments that Kathy was "more comfortable" with him and had "less fear of him" now that he tried to control his temper. Heatly's professional notes, from a first-time, one-hour session, failed to question how Charlie's "hostility" might manifest itself in public—never mind in the car, the kitchen, or the bedroom.

A tangle of disturbing moments witnessed by others that spring, impossible to sequence perfectly now, further broke the façade of tranquility. At one point of distress, a classmate found Charlie in the apartment packing clothes, muttering about leaving Kathy, dropping out of UT, and moving to Japan, where he could work on his black belt in Karate. He disappeared for an entire day to an unknown location without telling Kathy. In one evening of panic, he showed up on Professor Riley's doorstep, ostensibly for help with an architectural engineering problem, only to take a seat at the living room piano and play a beautiful, if manic, version of "Clair de Lune."[18] Family distress, academic pressure, and a desperate fear of losing control of Kathy overlapped with another quiet reality: his friend and mentor, Father Gil, was preparing to leave Texas for a US Air Force chaplaincy assignment in Alaska. The priest also defaulted on the promissory note for his Liverpool cabin.[19]

At some point, likely between March and May, Kathy visited Needville alone and spoke candidly to her parents around the kitchen table about divorce. She wanted their support if it came to that choice, which had never happened in the Leissner family. She would not have had an easy time explaining it all: how the problem was not one or two incidents but a tangle of humiliations and subjugating patterns that would be exhausting if not impossible to summarize briefly—and shame-inducing to repeat. Even with family she trusted, would they believe these years of marriage had been worse than she ever let on, much worse than anyone imagined?

Kathy's brother Nelson overheard the main points plainly enough. Kathy loved Charlie but wished she had never met him. When Raymond asked if her husband had ever hurt her, Kathy conceded only in the broadest terms that Charlie could be violent. Her father did not mince his words, Nelson recalled, and they burned indelibly into his memory. Kathy should waste no time, Raymond said. She had better leave before Charlie killed her.[20]

REASONING WITH CHARLIE HAD NEVER BEEN easy, even with straightforward subjects: the cost of a stove, her access to a telephone, her distaste for certain beers. Ample evidence suggests that the more serious Kathy was about a final break, the more cautious she would have chosen to be. In summer 1963, she had been able to justify a separation that fit well into accepted military practices and aligned with her husband's economic motivations. Divorce now would not do that. Unlike her husband, Kathy was not impulsive. She would need allies, but trusting the wrong person could be dangerous. Her short-lived personal bank account suggested a desire to separate monetary choices from Charlie's scrutiny and control (For an appointment with a lawyer? To see a gynecologist or counselor of her choosing?) followed by a recalibration. Did she withdraw all the money to prevent discovery or because her husband had discovered it?

For nearly four years she had seen, heard, and felt what he was capable of. Charlie resembled his father as much as he—and the entire Whitman family—had been victimized by him. Yet it is also crucial to understand how Kathy and her mother reportedly recoiled when Raymond suggested Charlie might kill her.[21] The blunt statement may well have felt alarmist, as if the threat were too true to verbalize or could perhaps be contained if left unspoken. Kathy may also have sought to assuage her father's worst fears as a means of forestalling any direct physical confrontation with her husband. While prescient, Raymond's statement also begged the question: How bad did it need to be?

Charlie had long cultivated Kathy's doubts about which of her perceptions were valid. The full record speaks for itself, but it was stored away on hundreds of pages like an apocryphal codex—in envelopes, in shoeboxes, in a closet—detailed patterns invisible to anyone but her. Even as Margaret Whitman's experience suggested a premonition of her own future, Kathy likely minimized her problems in comparison to her mother-in-law's. Margaret was a devout Catholic seeking divorce after twenty-five years of marriage and three children. Had Kathy really suffered enough for the right to enjoy happiness beyond Charlie? Had she learned enough in four years about her marriage, her husband, and herself to trust her own reasons for leaving?

A change of location offered one last reach for renewal—or distraction. Kathy and Charlie moved again, one final time, to a small house in a quaint neighborhood south of Town Lake, on Jewell Street. A receipt for furniture moved by Central Freight on April 5 listed among the couple's sparse belongings one table base and tabletop, four chairs, two tables, one dresser, one mirror, one bed, two rails, one chest. Here would be the last living room Kathy would decorate, the last kitchen and bedroom for which she would sew curtains.

Kathy wrote to her family as she settled into the new house. By June 1966 Charlie's interference as communications middleman was again sowing insidious confusions. Kathy first clarified about a Father's Day card Charlie said he had mailed, unbeknownst to her, "a week early," leaving her feeling the need to "remind Daddy that he did receive [it]," perhaps doubting whether it had been sent at all. Continuing, Kathy was "so sorry" to have missed her parents' phone call the previous night—Father's Day evening—but, notably, she did not offer any reason for not being able to talk. She repeated what Charlie had relayed from the conversation as if for verification. One of her uncles was very ill and in need of surgery: "Charlie said he was so sick they couldn't even move him to Houston. . . . I sure hope they haven't let it go too far." She also intimated that Charlie had not informed her about his latest suggestion to visit Needville, and she seemed braced for a sudden change of plan. "He hadn't mentioned it to me, but I sure hope we can," Kathy said. "I don't think he has any big project due." She went on, "He asked me last week to ask you to come down to see our house. I wish you could come see it before it gets old looking."[22]

Meanwhile, she stretched their budget, buying "a great big plant (fake) for the dining room corner" and "a big black Mexican pot that I'm going to put a fern in." The couple built a bookcase "that sort of partitions off the dining room and living room." Their dog, Scocie, had absorbed every rule of the house, and Kathy emphasized the animal's obedience and confinement—a stark contrast to her childhood, where the antics of dogs, cats, and even horses were a silly, imperfect, even joyful part of family lore. "Scocie has never been on the rugs. He knows better," Kathy wrote. "He is allowed in the kitchen, study, + bath. He just sits and watches us when we are in the bedroom or living room." How Scocie had learned to "know better" one can reasonably imagine.[23]

Kathy included a brief update on the Whitmans, and she empathized with her mother-in-law's new reality. "[She] is still quite determined to stay [in Austin]," Kathy wrote. "All reports say Mr. Whitman has lost 30 lbs. and is about to crack. She doesn't seem to care. It's not unusual that she doesn't have one ounce of feeling for him after all she's been through. She likes her job real well." Charlie's brother Patrick—now married for almost a year—had also taken up temporary residence with his wife in Austin and was preparing to return to Florida. Before their departure the family celebrated Patrick's twenty-first birthday together at a restaurant, the Barn, located on the north side of Austin. Patrons sat down to tables serving a giant block of Swiss cheese and glasses of complementary rosé wine. The chefs cooked steak and seafood on an open grill at the center of the restaurant, and a live cowgirl lolled in a swing over the bar. Charlie remounted a diamond ring and gave it to Patrick as a gift. It was a strangely sentimental gesture for their fraught relationship, more than he had ever given Kathy.[24]

A week later, on a Sunday, Kathy wrote that she had been relieved to talk with her parents Friday night—especially since the weekend visit Charlie suggested did not materialize after all. She composed her letter in Taylor Hall, where Charlie drafted drawings for a project, the same building where he had strangled a classmate (although she didn't see it). She had viewed *Meet the Press* that morning with particular interest because of the medical guest, Dr. Michael DeBakey, a Houston surgeon and pioneer in the field of cardiovascular procedures. "Do you know if he is the one that will perform the surgery . . . ?" Kathy asked, referring to her uncle. "It would be wonderful if he is, as he must be *the* best!" Looking ahead to summer, she yearned for more time with her family. The weather had been "miserable," and she was consumed by chores. "I have done absolutely nothing but clean house + iron," she wrote, adding sardonically, "Lots of excitement to start another week on!" Married friends were planning a weeklong summer trip in California, but Kathy had her sights set to join her family for a camping trip in early June. "That's just about the only break we could afford!" she wrote, noting that the timing would fit well with Charlie's summer school start date of June 9.[25]

Most of all, Kathy was excited about the new high school campus being built. She visited the construction site after work and observed the beauty of the innovative instructional design: "[I]n the science dept., the classrooms (6) are centered around a large room containing the 3 lab storerooms and partitioned offices for each teacher. Every teacher will have a desk, bookshelf, and bulletin board in a central office room. There will be no desks (teacher) in the classrooms, only demonstration tables." Kathy's teaching assignment would be four sections of biology and one class in physiology for seniors—the latter requiring new preparation. "Help!" she wrote.[26]

In an undated note, Kathy highlighted the "features" of a floral stationery set she enclosed as a gift to Frances. "Notice that it is purse size and will allow you to carry it to school," she wrote, "so that on the many occasions you relax in the lounge, you may drop your poor lonesome daughter a note." Only four cream-colored envelopes remain, their tissue-paper linings dotted with purple butterflies and yellow wildflowers. Frances would preserve the note and its packaging alongside Kathy's official death certificate.[27]

FATHER GIL VISITED THE COUPLE'S NEW house that spring and observed that Charlie seemed "in turmoil" about religion and showed off the guns he now stored in the garage rather than the house (likely a boundary Kathy had drawn during the move). Kathy never mentioned the priest in letters at this time, nor in June when she accompanied Charlie and Margaret to visit him on the base in San Antonio for dinner at the Officers' Club. He had been no help during their separation, as she had discovered in 1963. Even now, she likely hoped for the best possible influence on her husband from any man wearing a collar.[28]

As summer arrived, just in time for Charlie's twenty-fifth birthday, the couple took out a loan at the Teacher's Credit Union for a new Chevy Impala, reportedly yet another "gift" from his father that needed to be repaid.[29] They drove to Needville at some point in early June, though it was unclear whether they joined the Leissner camping trip. Afterwards, Kathy observed, "It seems like it's been much longer than two weeks since we were home." She had resumed work at Southwestern Bell and was happy to have summer employment, although this time she trained as an information operator. "I'm sitting in the lounge of the telephone company waiting to go to the board at 1 o'clock," she wrote. "Can you believe they spent two weeks teaching me how to look things up in the telephone book." She worked a split schedule her first week, one to six p.m. and seven to ten p.m. each day.[30]

Kathy's notes regarding Charlie and his imminent birthday were subdued, touching more on his academics, which included a part-time research project about traffic control.[31] "Charlie is in school and working his head off again," she wrote. "He's as brown as a berry from being in the sun all day counting cars. We ate dinner with Mrs. Whitman yesterday to celebrate his birthday. It's hard to believe he will be 25 years old."[32] She wrote of a welcome visit with a cousin who had started classes in Austin and was now working in the Peace Corps office. Kathy did not mention, or did not know, that Charlie had visited her cousin privately, leaving a disturbing impression. Kathy remarked again on the lives passing her by, noting about another couple, "It's hard to believe that they got married after we did and already have two children."[33]

With Frances, Kathy hatched plans for her brother Ray to visit Austin in early July. A teenager now, he would help wash the car, attend classes with Charlie, and swim at Barton Springs—not far at all from the little house on Jewell Street.[34] When he left a pair of pants and his bathing suit behind, Kathy sent them in a package to Frances, along with a special gift for baby Adam. Austin prepared to host the world premiere of the new *Batman* film, a campy extension of the popular television series, and the stores were filled with movie-themed merchandise. "I thought Adam Kyle would get a kick out of the placemat," she wrote. "I hope it will fit on his table."[35]

The last letter Kathy ever composed began as a thank

you the day before her twenty-third birthday, in a few quiet moments before she "hit the ironing board." Her parents had arranged for Charlie to deliver their gift: a makeup mirror. "[He] felt sorry for me trying to balance my hand mirror between bottles of makeup this morning so he brought it out and surprised me," Kathy wrote. "It's just great! It's gold and has six lights around it. The mirror itself turns over as one side is small + the other large magnification. It also has a little drawer for your makeup and stuff. . . . I've already taken my make-up off this afternoon, just so I could use it."[36]

Kathy reported other gifts, too. Margaret Whitman had given her a favorite lotion and bath powder. Charlie had simply given her money, which Kathy earmarked for material. "So I can get busy sewing," she wrote. She added that she was still on a weight control program, neither losing nor gaining any pounds, but she liked how she looked in the clothes her mother had sent. "I got at least 5 compliments on that brown dress," she wrote. "I can't get over how comfortable it is." Her age continued to puzzle her, as it had since she left Texas for the first time. "It sure doesn't seem like I should be 23 years old, does it?"[37]

Kathy lived twenty more days. Her fifth-year NHS reunion was approaching, and she was eager to sew new outfits for the upcoming getaway. There was also a Lanier student picnic to plan for, and Kathy took care to arrange a switched schedule with a coworker so that she could attend. On July 24 Kathy and Charlie traveled to San Antonio once more along with his brother Johnnie Mike, who was passing through on a road trip. It is unknown whether they intended one last visit with Father Gil. Military records show that the priest reported for duty the same day at Elmendorf Air Force Base in Alaska.[38]

July wound down with Nelson bringing baby Adam, their cousin Carol, and Mama Leissner to Austin. They visited

Barton Springs and splashed with Adam in the water. They joined Margaret Whitman for lunch at Wyatt's Cafeteria. The last pictures taken of the family together were likely snapped by Kathy herself: on the street outside their new house, on the walkway outside a small strip mall. She appeared in none of these images, already a ghost behind the frame.[39]

IN ROUGHLY 180,000 WORDS COMPOSED BETWEEN 1962 and 1966, Kathy demonstrated that she was a highly fluent writer whose letters, regardless of mood or subject matter, contained only occasional grammatical slips or minor misspellings (what composition scholars and English professors often call first-draft mistakes that do not undermine coherence). She often identified these herself but generally did not overworry them. Two small annotations in Kathy's final letters—easy to miss without the full context of correspondence—suggest intense hypervigilance about even the most minor misstep. These are subtle but profound indicators of how self-trust can be warped over time by a domineering partner, doubts flaring like a deep-tissue injury that does not heal.

Dated June 20 and July 11, both letters contain a tiny mark that referenced the casual scolding Charlie gave Kathy in the unsettling early days of November 1964, shortly before his return to Austin, when he lectured that she confused spellings of "to" and "too" in asking him not to be rough with her. The manipulative critique now manifested in Kathy's language. In the June letter Kathy said of her cousin, "She dropped the math course because she was just trying to do too much." In the July letter, explaining her gift for Adam, Kathy wrote, "They had Robin mats too but I thought Adam would prefer Batman." In both cases, Kathy crossed out the second o. But here—as on hundreds

*and honestly do think she needs counseling. I saw
her again last Wednesday and she looks a little
better. She dropped the math course because
she was just trying to do too much. She is
working 7 hrs. a day at the Peace Corp Office.*

of occasions before—she had spelled and used the word correctly the first time.[40]

This tiny edit betrayed an existential pressure point and distortion of Kathy's actual knowledge, suggesting that Charlie had continued to wage a campaign of what experts in coercive control refer to as "perspecticide."[41] Whatever independence she previously felt or asserted, Kathy was again subsumed by Charlie's rules and fixations. Under the circumstances, any intelligent person could easily misspell herself—one small line through one small letter—even for the most open and supportive audience she knew.

BRUTALITY AGAINST WOMEN MADE HEADLINES TWO days after Kathy's birthday. In Chicago, drifter Richard Speck broke into a group residence shared by nursing students and murdered eight of them, one by one, in a separate room—some killed with his bare hands, some stabbed, some both. The lone survivor saved herself by hiding under a bed, aware of every death.[42]

Kathy wanted her own life to go on, and for now she simply sought to endure. On July 22 Kathy dropped by Lanier one last time to pick up some teaching materials. The principal's secretary, Mrs. Doris Kreuz, later recalled in a letter to the Leissners how much Kathy loved her profession and could not wait for school to start again. Meanwhile she looked forward to the five-year reunion of her own graduating class. On July 30 she purchased fabric for a new dress at Kraft Corner. A day later her husband purchased a Bowie knife at Academy Surplus.[43]

Kathy rose early the last day of July to prepare for the morning segment of her split shift at Southwestern Bell, starting at nine a.m. Charlie picked her up shortly after one p.m. for lunch with her mother-in-law. He then took Kathy to see a movie matinee—not of *Batman*, but a tired remake of *Stagecoach* starring Ann-Margret as a dancehall hostess, outnumbered in a cast of men playing cowboys, cons, and drifters. The film concludes with a predictable shoot 'em up and with Ann-Margret's character riding into the night with the gunman in a carriage. Before Charlie returned Kathy for the second half of her shift at six p.m., he took her to visit friends for an hour. He had programmed her entire day.[44]

Kathy's last night on the switchboard concluded quietly, only a few blinks of light left behind—no hint of the bulbs that would flash a massive wall of light fourteen hours later.[45] Charlie picked her up at ten p.m. as usual and steered the Impala down Congress Avenue, the glow of the Capitol receding behind them as they approached Town Lake then crossed it. Charlie was likely very quiet, and perhaps Kathy hesitated if he encouraged her to turn the radio dials to whatever station she wanted. The previous day, Congress Avenue had been renamed "Batman Boulevard" in honor of the celebrity-studded movie premier.[46] The gibbous moon was heavy in the sky, but there was no superhero signal, no radar, no civil defense siren that night. No bulletin to tell Kathy: this is your last chance to go.

For now, relieved to be home, she would respond to immediate things: the long day, its lingering heat. She would remove her shoes. Perhaps she opened the window near the headboard of the bed before taking a shower. She wiped away makeup and clipped a few strands of hair—darker again—into waves, securing a gauzy nylon net (not too tight) to protect them.[47] There was a phone call with her parents. Perhaps she closed the sewing basket, smoothed the new fabric already trimmed and laid out on the table for her new dress. Sewing had such predictable elements: materials to gather, tissue paper patterns to pin, the perfect thread in the proper needle. Did Charlie mention that her cousin phoned earlier to say she would arrive tomorrow morning instead of tonight? Did Kathy hear the phone when a friend from Needville called, then rang again, to talk about plans and outfits for the reunion?[48]

Before bed, maybe a simple glass of water. Perhaps Charlie suggested a pill—For nerves? For better sleep?—before he left to study at his mother's air-conditioned apartment. But no: Kathy was exhausted, with memories that could soothe her to rest as she heard the door close, as she heard her husband's footfalls on the path outside, the ignition as he started the car and pulled from the curb (or was he returning already?). There was Adam's little squint when he smiled and kicked in his chair. The way her mother's chin tilted slightly when she showed tender feelings. Lately, zooming on a boat with friends across Lake Austin, how it could feel like flying to lean out and smile into the humid breezes that tousled her hair, the sunset winking orange.[49] And years ago, those long summer days after hauling rice, the artesian spring such relief for burning shoulders in a season when the biggest secrets were only sharings between girls, and Kathy could reach one arm back past her ear in a swim stroke that curled her body over in the cool water.

Charlie had been sweet today, hadn't he? It was more that he seemed less agitated, even with all those final exams coming. She would not have to leave him, not quite yet. Maybe she could love her husband the way a woman could come to love a scar on her own body, like that mark she touched where her ovary had been. If Kathy could just find a way, sometime, maybe soon, where letting go would not need to hurt him, where he could fade to a silver shadow as she went on to discover—what exactly? How would it feel again to trust her own words, placing the o she wanted where she knew it belonged, those easy sounds she knew in all their lovely variations: the end of two, the middle of joy—

Epilogue

Recovery and Response

KATHY, LIKE HER MOTHER-IN-LAW MARGARET, WAS already dead as the earliest hints of August sunlight graced the surface of Town Lake. Her fatally wounded body remained unattended for hours before any person on the UT campus heard that first terrible crack in the sky. When her cousin arrived midmorning, she knocked at the door of the Jewell Street house and waited, then knocked again in the strange stillness. When she looked through the screen of the open window, Kathy lay motionless in bed.[1]

The reality dawned slowly; friends and authorities did not immediately connect the Tower mayhem to the two women who did not answer their doors or phones. As radio and television broadcasts reached Needville, folks initially assumed that Charlie and Kathy would be safe—he in a classroom, she at Southwestern Bell. Nelson had heard the

Interior view from the UT Tower, looking south toward the Austin Capitol dome and toward Kathy's final home on Jewell Street. By Paralta Studios, Prints and Photographs Collection, di_02200, Dolph Briscoe Center for American History, The University of Texas at Austin.

first startling reports while washing his mother's car, but the violence seemed distant. When Ray and a friend announced that they wanted to go swimming in the rice fields, Nelson offered a ride.

By the time the boys returned home, the scene had changed forever. Nelson remembered the chaos of cars and trucks filling the circular driveway and parked hastily along the road. Reporters and police seemed to be everywhere. Nelson's first thought was that something happened to Adam. As he pushed through the door, his senses flooded. He scrambled through packed rooms, looking for his parents. In the living room, the television flashed a horrible image: ambulance attendants removing a blanket-covered body from the house he recognized.

His father had disappeared. As soon as she realized Raymond was missing, Frances raced in a car out to the farm. She found him alone in the barn, in total darkness, crying and holding a gun.[2]

Not since Hurricane Carla had Needville confronted such widely broadcast devastation, but this time the damage was personal, and a curtain of unspeakability descended. Kathy's brutal death at the hands of Charlie, the murder of his own mother, and his suicidal attack from atop the Texas Tower were unnatural and irreconcilable acts. In ninety-six-minutes Charlie killed fifteen and wounded thirty-one—traumatizing an entire country—while Carla's death toll, even as a Category 4 storm lasting many hours, had been contained to forty-six. Advance tracking and community mobilization had made all the difference.[3]

Kathy returned home in a casket. Nelson accepted the solemn duty of selecting his sister's burial clothing at a small Rosenberg women's boutique she had known well. Saleswomen at Etta Mae's Shop laid aside items for him to consider in a private visit. Nelson selected a pink knit suit with gold buttons and a gold chain detail, only later realizing that their cousin Cheryl had also been buried in pink and that the style of the suit resembled Jackie Kennedy's clothing the day of her husband's assassination.[4] On August 3 Kathy's classmates carried her coffin down the steps of the First Methodist Church after the funeral. It had not been the reunion they planned. Mourners overflowed from the main sanctuary to the vestibule, onto sidewalks and adjacent streets. Cars and media vans claimed space everywhere. Cards and letters

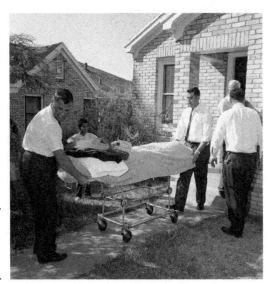

Draped with a sheet, Kathy's body was removed from the house on Jewell Street on August 1, 1966. AP Photo/DO.

from strangers flooded from across the world, some messages lashing out with blame.

The day that Raymond and Frances Leissner witnessed their beloved daughter's coffin lowered into the ground at Rosenberg Cemetery, they received another letter. When Nelson saw the envelope, he recognized the author immediately. Written coldly and tidily on two pages of graph paper, the contents traced Kathy's last hours and moments alive. The letter was one final triangulation, Charlie's last cruel attempt to alibi himself as the good boy who always meant well when he did wrong—like so many messages Kathy received in letters and notes, written traces of how she was treated in daylight and in darkness. "I tried to be as sweet as possible to her on this her last day," he wrote. "Tonight after she talked with you we shared a last interlude together, she has always been a fine lover. Then I tried my best to kill her as painlessly as possible, however I have my doubts about how painless it was. She was a very strong girl."[5]

Raymond and Frances kept the document to themselves under lock and key, where it remained until their deaths.

In January 2015, sitting with Nelson one evening at his home, the first time we ever met in person, I removed that letter from its envelope and held it in my hands. The chill that overcame me as I read was unmistakable: Kathy's last moments—naked, terrified—were far from painless. She had known her attacker, and she had fought.[6]

IT IS KATHY'S VOICE—HER SHIMMERING EAGERNESS for connection—that stays with me, as when she wrote to her family before returning to Texas in summer 1963. "I guess you all have sore ears from listening to Nelson's tales of his world travels. I hope they feel better because when I get home you will have to listen to me." Her letters and their expressions of life did not simply end: they were brutally interrupted.[7]

In writing this book I have reflected often about the summer after I turned twenty-three. I, too, had just completed my first year in the classroom. My parents had separated, soon to divorce. Aside from a brief trip to childhood music camp across the Canadian border, I had never traveled outside the country. I had not yet attended graduate school. Aside from school-related projects and an occasional letter to the editor, I had never published a word. I had prematurely committed myself to an unhealthy relationship I would take seven years to leave, even though I knew early on that it was not good for me. I allowed myself little room for error and remained deeply motivated by anxiety and guilt, a need to prove I was a good girl. My childhood choice of patron saint—Maria Goretti, an eleven-year-old girl stabbed to death as she resisted a sexual assault—haunted me. I had never had a pap smear but remained paranoid about accidental pregnancy though my risk was low. It would be thirty years before I could name and address the sexual traumas of my childhood. My religious questions and political rebellions were only beginning to evolve, and I had not met the man I would eventually—very happily—marry.

What about you, dear reader? Where were you at twenty-three—or does that age yet elude you on a close horizon? The people nearby, those who felt inevitable in your life: Who encouraged you and who stifled your spirit? How did you know the difference? What did you swear would "never" happen to you, that you would "never" tolerate or do? What have you learned to see and articulate about your life that once felt impossible to translate?

Kathy was robbed of all possible futures at the onset of adulthood, as Margaret was robbed in middle age. Such victimization was not a choice. Throughout her marriage, Kathy adapted different forms of resistance within her social circumstances—just as her mother-in-law fought back within hers.[8] Like thousands of women before and since, Kathy was only precious as a possession until her husband deemed it necessary to discard her. As of this date, the Domestic Violence Prevention Centre estimates that it takes an average of seven attempts to leave a violent relationship permanently. Research warns that the abused partner is most vulnerable to fatal assault around the time of the most serious attempt to leave—and for up to two years afterward.[9]

Although Kathy dared speak of divorce in the last year of her life, the practical realities of the time did not help. Apathy about violence in marriage was stoked by what legal scholar Carolyn B. Ramsey terms the "exit myth," wherein popular theorists pathologized wives who did not leave as "masochistic." No-hassle, "migratory" divorces were available for those who could fly to Nevada, but it was not until 1969, under Gov. Ronald Reagan, that California became the first state to adopt no-fault divorce laws. Kathy would have been required to delve into details with lawyers and judges to justify cause (or "fault") for her divorce from a volatile man who rarely accepted responsibility and knew well how to charm and manipulate strangers. In Texas, as in many states at the time, it was still not a crime for a husband to sexually assault his wife. There was no 911 emergency number for any American in 1966, nor did secure, anonymous abuse hotlines exist. There were no community resources for people in Kathy's position. The Austin Center for Battered Women and Rape Crisis Center would not form until the next decade, eventually merging with local groups supporting abused and neglected children to create Stop Abuse for Everyone (SAFE) and the SAFE Alliance. The Texas Council on Family Violence (TCFV) and National Domestic Violence Hotline are now based in Austin, making the location a national leader in education, activism, and practical support for survivors with differing needs across demographic groups.[10] Kathy, like her contemporaries, could not access these networks.

Current resources address a need that seems sadly to grow. Statistics of violence in the home during the 1950s and 1960s are difficult to come by, due to lack of terminology and systemic inquiry. Prior to 1977, the FBI's Uniform Crime Reports (UCR) grouped all killings "committed by spouses" together by gender, suggesting a misleading equivalency.[11] With data no longer restricted to marital status and now disaggregated by many factors, in addition to gender (including race, sexual orientation, economic status, and geographical region), we can see that the decade of 2010–2020 does not reflect a positive trajectory. The National Coalition Against Domestic Violence (NCADV) reported in 2020 that one in four women and one in ten men experience some form of IPV during their lifetimes—a total of 10 million adults annually in the US—with the number of such victimizations increasing a whopping 42 percent between

2016 and 2018. NCADV also estimates that 51.3 percent of Black adult female homicides are related to IPV and that American Indian and Alaska Native women experience IPV at higher rates than women of any other ethnicity. Early studies suggest that LGBTQ people are targets as often, if not more often, than their heterosexual counterparts.[12]

Even with the private murders of Kathy and Margaret proximate to such a notorious and public crime, official documents minimized the context of their deaths—most maddening given official investigative summaries and early media reports that simultaneously documented Kathy's fear of her husband while glossing over its patterns, substance, and cumulative impact. The public report of the grand jury declared surprise at Whitman's attack, referring to him as a "previously peaceful individual" who had "suddenly gone completely berserk with no warning to his family or friends." Similarly, the panel of experts assembled by Texas governor John Connally presented twelve public assessments about the crimes and offered ten powerful recommendations, none of which addressed abuse. The commission only generally referenced "marital problems" and "discord" between Whitman's own parents and romanticized "strong loving ties" with Kathy, despite his "inconsistent" behavior.[13]

In this story, as in so many, the primary investigation and analysis of the crime unwittingly perpetuated the logic of the killer himself. Erasure and collective forgetting are common results among thousands of cases that do not make the news. Imagine for a moment that Kathy was her husband's sole victim. Her death would have been shrugged quietly into other mortality statistics of 1966, when 2,877 women in the US were victims of homicide—193 women in Texas alone, with six white and fifteen nonwhite women fatally assaulted by "cutting and piercing instruments."[14]

Permanent escape would not have been simple or smooth, but I have pictured so many futures for Kathy without or beyond Charlie—futures where I would have likely never known her name. The friends she would have met at Grace Hall in 1962 if she had not married so quickly. The graduate work she dared to dream about in biology or education. The students and colleagues she could have known as a teacher. All those nights she could have come home after work without bracing for the ridicule, the angry lecture, that tell-tale flash in his eyes when he turned on her. The partners who would have cherished her, reciprocating tenderness without conditions. A baby or babies, or no children, if she wanted. The right to disagree, to change her mind, to grow without fear. The chance to hear her father admit a longtime affair, then to know her parents in new marriages and, when the time came, to mourn their deaths. All the moments to savor with her brothers as adults: listening to Adam play guitar and ukulele; trading science talk with Ray; enjoying Nelson's Mardi Gras gatherings with a sparkle of yellow, purple, and green plastic beads at her neck. At least once in her life— alone in a car or in the shower, or shoulder-to-shoulder with friends at a party—belting out Gloria Gaynor's chorus, "I Will Survive." Meeting others who pulled through, no longer carrying secrets for people who hurt them. Wondering from the safe distance of a different life: Did Charlie ever get help? In 2023, Kathy would have celebrated her eightieth birthday.

Kathy's husband treated letters as trophies, but she used writing to express autonomy, learning, and creativity in a life she sought to understand and transform. In the investigative aftermath of the UT massacre, a police report included this statement: "Two packages of personal letters between [Charlie] and his wife, Kathy, were taken back to the residence . . .

Kathy Leissner in 1962, before she was married. Private archive of Nelson Leissner.

as it was felt that these letters should not be read by this department."[15] At the time this was a wise choice, leaving the texts for family to tend. And now, because of Nelson, these letters have been delivered when we need them more than ever.

Kathy's words leave their own signal—a steady SOS undetected in time to save her life. The patterns are always there if we pay attention. Survivors may recognize flickers of their own knowledge, their ways of reasoning and beseeching, sharing and hiding, coping and resisting, fighting, biding time. There is room for every voice: no one must remain ·

locked away inside this very old story of aloneness. For my part, it is hard to let Kathy go. In her letters I feel a pulse reminding me how memory can be restored when agency is respected—how hope and even healing, as she might say, *sometime*, can reach beyond the grave.

Acknowledgments

THIS BOOK WOULD NOT BE POSSIBLE without the trust and support of Nelson Leissner. He was generous not only in sharing archival materials but also in assisting with countless clarifications during formal interviews as well as follow-up emails and conversations, in person as well as by phone and text. When I first began to write about Kathy's life in 2015, he helped connect me with surviving family members and friends. While Nelson was always frank with his perspective and his unflinching commitment to Kathy's memory, he never attempted to shape my interpretations or my writing. I am humbled by his openness. I have done my very best to honor all materials containing such indispensable and deeply traumatic history.

Although this book is not intended as a collage of memories by those who loved Kathy and knew her during happier times, I am indebted to so many who were willing to be interviewed. Their perspectives helped me immensely to understand Kathy's character, spirit, and lasting impact on others. Much appreciation to Ray Leissner, Adam Leissner, Nancy Leissner Bartosh, Woody Bacica, Marje Janacek, and Betty Giese; as well as to Darleen Hibbs Koenig and Linda Damerau Cipriano, who both worked with Kathy at Southwestern Bell in Austin. A special thank you to Elaine (Fuess) Brazzell, whose voice I included in the introduction. For those individuals to whom I reached out over the years and who chose not to respond for various reasons, I respect and appreciate that choice.

Two women who remembered the Whitman family vividly offered perspectives from Lake Worth: Judith Fabris and Jane (Spotts) Conway. Needville resident and Fort Bend historian Mable Huff York provided many memories of Needville and the Houston region by telephone as well as in follow-up questions through Ancestry.com messaging.

I was grateful for the opportunity to speak with individuals who generously provided so many insights about UT Austin campus life, activities, and dynamics in the city in the early to mid-1960s. A chain reaction of sorts evolved as I began talking with people who connected me with others. John Reetz showed me how to locate the *Daily Texan* electronic archives and introduced me to Dave McNeely, who shared his wealth of knowledge about Austin history and introduced me to Greg Lipscomb and Dr. Leon McNealy. Greg Lipscomb helped me connect subsequently with Suzan Glickman, Dr. Anitha Mitchell, Cindy Keever, Susan Morehead, Bea Ann Smith, Wilda Campbell (who happened to room for a time with Kathy's cousin Margie Ann), Michael Gillette, and Susan Wiltshire. Forrest Preece, whom I had met at the fiftieth memorial for the UT shooting, also shared his recollections of Austin and his harrowing experience of the Tower shooting.

The gestation of this book began with "Listening to Kathy," published in *Catapult* in 2016, and I thank my original editors, Mensah Demary and Yuka Igarashi, for helping me bring the story into the world. The opportunities to deepen my understanding and refine my questions about the archive were subsequently afforded by editors at the following academic publications: *Pacific Coast Philology* (special gratitude to Dr. John Ganim), *American Studies Journal*, and Demeter Press's anthology, *Critical Perspectives on Wives:*

Roles, Representations, Identities, and Work, edited by D. Lynn O'Brien Hallstein and Rebecca Bromwich, 2019.

Feedback I collected on cards during presentations about the archive during 2017–2018 helped me to envision a much broader audience for Kathy's story, and to see how her voice might connect with contemporary readers across a spectrum of experiences. The opportunity for multimedia discussion was invaluable. I thank students and faculty of Riverside City College, Norco College, Moreno Valley College, Claremont McKenna College, and La Sierra University, as well as staff and volunteers at Austin SAFE and Austin Unitarian Universalist Church for their honest comments, questions, and suggestions. Special thanks go to individuals who served as primary hosts, organizers, and discussants at these events: Daniel Cox Malyszka, Derrick Crowe, Scott Butki, YiShun Lai, Dr. Larry Geraty, Laura E. Geriguis, Chrissy Crockett Sharp, and Priya Junnar.

During a pandemic research process, I was especially grateful for the quickly generated information provided by experts at many institutions: Doug Parker, Educational Data Center Texas Higher Education Coordinating Board; Barbara Kievit-Mason, University Archivist, Newton Gresham Library, Sam Houston State University; Kristi Cantu, Exhibit Specialist, Austin Nature & Science Center; Roxanne Puder, Onslow County Public Library, Jacksonville, North Carolina; Rebecca A. Baugnon, Special Collections Librarian, William M. Randall Library, UNC Wilmington; Gaby Gomez, Travis County Tax Office, Voter Registration Division. Siobhan Fleming's assistance navigating Texas academic records systems was deeply appreciated, as were her keen eye for historical connections and her ear for good titles.

For guidance in parsing historical patterns of gendered participation in twentieth-century American elections, I give special thanks to Kelly Dittmar, Rutgers University;

and Christina Wolbrecht, University of Notre Dame. And for their insights about recognizing the idiosyncrasies and scope of private epistolary archives, I am ever grateful for Dr. Robert Hudspeth (who I did not realize until recently is himself a UT alumnus), Claremont Graduate University; and Professor Margaretta Jolly, University of Sussex, UK.

Aryn Glazier and Caitlin Brenner in Duplication Services at the Dolph Briscoe Center for American History were both immensely helpful in locating historical images during the center's update of its digital collection system. I appreciated every chance to "nerd out" and consult with graphic designer Dean A. Vergara about image preservation, scanning, and file resolutions.

Indexing costs as well as licensing fees for all photographs selected from Briscoe, Getty, and the Associated Press were made possible by a generous gift received from artist Norma Jo Huron Lipsett (1935–2020) after her passing.

It is powerful that this book finds its home with the University of Texas Press, given that Kathy graduated from the university in 1965 despite all she endured. The respect and attention from the publishing team at every layer and level has been a true gift. I had the pleasure to work with three editors, first Sarah McGavick, who acquired the manuscript and helped me envision its structure; then Dawn Durante, who helped bring the book through peer review and revisions; and lastly, Casey Kittrell, who advanced the book to completion. Their thorough communication and encouragement always kept me on track, as did the meticulous work of Mia Uribe Kozlovsky, Robert S. Kimzey, and my brilliant copy editor, Leslie Tingle. I would also like to extend my appreciation to my peer reviewers for their time and feedback.

The concentration needed for any book, particularly a book of this kind, requires more than a fair amount of solitude. I am incredibly lucky to have a life partner, Justin, who understood and respected the value of Kathy's story as much as I did and who served often as a sounding board, insightful editor, and technical guru. More than that, he helped me keep my bearings when the heaviness would sometimes overwhelm. I could not have made it without him.

Questions for Book Groups or Classroom Discussion

The story of the UT Austin shooting, and that of many other shootings, tends to center the perspective of the perpetrator. Consider another story of a mass shooting. Whose experiences could we be more curious about, and what would be able to learn?

This book relies on access to written artifacts—paper and envelopes—preserved and reread over time. Imagine that Kathy's story took place during the age of email, personal messaging, and social media. What would be similar or different about an electronic dialogue of abuse? What additional barriers or tools would come into play for synthesizing the conversational history? How does technology impact abusive relationships?

Consider the elements of coercive control identified in the introduction. Where do you see them most vividly inside Kathy's story, and what elements might you add? Which situations would be most challenging to describe, and why?

Imagine that you have a close friend who confides that their longtime partner scares them at times, but then later minimizes that statement. How might Kathy's story help us understand what could be going on? What could you do?

Most college students in the twenty-first century have much more access to information about gender and sexuality than students in the mid-twentieth century, and most are not married to or even living with their intimate partners yet. However, this demographic remains at a high risk of IPV, including coercive control. How would you explain this enduring reality? What social and behavioral understanding are we missing, and what changes are needed?

Abusive behavior may be rationalized in cases where the perpetrator has a traumatic background of some kind. How can we acknowledge past trauma without making excuses for abuse in the present?

The National Domestic Violence Hotline has created an interactive "safety plan." Go to https://www.thehotline.org/plan-for-safety/create-a-safety-plan. Imagine you are helping Kathy consider this plan. At what point(s) in her story do you see potential off-ramps or opportunities? What skills, assets, or allies were available? What barriers would be most challenging?

Kathy's husband often referred to her as his "most precious possession," a phrase repeated in retellings of this story that relegate her to background. What details in Kathy's story reveal this attitude as dangerous rather than romantic? How or why might this be easy to confuse?

"Magical thinking" is a common coping mechanism when there may seem to be no way out of an abusive situation, particularly in childhood or intimate relationships. Without simply dismissing this as illogical, consider how it serves a temporary function. Where do you see examples of this in

Kathy's story—and where do you see her clarity breaking through?

Even though today we have more terminology and more knowledge, abuse remains difficult to name for those who are living through it. Consider films or TV series where characters struggle at first to find words that match the reality of their experience—or whose stories are dismissed. Who or what makes a difference in finding the words? How can you connect these patterns to Kathy's writings?

Bystanders often ask, rhetorically, "Why didn't you call the police?" Being more curious about the real answer to this question may help us find solutions. In Kathy's story, what are the most likely explanations for no phone calls to police in various situations? In the twenty-first century, what are real reasons family members hesitate to call law enforcement or social services? What must we learn from this hesitation—and how could it impact training for first responders?

Stories of violence not only may neglect to understand private survivors and targets but also omit the powerful role bystanders can play. Programs such as StepUP! educate individuals about safe, appropriate ways to intervene. Review some of the key ideas at stepupprogram.org and put yourself into a specific situation in the book as a neighbor, trusted friend, or family member. Who do you see trying to implement these strategies? Who struggles? What could you do now to assist someone else?

Notes

Author's note: All correspondence referenced below, unless otherwise indicated, is from the private archive of Nelson Leissner.

Notes below include a significant number of references to the letters between Kathy Leissner (prior to marriage) or Kathy Leissner Whitman (after marriage) and Charles J. Whitman (he regularly included his middle name "Joseph" or initial). For purposes of brevity, all correspondence citations reference Kathy Leissner as "KL," Kathy Leissner Whitman as "KLW," Charles J. Whitman as "CJW," and Frances Leissner as "FL."

Additional abbreviations are indicated after first use. Longer month names are also abbreviated.

Introduction

1. Charles Whitman's fatalities from the Tower (not including his wife, Kathy, and mother, Margaret) were updated from fourteen to fifteen to include the death of David H. Gunby, who succumbed to his injuries in 2001. With this revision, the final total of all casualties (not counting Whitman himself) is seventeen dead, thirty-one wounded.

2. Kathy Leissner Whitman (hereafter KLW) letter to parents, 14 Feb. 1963; Jackie Gu, "Deadliest Mass Shootings Are Often Preceded by Violence at Home," Bloomberg.com, 30 June 2020, https://www .bloomberg.com/graphics/2020-mass-shootings-domestic-violence -connection; National Coalition Against Domestic Violence (NCADV), "Domestic Violence," 2020, https://assets.speakcdn.com/assets/2497 /domestic_violence-2020080709350855.pdf; see also "Guns and Violence against Women" (report updated 27 April 2021), Every-town for Gun Safety, https://everytownresearch.org/report/guns-and -violence-against-women-americas-uniquely-lethal-intimate-partner -violence-problem. I wrote about the pattern in the wake of the Sandy Hook shooting, several years before this angle of analysis was widely

discussed: "Shooting Sprees Start with Women," *Salon*, 21 Jan. 2013, https://www.salon.com/2013/01/21/mass_killers_start_with_women, syndicated from "Supersex Me," *The Nervous Breakdown,* 17 Jan. 2013, https://thenervousbreakdown.com/jscottcoe/2013/01/supersex-me.

3. Charles Joseph Whitman (hereafter CJW) letter to Leissners, 1 Aug. 1966; see also Daily Record of C. J. Whitman, 23 Feb. 1964; and CJW, typed untitled letter dated 31 July 1966, Austin Police Department (APD) Files, Austin History Center (hereafter AHC); Sylvia Hubel, "The Deconstruction of Clerical Hegemony: Ending the Moral Dissonance and Abuse of Power," in *Crisis and Challenge in the Roman Catholic Church*, edited by Debra Meyers and Mary Sue Barnett (Lexington Books, 2020), 103.

4. For a thoughtful introductory analysis of Nils Christie's critical victimology and its interdisciplinary relevance, see Sandra Walklate's "Nils Christie: On the Periphery but in the Centre," *TEMIDA* 19, Br. 2 (2016): 243–256, doi:10.2298/TEM1602243W.

5. Jo Scott-Coe, *MASS: A Sniper, a Father, and a Priest* (Pelekinesis, 2018); see also Archdiocese of Galveston-Houston Clergy Disclosure List, released 31 Jan. 2019, https://www.archgh.org/clergylist; Jo Scott-Coe, "Priest Named on Molestation List Was Texas Sniper's Scoutmaster, Friend, and Confidant," *Press-Enterprise,* 16 Feb. 2019, https://www.pe.com/2019/02/16/priest-named-on-molestation-list-was -texas-snipers-scoutmaster-friend-and-confidant.

6. Peter Wydn, "The Revolt of Texas Women," *Saturday Evening Post*, 14 Jan. 1961, pp. 25, 55–56; Sierra Juarez, "How Polly Abarca Fought to Bring Birth Control to South Texas," *Texas Monthly*, 9 March 2021, https://www.texasmonthly.com/being-texan/how-polly-abarca -fought-to-bring-birth-control-to-south-texas.

7. Jo Scott-Coe, "Listening to Kathy," *Catapult*, 30 March 2016, https://catapult.co/stories/listening-to-kathy.

8. Megan L. Evans, MD, MPH, Margo Lindauer, JD, and Maureen E. Farrell, MD, "A Pandemic within a Pandemic—Intimate Partner Violence," *New England Journal of Medicine*, 10 Dec. 2020, https://www .nejm.org/doi/full/10.1056/NEJMp2024046; TCFV, "Honoring Texas Victims: Analysis of Family Violence Fatalities in 2020," 4–5, https:// www.familyabusecenter.org/wp-content/uploads/tcfv_htv_rprt_2020 -1.pdf.

9. See Katie Barclay, "Falling in Love with the Dead," *Rethinking History* 22, no. 4 (2018): 460–461, 464.

10. Svanhildur Bogadottir, "Searching for Women in the Archives:

Collecting Private Archives of Women," in *Teaching Gender with Libraries and Archives: The Power of Information*, ed. Sara De Jong (ATGENDER: European Association for Gender Research, Education and Documentation, Central European University Press, 2013), 66.

11. See Lenore E. A. Walker, *The Battered Woman Syndrome*, 4th ed. (Springer, 2017); Diana E. H. Russell, *Rape in Marriage* (Macmillan, 1982); and Evan Stark, *Coercive Control: How Men Entrap Women in Personal Life* (Oxford University Press, 2009).

12. See the Duluth Model for the original wheel model and variations, as well as a video explaining the models, https://www.theduluthmodel.org/wheels; KLW letter to CJW, 5 Nov. 1963.

13. Interview with Elaine Brazzell (Fuess), 12 Jan. 2021.

14. Walker, *The Battered Woman Syndrome*, 105.

15. Russell, *Rape in Marriage*, 289; Walker, *The Battered Woman Syndrome*, 105.

16. Jane Monckton Smith, *In Control: Dangerous Relationships and How They End in Murder* (Bloomsbury Circus, 2021), 102.

17. Jillian Peterson, Gina Erickson, Kyle Knapp et al., "Communication of Intent to Do Harm Preceding Mass Shootings in the United States, 1966–2019," *JAMA Network Open* 4, no. 21 (2021), doi:10.1001/jamanetworkopen.2021.33073.

18. See Stark, *Coercive Control*, 362–388. One nationally recognized program of Bystander Intervention Training that focuses on the college-age demographic is StepUP!, developed by Becky Bell in partnership with the University of Arizona and the NCAA, https://stepupprogram.org.

19. In addition, words and phrases that were underlined for emphasis in the letters are reproduced here with italics.

20. Greta Anderson, "Intimate Partner Violence Common among Students," *InsideHigherEd*, 9 Sept. 2020, https://www.insidehighered.com/quicktakes/2020/09/09/intimate-partner-violence-common-among-students; see the original study by Hyunkag Cho et al., "Gender Differences in Intimate Partner Violence Victimization, Help-Seeking, and Outcomes among College Students," *Advances in Social Work* 20, no. 1 (Spring 2020): 22–44, http://134.68.190.31/index.php/advancesinsocialwork/article/view/23675/23119.

21. Holman W. Jenkins Jr., "Red Flag Laws Are as Good as the Data," *Wall Street Journal* opinion, 27 May 2022, https://www.wsj.com/articles/red-flag-laws-are-as-good-as-the-data-guns-weapons-ban-private-email-mass-shooting-texas-11653685209.

Danger, 1961

1. Nelson Leissner emails, 7 Aug. 2019.

2. *Austin American-Statesman*, 12 Sept. 1961, p. 1.

3. Nelson Leissner emails, 7 Aug. 2019.

4. "Dan Rather: American Journalist," Briscoe Center for American History, University of Texas (UT) at Austin, 2020, https://danratherjournalist.org/ground/natural-disasters/hurricane-carla/video-hurricane-carla-us-weather-bureau; see also Megan Garber, "Dan Rather Showed the First Radar Image of a Hurricane on TV," *The Atlantic*, 29 Oct. 2012, https://www.theatlantic.com/technology/archive/2012/10/dan-rather-showed-the-first-radar-image-of-a-hurricane-on-tv/264246.

5. "Hurricane Carla Aftermath No. 1," Texas Department of Public Safety Historical Museum and Research Center (1961), and "About the Video," Texas Archive of the Moving Image, https://texasarchive.org/2009_00883; Nelson Leissner emails, 7 Aug. 2019.

6. Kathy Leissner bank statements and cancelled checks, envelope #1 (July–Aug. 1961), private collection of Nelson Leissner; Nelson Leissner text messages, 3 April 2020.

7. Nelson Leissner emails, 7 Aug. 2019; Nelson Leissner interviews 27 and 30 Oct. 2015.

Country Life, Only Daughter

1. Interview with Nelson Leissner, 30 Oct. 2015; Frances Leissner family tree documents, n.d., private archive of Nelson Leissner.

2. Personal papers and "Life Letter" (n.d.) of Raymond Leissner, private archive of Nelson Leissner; Nelson Leissner interview, 30 Oct. 2015.

3. *Handbook of Texas Online* (hereafter *HTO*), s.v. "Velasco, TX," 2021, https://www.tshaonline.org/handbook/entries/velasco-tx; Nelson Leissner interview, 30 Oct. 2015. For historical references, see J. U. Salvant and David G. McComb, *The Historic Seacoast of Texas* (University of Texas Press, 1999), 39; see also Dina Cappiello, "Dow Chemical Brought Growth, Regrets to Freeport," *Houston Chronicle, 19 Jan 2005*, https://www.chron.com/news/article/Dow-Chemical-brought-growth-regrets-to-Freeport-1922627.php; as well as "Mining the 'Blue Economy,'" Dow Chemical Corporation 1995–2020, https://corporate.dow.com/en-us/about/company/history/mining-blue-economy.html.

4. Raymond Leissner, "Life Letter" (n.d.), private archive of Nelson Leissner.

5. Leissner baby books for Kathleen, private archive of Nelson Leissner.

6. *HTO*, s.v. "Fourth Ward, Houston," by Cary D. Wintz, n.d., https://www.tshaonline.org/handbook/entries/fourth-ward-houston; see also Willa Granger, "'Order, Convenience, and Beauty': The Style, Space, and Multiple Narratives of San Felipe Courts," Rice Design Alliance, 3 Nov. 2020, https://www.ricedesignalliance.org/sanfelipecourts.

7. Raymond Leissner, "Life Letter" (n.d.), private archive of Nelson Leissner; H. A. Leissner and Linda Leissner, Warranty Deed, State of Texas, 27 Aug. 1951, Vol. 219, p. 63, Deed Records of Fort Bend County Texas.

8. Sam Houston, Vocational Agriculture course requirements and course catalogs, 1942–1943; Nelson Leissner interview, 8 April 2020.

9. Leissner photos, c. 1948–1950, private archive of Nelson Leissner; Nelson Leissner interview, 30 Oct. 2015.

10. Nelson Leissner interview, 30 Oct. 2015.

11. 1950 Census Report, "Number of Inhabitants: Texas," https://www2.census.gov/library/publications/decennial/1950/population-volume-1/vol-01-46.pdf; see also *HTO*, s.v. "Needville TX," by Mark Odintz, Needville State Historical Association, https://www.tshaonline.org/handbook/entries/needville-tx.

12. Mable Huff York interview, 7 Aug. 2020.

13. Ibid.; see also Fort Bend County Historical Commission, Oral History Committee, Interview of Mable Huff York, 19 Aug. 2014, https://historicalcommission.fortbendcountytx.gov/Oral-Histories/Mable-Huff-York-Interview.pdf.

14. Details of the original lots are explicated on the warranty deed from Raymond to Frances Leissner following their divorce in 1973; Nelson Leissner interviews, 30 Oct. 2015 and 8 Nov. 2020.

15. Nelson Leissner interviews, 30 Oct. 2015 and 8 Nov. 2020.

16. Inscription at end of the *Blue Jay* NHS yearbook, 1961, private archive of Nelson Leissner.

17. Letters and artifacts from Kathy Leissner, *Things and Stuff* scrapbook, private archive of Nelson Leissner.

18. Nelson Leissner interview, 30 Oct. 2015.

19. *Things and Stuff* scrapbook, private archive of Nelson Leissner.

20. *Blue Jay* yearbook, 1961, private archive of Nelson Leissner; Eric Hanson, "Teen Admits to Needville School Fire," *Houston Chronicle*, 8 May 2007, https://www.chron.com/news/article/Teen-admits-to-Needville-school-fire-1565957.php; Fort Bend County

Historical Commission, York interview, 19 Aug. 2014; see also *HTO*, "Needville, TX."

21. *Blue Jay* NHS yearbook and the *Blue Jay Chatter* newspaper, 1961, private archive of Nelson Leissner; written notes by Nelson Leissner, 2015.

22. Nelson Leissner interview, 30 Oct. 2015.

23. Family photos, private archive of Nelson Leissner; interview with Marje Janacek, 10 Dec. 2015.

24. Tracing changes in the profession over time, Jay Fitzgerald notes that only 8 percent of pharmacists in the mid-1960s were women: "Pharmacy and the Evolution of a Family-Friendly Profession," *The Digest* No. 2, National Bureau of Economic Research, February 2013, https://www.nber.org/digest/feb13/pharmacy-and-evolution-family -friendly-occupation; content and inscriptions from *Blue Jay* NHS Yearbook, 1961, private archive of Nelson Leissner.

25. Kathy Leissner bank statements and cancelled checks, Sept. 1961, private archive of Nelson Leissner.

26. Associated Press (AP), "Disturbance Reported in Atlantic," *Corpus Christi Caller Times*, 3 Sept. 1961, p. 3; AP, "Slowly Growing: Tropical Storm Carla Veers Towards U.S.," *Victoria Advocate*, 6 Sept. 1961, p. 1; AP, "Texas Coast Eyes Carla as Storm Aims for Gulf," *Victoria Advocate*, 7 Sept. 1961, p. 1; "City in Target Area of Hurricane," *Corpus Christi Caller Times*, 10 Sept. 1961, p. 1; see also inland coverage: "Powerful Carla Plows toward Texas Coast," *Austin American-Statesman*, 9 Sept. 1961, p. 1.

Pulled Off Course

1. John Burnett, "The Tempest at Galveston: 'We Knew There Was a Storm Coming, But We Had No Idea," NPR, *Morning Edition*, 30 Nov. 2017, https://www.npr.org/2017/11/30/566950355/the-tempest -at-galveston-we-knew-there-was-a-storm-coming-but-we-had-no-idea; National Weather Service, "Hurricane Carla—50th Anniversary," https://www.weather.gov/crp/hurricanecarla.

2. "SP-168: Exploring Space with a Camera," NASA.gov, https:// history.nasa.gov/SP-168/section1.htm; and Bryan Norcross, *Hurricane Almanac: The Essential Guide to Storms Past, Present, and Future* (St. Martin's Griffin, 2007), 62–63; coverage of Rather's one-year anniversary at KHOU in the *Baytown Sun*, Thursday, 7 Sept. 1961, p. 2; see also Garber, "Dan Rather Showed the First Radar Image."

3. AP, "Mass Evacuation from Danger Zone Called Greatest in Modern History," *Kilgore News Herald*, 10 Sept. 1961, p, 1; *Corsicana Daily Sun*, 11 Sept. 1961, p. 8.

4. Mattie E. Treadwell, Texas State Director for Field Operations, Office of Civil Defense, *Hurricane Carla, September 3–14, 1961*, study commissioned by the Department of Defense, 22 Dec. 1961, p. 70, https://books.google.com/books?id=KYdMxHzbUeYC&pg=PA70&lpg =PA70&dq=hurricane+carla+bell+telephone&source=bl&ots=fwjfMg VQrK&sig=ACfU3U1ct5WETMFDpsXU4zX8dxr6gjc9Fg&hl=en&s a=X&ved=2ahUKEwiogI6Ek7nqAhUVO30KHR0GCsIQ6AEwAXoE CAgQAQ#v=onepage&q=hurricane%20carla%20bell%20telephone &f=false; testimony of R. A. Goodson, Vice President of Operations for AT&T, former VP of Operations in Texas for Southwestern Bell, regarding Overtime Penalty Pay Act of 1964, Joint Hearings before the General Subcommittee on Labor, the Select Subcommittee on Labor of the Committee on Education and Labor, Eighty-Eighth Congress, Second Session (US Government Printing Office, 1964), 481–485; see also *When Carla Called*, industrial film produced by Southwestern Bell Telephone Company, 1960s, Texas Archive of the Moving Image, https://texasarchive.org/2012_00226.

5. Milton I. Rudd, US Weather Bureau, Galveston, "Tornadoes during Hurricane Carla at Galveston," *Monthly Weather Review 92, no. 5* (May 1964): 251–254, http://citeseerx.ist.psu.edu/viewdoc/download ?doi=10.1.1.395.1330&rep=rep1&type=pdf; *Austin American,* 14 Sept. 1961, p. 27; *Galveston Daily News*, 11 Sept. 1961, p. 1.

6. *Austin American*, 14 Sept. 1961, p. 27; Texas Coast Aerial Photography, http://texascoastgeology.com/passes/rollover.html; Richard D. Watson, "Texas Coast Geology," http://texascoastgeology.com /pabeach/naturalduneseawall.html; Craig Hlavaty, "Mighty Hurricane Carla Battered the Texas Gulf Coast in 1961," *Houston Chronicle*, 11 Sept. 2018, https://www.houstonchronicle.com/news/houston-weather /article/Hurricane-Carla-in-1961-was-the-worst-hurricane-13220372 .php#photo-13905324; Keith Heidorn, "Hurricane Carla: Texas-Sized," The Weather Doctor: Weather Almanac for September 2011, 1 Sept. 2011, http://www.heidorn.info/keith/weather/almanac/arc2011 /alm11sep.htm; "Islanders Get almost 2,000 Typhoid Shots," *Aransas Pass Progress*, 20 Sept. 1961, p. 1.

7. Kathy Leissner bank statements, Sept. 1961, private archive of Nelson Leissner.

8. "Giant Unmade Bed" of refugees on Highway 290 in *Austin American-Statesman*, 11 Sept. 1961, p. 11; *Austin American*, 11 Sept. 1961, pp. 2, 3, 11; *Austin American-Statesman*, 12 Sept. 1961, p. 3.

9. Kathy Leissner, "Memories of School Days" senior souvenir book, spring 1961, private archive of Nelson Leissner.

10. Table 187, "College Enrollment rates of High School Graduates

by Sex, 1960–1998," National Center for Education Statistics, https://nces.ed.gov/programs/digest/d99/d99t187.asp.

11. The Texas Higher Education Coordinating Board, "Head-Count Enrollment by Sex, Fall 1959–1971, Public Senior Colleges and Universities," table, p. 6; Denise Gamino, "MLK's Mark on UT," *Austin American-Statesman*, 16 Jan. 2011 (updated 12 Dec. 2018), https://www.statesman.com/story/news/local/2011/01/17/mlk-s-mark-on-ut/6701060007.

12. *Austin American-Statesman*, 12 Sept. 1961, p. 3; *Daily Texan*, 12 Sept. 1961, pp. 1, 32; ibid., 15 Sept. 1961, p. 1.

13. *Austin American-Statesman*, 15 Sept. 1961, p. 1; *Daily Texan*, 13 Sept. 1961, p. 1.

14. *Daily Texan*, 14 Sept. 1961, p. 7; Dr. Gregory J. Vincent, Virginia A. Cumberbatch, and Leslie A. Blair, *As We Saw It: The Story of Integration at the University of Texas at Austin* (Tower Books, 2018), 84; UT Austin Division of Diversity and Community Engagement, "The Intersection of Athletics and the 40 Acres," *The History of Integration at the University of Texas at Austin*, 18 Nov. 2014, https://diversity.utexas.edu/integration/2014/11/the-intersection-of-athletics-and-race-on-the-40-acres.

15. Kathy Leissner first semester transcript, fall 1961, private archive of Nelson Leissner; *Daily Texan*, 13 Sept. 1961, p. 1.

16. Kathy Leissner bank statements and cancelled checks, Sept. 1961, private archive of Nelson Leissner.

17. See Judith N. MacArthur and Harold L. Smith, *Texas through Women's Eyes: The Twentieth Century Experience* (University of Texas Press, 2010), 61: "There were no 'women's jobs' in working cattle"; *Daily Texan*, 13 Sept. 1961, p. 1; ibid., 17 Sept. 1961, p. 1; *Austin American-Statesman*, 15 Sept. 1961, p. 1.

18. Anitha Mitchell interview, 2 April 2021. Mitchell described her experiences of sexism as well as racism as a pre-med student studying science at UT; see also Vincent, Cumberbatch, and Blair, *As We Saw It*, p. 89.

19. *Daily Texan*, 17 Sept. 1961, pp. 2, 9.

20. Asher Price, "Memo by Secret Memo, The University of Texas Kept Segregation Alive into the 1960s," *Mother Jones*, 12 Jan. 2020, https://www.motherjones.com/politics/2020/01/memo-by-secret-memo-the-university-of-texas-kept-segregation-alive-into-the-1960s; Vincent, Cumberbatch, and Blair, *As We Saw It*, 36–37; see also Joseph Leahy,

"The Night Hawk's Final Flight," KUT 90.5, 27 July 2018, https://www
.kut.org/life-arts/2018-07-27/the-night-hawks-final-flight-diners-bid
-farewell-to-a-piece-of-austins-culinary-past.

21. See Jo Eickmann's recollections in "A Decade of Change,
1960–1970," in *The Daily Texan: The First 100 Years* (Eakin Press,
1999), 77; *Daily Texan*, 17 Sept. 1961, p. 8.

22. "Little Man on Campus," *Daily Texan*, 12 Sept. 1961, p. 2;
"Little Man on Campus," Daily Texan, 3 Oct. 1961, p. 2; "Little Man on
Campus," *Daily Texan*, 29 March 1962, p. 2; "Little Man on Campus,"
Daily Texan, 25 Sept. 1962, p. 2; sample ads appearing in fall 1961:
Daily Texan, 12 Sept., p. 10; 19 Sept., p. 6; 20 Sept., p. 4.

23. *Daily Texan*, 15 Sept. 1961, p. 6.

24. Jim Berry, "Story Brings UT Prowler's Arrest," *Austin American-Statesman*, 15 Sept. 1961, p. 1.

25. *Daily Texan*, 19 Sept. 1961, p. 3.

26. KLW letter to CJW, 12 Feb. 1964. For historical analysis of stereotypes and myths in twentieth-century American representations of
criminality, see Calvin John Smiley and David Fakunle, "From 'Brute'
to 'Thug': The Demonization and Criminalization of Unarmed Black
Male Victims in America," *Journal of Human Behavior in the Social
Environment*, Vol. 26, Nos. 3–4, pp. 350–366, 2016; as well as Joann
Conrad, "Stranger Danger: Defending Innocence, Denying Responsibility," *Contemporary Legend*, n.s. 1, pp. 55–96, 1998; for context
about sexual assault at colleges and universities, see Anya Kamenetz,
"The History of Campus Sexual Assault," National Public Radio, 30
Nov. 2014, https://www.npr.org/sections/ed/2014/11/30/366348383
/the-history-of-campus-sexual-assault.

27. Bill Woods, "Priest Pointed Out as Girl's Attacker," *Austin
American-Statesman*, 12 Sept. 1961, pp. 1, 6; AP, "Feit Trial for Rape
Is Opened," *Austin American-Statesman*, 12 Sept. 1961, p. 20; Bill
Woods, "Feit Case Heads to Jury Today," *Austin American-Statesman*,
14 Sept. 1961, p. 18; Bill Woods, "Feit Case a Mistrial," *Austin Ameri-
can-Statesman*, 15 Sept. 1961, p. 1.

28. *Austin American-Statesman*, 15 Sept. 1961, p. 1.

29. AP, "Priest Case Concluded," *Daily Texan*, 29 March 1962,
p. 1; AP, "Ex-Priest Gets Life for 1960 Murder," *Austin American-
Statesman*, 9 Dec. 2017, p. B1.

30. Information on the now-closed dormitory is archived at http://
www.goodallwooten.com; At-a-Glance Diary of Charles Whitman,
entries 6–10 Sept. 1961, AHC.

31. Kathy Leissner bank statements and cancelled checks from September 1961, private archive of Nelson Leissner.

32. Skip Hollandsworth, "The Greek Way," *Texas Monthly*, March 1991, https://www.texasmonthly.com/articles/the-greek-way; Steven McBrearty, "Jack's Party Pictures," *The Alcade*, March/April 1977, pp. 51–53; Kathy Leissner cancelled checks Oct. 1961, private archive of Nelson Leissner.

33. KLW letters to CJW, 15 and 17 Feb. 1964.

34. "Sirens to Signal Alert," *Daily Texan*, 3 Nov. 1961, p. 1; David T. Lopez, "2,500 Coax Pretties to Part with Panties," *Daily Texan*, 3 Nov. 1961, p. 1; for reference to the fire alarm that drove men from their dorms, see "The Year 1961–1962 at the University of Texas," *The Cactus*, 2 Nov. 1962, pp. 529–530.

35. See Paul Lomartire, "Demons and Doom: The Whitmans of Lake Worth," *Palm Beach Post*, 28 July 2016 (republished from 2006), https://www.palmbeachpost.com/story/news/crime/2016/07/28/demons-doom-whitmans-lake-worth/7212403007. For synthesis of early biographical details, see Gary Lavergne, *A Sniper in the Tower* (University of North Texas Press, 1997), 1–9; for the religious structure of Whitman's childhood, see Jo Scott-Coe, *MASS*, 45–49.

36. See Bill Kimmey, "UA Professor Recalls Whitman as Student with Many Problems," *Tucson Daily Citizen*, 5 Aug. 1966, p. 2.

37. Official Catholic Directory, 1955–1962; Joseph G. Leduc deeds and promissory note, Brazoria County 1960 and 1961; see also FBI Statement of Father Joseph G. Leduc, 15 Aug. 1966, APD Files, AHC. I documented for the first time Leduc's biographical and clerical time-line, property details, and association with Whitman in *MASS*.

38. CJW letters to KLW, 13 Jan. and 9 Feb. 1964; At-a-Glance Diary of Charles Whitman, entry 19 Sept. 1961, AHC.

39. Joselyn Lopez and Ben Farrell, "Watch Van Cliburn Play the Piece that Made Him Famous," WQXR Editorial, 11 July 2018, https://www.wqxr.org/story/van-cliburn-tchaikovsky-first-piano-concerto; see also Bill Zeeble, "Remembering Van Cliburn: A Giant among Pianists and a Cold War Idol," *Deceptive Cadence,* NPR Classical, 27 Feb. 2013, https://www.npr.org/sections/deceptivecadence/2013/02/27/173061668/remembering-van-cliburn-a-giant-among-pianists-and-a-cold-war-idol.

40. CJW letter to KLW, 30 Jan. 1964; KLW letter to CJW, 12 Sept. 1963. Regarding short courtship among men who kill their intimate partners, see David Adams, *Why Do They Kill?* (Vanderbilt University Press, 2007). Adams observes, "Besides beginning and ending

[through murder] more quickly, relationships with shorter courtships appeared to be less stable, faster-paced, and possibly more violent," and he goes on to highlight the need to examine specific elements in case studies, including alcohol and drug use, frequent sex, frequent violence, instability, and hidden pasts, "since this may help us to identify more specific violence and homicide prevention strategies" (139–147).

41. For initial reports, see "Students Fined $390," *Austin American-Statesman*, 21 Nov. 1961, p. 13; see also court blotter "County Court at Law," *Austin American-Statesman*, 1 Dec. 1961, p. 28.

42. Primary source descriptions of the deer incident: FBI Statement of Father Joseph G. Leduc, 15 Aug. 1966, as well as FBI Statement of Francis J. Schuck Jr., 13 Sept. 1966, both in APD Files, AHC; for secondary discussion, see Lavergne, *Sniper in the Tower*, 20; and Scott-Coe, *MASS*, 213.

Whirlwind

1. Nelson Leissner interview, 30 Oct. 2015; *Daily Texan*, 17 Sept. 1961, p. 8; "Tickets Still Available for Ferrante, Teicher," ibid., 13 Feb. 1962, p. 1.; Bill Hampton, "Ferrante and Teicher Pound," ibid., 14 Feb. 1962, p. 4; KLW letter to parents, 19 Sept. 1962. CJW was fixated on the "drop" date, which Kathy often apologized for forgetting, even much later: see KLW letter to CJW, 12 Feb. 1964.

2. Lavergne, *Sniper in the Tower*, 21–23; FBI Statement of Francis J. Schuck Jr., APD Files, AHC.

3. CJW letter to KLW, 30 Jan. 1964; KLW letter to CJW, 23 Feb. 1964.

4. Regarding Charles Whitman's casual and regular use of amphetamines as well as tranquilizers, see affidavits of Richard Owen Clark and Robert Don McCrary to J. W. Hand of the US Food and Drug Administration, 8 Aug. 1966, AHC; for the report about Charles Whitman's pranks as well as a student matching Charles Whitman's description trying to sell off pornographic photos to a merchant on the Drag, see "Who Was Charles Whitman?," *Texas Observer*, 19 Aug. 1966, p. 3.

5. "Martin Luther King to Lecture Tonight," *Daily Texan*, 9 Mar. 1962, p. 1; Gamino, "MLK's Mark on UT."

6. Bank statements, May 1962; CJW car accident release document, 23 May 1962, private archive of Nelson Leissner.

7. KL letter to CJW, 10 June 1962; bank statements, May 1962, private archive of Nelson Leissner.

8. See Scott-Coe, "Listening to Kathy."

9. KL letter to CJW, 10 June 1962; CJW letter to KLW, 3 July 1964.

10. KL letter to CJW, 18 June 1962.

11. Ibid.

12. KL letter to CJW, 11 June 1962.

13. KL letter to CJW, 18 June 1962; CJW letter to KL, 19 June 1962.

14. KL letters to CJW, 25 and 26 June 1962; KL checks and bank statements, June 1962, private archive of Nelson Leissner.

15. KL letter to CJW, 5 July 1962.

16. KL letter to CJW, 10 July 1962.

17. KL letter to CJW, 11 June 1962.

18. KL letters to CJW, 3 July and 16 July 1962.

19. KL letter to CJW, 26 July 1962.

20. KL letter to CJW, 18 July 1962.

21. See Carolyn Herbst Lewis, *Prescription for Heterosexuality: Sexual Citizenship in the Cold War Era* (University of North Carolina Press, 2010).

22. KL letters to CJW, 12 and 18 June 1962; CJW letters to KL, 9 and 15 June 1962.

23. CJW letter to KL, 12 June 1962.

24. CJW letters to KL, 19 June and 24 July 1962.

25. CJW letter to KL, 12 June 1964; KL letter to CJW, 10 June 1962.

26. Charles Whitman, At-a-Glance Diary, entries 16 and 27–29 Oct. and 15–17 Dec. 1961, AHC.

27. For context on bride's and groom's expenses, see Kay Toy Fenner, *American Catholic Etiquette* (Newman Press, 1961 and 1965), 189–195.

28. CJW letters to KL, 15 and 20 June and 10 July 1962.

29. KL letter to CJW, 6 July 1962.

30. CJW letter to KL, 24 July 1962; KL letter to CJW, 25 July 1962; Goodrich Schauffler, "The Need for a Premarital Examination," *Modern Bride*, Aug./Sept. 1962; see also Carolyn Herbst Lewis, "Waking Sleeping Beauty: The Premarital Pelvic Exam and Heterosexuality during the Cold War," *Journal of Women's History* 17, no. 4 (2005): 86–110, https://muse.jhu.edu/article/190427; and Carolyn Herbst Lewis, "The Premarital Pelvic Examination," in Lewis, *Prescription for Heterosexuality*, 95–112.

31. CJW letter to KL, 24 July 1962.

32. CJW letter to KL, 24 July 1962; KL letters to CJW, 25 and 26 July 1962.

33. KL letter to CJW, 30 July 1962; Kathy Leissner bank records and checks, August 1962, private archive of Nelson Leissner.

34. See Fenner, *American Catholic Etiquette*, 189–195.

35. Nelson Leissner interview, 30 Oct. 2015.

36. CJW letter to KL, 19 July 1962.

37. CJW letter to KL, 11 Aug 1962.

38. For full explication of Reverend Leduc's biography and its intersection with Whitman's history, see Scott-Coe, *MASS*. Nine months after *MASS* was published (in 2018), Leduc's name appeared posthumously on a list of priests "credibly accused" of sexually abusing children in the Archdiocese of Galveston-Houston: https://www.archgh .org/clergylist.

39. KLW letter to family, 18 Aug. 1962; KLW postcard to her family, 20 Aug. 1962.

40. KLW letter and enclosures to Mom and Dad, 24 Aug. 1962.

41. Ibid. United Press International (UPI) reports of the New Orleans raids were syndicated in early August 1962: see UPI, "21 Persons Held after Vice Raid," *Town Talk*, 16 Aug. 1962, p. 19; and UPI, "Orleans Vice Raids Amuse," *Monroe Morning World*, 12 Aug. 1962, p. 4.

42. Nelson Leissner interview, 27 and 30 Oct. 2015. I also quoted this memory in "Listening to Kathy."

43. Ibid.

44. Nelson Leissner interview, 19 April 2020.

45. Ibid.

46. Margaret Whitman letter to Frances Leissner, 14 Sept. 1962.

47. KLW letter to CJW, 23 Jan. 1964.

Trouble Starts at Home

1. *Austin American-Statesman*, 9 Sept. 1962, p. 1; Frances Leissner (hereafter FL) letter to KLW and CJW, 28 Aug. 1962; KLW letter to family, 18 Aug. 1962.

2. *Daily Texan*, 18 Sept. 1962, pp. 1–2; Roddy Stinson, "Gilbreth Views Working Wife: Place in Home, Job, Noted Woman Says," *Daily Texan*, 1 Nov. 1962, p. 1; "Ledbetter Tells Role of Women," *Daily Texan*, 26 Oct. 1962, pp. 1, 8.

3. KLW letter to Mom and Dad, 19 Sept. 1962.

4. Ibid.; KLW letter to family, 28 Sept. 1962.

5. KLW letters to family, 19 and 28 Sept. 1962.

6. KLW letter to Mother and Daddy, 4 Nov. 1962.

7. CJW note and map enclosures to FL, 2 Oct. 1962.

8. CJW letter to Mother and Dad, 4 Dec. 1962.

9. KLW letter to Mom and Dad, 19 Sept. 1962; CJW letter to KLW, 4 Aug. 1963; KLW letter to CJW, 12 Aug. 1963.

10. A chronology, including audio of the speech, is stored in the John F. Kennedy Presidential Library and Museum, https://microsites .jfklibrary.org/cmc/oct22; for contemporary political analysis of the argument, see Andrew J. Bacevich, "Take It from JFK: Appeasement over Confrontation," *The Nation*, 3 March 2022, https://www.thenation .com/article/world/kennedy-biden-ukraine-russia; and Chris Matthews, "How John F. Kennedy's Appeasement Strategy Averted a Nuclear Holocaust," *New Republic,* 13 Oct. 2012, https://newrepublic.com /article/108575/how-john-f-kennedys-appeasement-strategy-averted -nuclear-holocaust.

11. KLW letter to family, 28 Sept. 1962.

12. FL letters to KLW and CJW, 7 Dec. 1962 and n.d., Dec. 1962.

13. KLW Christmas card to family, 12 Dec. 1962.

14. Margaret Whitman letter to KLW, 22 Dec. 1963.

15. In the student name list for St. John Vianney Seminary for the 1960s, compiled by alumnus Ray J. Vaughn, Patrick would have graduated with class of 1963, http://www.stjohnvianneyseminary.org/1960 %27s.htm. Following his transfer to Lake Worth High School, Patrick's graduation date as recorded in the announcement sent to Kathy's parents would be 5 June 1964; in a letter dated 20 Feb. 1964, CJW urged KLW to conceal that she knew of Pat's "problem" when engaging with his parents.

16. FL letter to KLW, "Tuesday night," n.d., Jan. 1962.

17. KLW letter to Mother, 8 Jan. 1963.

18. The sexism and homophobia reinforced within the field of psychiatry into the 1960s presented serious problems for anyone who did not conform to gender expectations in the home, including arbitrary rules of husbands or fathers. At times they could lead to involuntary commitment or treatment: see Alica Curtis, "Involuntary Commitment," *Bad Subjects* 58, Dec. 2001, http://psychrights.org/states/Maine /InvoluntaryCommitmentbyAliciaCurtis.htm; see also Phyllis Chesler's comprehensive analysis of misogyny in psychiatry and psychology in her formative work, *Women and Madness* (Lawrence Hill Books, 2018).

19. FL letter to CJW, 30 Jan. 1963.

20. KLW letter to Mother + Daddy, 2 Feb. 1963.

21. Ibid.; see also CJW letter to KLW, 30 Jan. 1964.

22. KLW letter to Mother + Daddy, 2 Feb. 1963.

23. Ibid.

24. See Evan Stark, quoting journalist Ann Jones's early analysis of the overlap between men's techniques of intimate partner battering and the treatment of hostages or POWs, in *Coercive Control*, 201.

25. KLW letter to Mother + Daddy, 14 Feb. 1963.

26. Ibid.

Mapping an Escape

1. KLW letter to Mother, Dad, and Boys, 1 March 1963.

2. KLW letters to family, 1 and 3 March 1963.

3. KLW letter to family, 3 March 1963.

4. Stephen R. Claggett, "North Carolina's First Colonists: 12,000 Years before Roanoke," Office of State Archaeology, North Carolina State Historic Preservation Office, revised 15 March 1996, https://archaeology.ncdcr.gov/articles/north-carolinas-first-colonists; Stratton C. Murrell and Billie Jean Murrell, *Jacksonville and Camp Lejeune* (Arcadia Publishing, 2001), 45, 73; *Wikipedia*, s.v. "Jacksonville, North Carolina," Demographics, US Census statistics, https://en.wikipedia.org/wiki/Jacksonville,_North_Carolina#Demographics). For emerging research on Jacksonville and USMC dynamics, see Crystal M. Johnson, "Blurring the Line between Civilian and Military: The Changing Nature of the Town-Base Relationship in Jacksonville, North Carolina," honors thesis, University of North Carolina at Chapel Hill, 5 April 2016, pp. 80–85, https://core.ac.uk/download/pdf/210594982.pdf.

5. "Two Local Concerns Face 'Shutdown,'" *Daily News*, 8 March 1963, pp. 1, 10, scans courtesy of Onslow Public Library; for Lejeune water contamination information, see "Camp Lejeune, North Carolina" on Agency for Toxic Substances and Disease Registry (ATSDR), 25 Sept. 2019, https://www.atsdr.cdc.gov/sites/lejeune/index.html; "Camp Lejeune Water Contamination Issues," US Dept. of Veterans Affairs, 22 Sept. 2020, https://www.va.gov/disability/eligibility/hazardous-materials-exposure/camp-lejeune-water-contamination.

6. KLW letter to Mom and Daddy, 9 March 1963.

7. KLW letter to Mother and Daddy, 13 March 1963.

8. Ibid.

9. KLW letter to Mother, 14 March 1963.

10. KLW letters to Mother and Daddy, 26 and 30 March 1963; also CJW letters to KLW, 14 and 15 Sept. 1963.

11. KLW letters to Mother and family, March 12, 14, 19, 25, 26, 28, 30, and 2 April 1963; CJW letter to KLW, 14 Sept. 1963.

12. KLW letter to Mother and Daddy, 28 March and 4 April 1963.

13. KLW letters to Mother, 25 and 28 March and 4 and 8 April 1963.

14. FL letters to KLW and CJW, 14, 15, and 18 March 1963.

15. FL letter to KLW, 18 March 1963.

16. FL letter to KLW and CJW, 15 March 1963.

17. KLW letter to Mother, 19 and 25 March 1963.

18. KLW letter to Mother, 25 March and 8 and 29 April 1963.

19. FL letter to KLW and CJW, 15 March 1963.

20. KLW letters to Mother, 19 and 25 March 1963.

21. KLW letter to Mother, 2 April 1963.

22. CJW letter to Leissners, 31 March 1963.

23. KLW letter to family, 10 April 1963.

24. KLW letters to Mother, 15 and 29 April 1963.

25. KLW letters to Mother, 25 and 30 March and 8 and 29 April 1963.

26. CJW letter to Leissners, 24 April 1963.

27. KLW letter to Mother, 15 April 1963.

28. Murrell and Murrell, *Jacksonville and Camp Lejeune*, photos of Court Street, 52, 79; CJW letter to KLW, 15 Sept. 1963; KLW letter to CJW, 29 June 1964; Naomi Whidden, "Court Street Community Remembers the Past, Looks to the Future," JDNews.com, 17 June 2017, https://www.jdnews.com/news/20170617/court-street-community-remembers-past-looks-to-future.

29. KLW letters to family, n.d., April/May and 16 May 1963.

30. KLW letter to Mother, 18 May 1963.

31. FL letter to KLW, 27 March 1963.

32. KLW letters to Mother, 10 and 18 May 1963.

33. FL letter to KLW, 20 March 1963; KLW letters to family, April through July 1963; see *Gaslight*, dir. George Cukor, Metro-Goldwyn-Mayer, 1944.

34. Morris W. Rosenberg, "The Trouble in Haiti: Hemisphere's Danger Spot," *News and Observer*, 28 April 1963, p. 36; see also Katrina Martin, "Duvalierism, With and Without Duvalier: Radio Haiti Commemorates the Massacres of April 26, 1963, and 1986," Duke University Libraries Blog, 26 April 2016, https://blogs.library.duke.edu/rubenstein/2016/04/26/duvalierism-without-duvalier-radio-haiti-commemorates-massacres-april-26-1963–1986; KLW letters to Mother, 26 March and 29 April 1963.

35. KLW letter to Mother, 10 May 1963.

36. KLW letter to Mother + Daddy, 16 May 1963.

37. Christopher Thomas, "Phone Company Workers Hold Reunion

for 17 Years," JDNews.com, 15 Dec. 2014; see also Venus Green, "Race and Technology: African American Women in the Bell System, 1945–1980," *Technology and Culture* 36, no. 2 (April 1995): S101-S144; *Supplement: Snapshots of a Discipline: Selected Proceedings*, Conference on Critical Problems and Research Frontiers in the History of Technology, Madison, WI, 30 Oct.–3 Nov. 1991.

38. Darleen Koenig interview, 3 Feb. 2021.

39. KLW letter to CJW, 1 Sept. 1963; see also Thomas, "Phone Company Workers Reunion," as well as "Women Telephone Workers and Changing Technology," US Department of Labor, Women's Bureau Bulletin 286 (Government Printing Office, 1963), 16–27.

40. KLW letter to Mother and Daddy, 16 June and 1 July 1963.

41. KLW letter to family, 16 and 22 May 1963.

42. KLW letter to family, 19 April 1963.

43. KLW and CJW letter to Leissners, 25 May 1963.

44. KLW and CJW letter to Leissners, 3 June 1963.

45. KLW and CJW letter to Leissners, 10 June 1963.

46. KLW and CJW letter to Leissners, 16 June 1963.

47. KLW letter to Mother, 20 June 1963; KLW letter to family, 1 July 1963.

48. KLW letter to family, 1 July 1963.

Separated and Almost Safe

1. KLW letters to CJW, 11 July and 1 Aug. 1963.

2. KLW letter to CJW, 11 July 1963.

3. KLW letters to CJW, 11 and 12 July 1963.

4. KLW letter to CJW, 11 July 1963; Alvin Fuhrman, "The Mark Sense Ticket," in *The Way It Was* (unpublished), Google Books, n.d., 103; see also US Dept. of Labor, Manpower Research Bulletin No. 13, Nov. 1966, "Technology and Manpower in the Telephone Industry 1965–1975," 17–18, https://files.eric.ed.gov/fulltext/ED015257.pdf.

5. KLW letter to CJW, 17 July 1963.

6. KLW letters to CJW, 23 and 17 July 1963.

7. Ibid.

8. KLW letter to CJW, 20 July 1963.

9. KLW letter to CJW, 22 July 1963.

10. KLW letters to CJW, 30 July and 1 Aug. 1963.

11. KLW letter to CJW, 20 July and 1 Aug. 1963.

12. KLW letters to CJW (back flaps of envelopes), 11, 12, 13, 15, 17, 22, 23, 27 (two letters), and 29 July 1963.

13. KLW letter to CJW, 27 July 1963.

14. KLW letter to CJW, 30 July 1963; also CJW notes on back flap of envelope. "Scripting" is a tool Jane Monckton Smith identifies as common among people with strong psychopathic traits: "[They] are rarely any good with intuitive dynamic conversations. They can certainly be manipulative and plausible, but these are often practised scripts and behaviors. . . . It is sometimes when they have to work 'off script' that they unknowingly reveal who they are." *In Control: Dangerous Relationships and How They End in Murder* (Bloomsbury Circus, 2021), 39.

15. CJW letter to KLW, 29 July 1963.

16. KLW letter to CJW, 1 Aug. 1963.

17. CJW letters to KLW, 4, 11, 14, 16, and 18 Aug. 1963.

18. KLW letters to CJW, 14, 15, and 18 Aug. 1963.

19. KLW letters to CJW, 2 and 8 Aug. 1963.

20. KLW letters to CJW, 15, 18, and 19 Aug. 1963.

21. KLW letter to CJW, 8 Aug. 1963; "Center of Attraction," *Daily Texan*, 24 Sept. 1963, p. 2.

22. KLW letter to CJW, 8 Aug. 1963.

23. CJW letters to KLW, 20 and 22 Aug. 1963.

24. KLW letter to CJW, 26 Aug. 1963.

25. Ibid.

26. KLW letter to CJW, 25 Aug. 1963.

27. KLW letters to CJW, 27 and 28 Aug. 1963.

28. CJW letters to KLW, 25 and 29 Aug. and 3 Sept. 1963.

29. KLW letters to CJW, 30 and 31 Aug. and 5, 7, 9, and 10 Sept. 1963.

30. KLW letter to CJW, 15 Sept. 1963; Nat Henderson, "At Last: Heavy Rains Drench Parched Austin Area," *Austin American*, 16 Sept. 1963, p. 1.

31. UPI, "Dynamited Church Fuels Bloody Riots, Four Girls Killed in Classroom," *Austin American*, 16 Sept. 1963, p. 1; "Local Group to Hold 'Birmingham Stand,'" *Daily Texan*, 17 Sept. 1963; PBS, *Black Culture Connection*, "The Birmingham Campaign," 2019, http://www .pbs.org/black-culture/explore/civil-rights-movement-birmingham -campaign.

32. CJW letters to KLW, 14 and 15 Sept 1963.

33. FL letters to KLW, 15 and 18 Sept. 1963.

34. KLW letters to CJW, 17 and 22 Sept. 1963; CJW letters to KLW, 19 and 23 Sept. and 23 Oct. 1963.

35. KLW letter to Mother + Daddy, 25 Sept. 1963.

36. Ibid.

37. Ibid.

38. Ibid.

39. CJW letters to KLW, 20 and 23 Sept. 1963.

40. KLW letter to Mother + Daddy, 25 Sept. 1963; KLW letters to CJW, 23, 25, and 26 Sept. 1963.

41. KLW letter to Mother + Daddy, 1 Oct. 1963.

42. KLW letter to CJW, 30 Sept. 1963.

43. KLW letters to CJW, 21 and 26 Oct. and 15 Nov. 1963.

44. KLW letters to CJW, 22, 23, 27, and 30 Oct. 1963.

45. KLW letters to Mother + Daddy, 31 Oct. and 1 Nov. 1963.

46. Ibid.

47. CJW letter to Leissners, 31 Oct. 1963.

48. Charles Whitman Memoranda notebook, Nov. 1963, AHC; date also confirmed on Brig Prisoner List, Daily Report of Prisoners Received 1 Nov. 1963, USMC Camp Lejeune, archive of Nelson Leissner.

49. CJW letter to KLW, 3 Nov. 1963.

50. Whitman Memoranda notebook, Nov. 1963; KLW letter to CJW, 3 Nov. 1963.

51. KLW letters to CJW, 4 and 5 Nov. 1963.

52. CJW letter to KLW, 8 Nov. 1963.

53. Whitman Memoranda notebook, Nov. 1963.

54. CJW letter to KLW, 11 Nov. 1963.

55. CJW letter to Leissners, 12 Nov. 1963.

56. Whitman, Memoranda notebook, Nov. 1963, AHC.

57. The dates of Thanksgiving break in fall 1963 were Nov. 28–30 according to Official Publications, Office of the Registrar, UT Austin (email 5 Jan. 2021); CJW letters to KLW, 16 and 17 Nov. 1963.

58. CJW letters to KLW, 16 and 17 Nov. (batch) and 22 Dec. 1963.

59. Whitman, Memoranda notebook, Jan. 1964, AHC.

60. Ibid., Nov. 1963; CJW letter to Leissners, 10 June 1963.

61. CJW letter to KLW, 14 Nov. 1964.

62. See Sharon Ashton, "Campus Grows Quiet as Death of JFK Told," *Daily Texan*, 23 Nov. 1963, p. 4; "TV Discontinues All Except News," *Daily Texan*, 23 Nov. 1963, p. 4; also "Programs Canceled throughout Austin," *Daily Texan*, 23 Nov. 1963, p. 4.

63. CJW letter to KLW, 4 Dec. 1963; KLW letter to CJW, 29 Nov. 1963.

64. KLW letter to CJW, 5 Dec. 1963; CJW letter to KLW, 7 Dec. 1963.

65. CJW letter to Leissners, 7 Dec. 1963.

66. KLW letter to family, 12 Dec. 1963.

67. Ibid.; CJW letter to KLW, 7 Dec. 1963.

68. KLW letters to CJW, 11 and 23 Dec. 1963; Margaret Whitman letter to KLW, 22 Dec. 1963.

69. KLW letters to CJW, 2 and 24 Dec. 1963.

70. KLW letter to CJW, 30 Dec. 1963.

Barometer Dropping

1. Complete footage included at beginning of *American Bandstand*, 4 Jan. 1964, https://www.youtube.com/watch?v=oat6EwQi0JQ&t=14s; partial NBC video also at "New Year's Times Square 1964," https://wwwyoutube.com/watch?v=t7T6-Za2hcA.

2. CJW letter to KLW, 2 Jan. 1964; see also "A Microcosm of the Cotton Bowl: Texas Makes Long Advance, Navy Is Held to Short One; Longhorns' Line Crushes Middies; Carlisle Runs for a Score, Passes for 2—Staubach of Navy Overshadowed," *New York Times*, 2 Jan. 1964, https://www.nytimes.com/1964/01/02/archives/a-microcosm-of-the-cotton-bowl-texas-makes-long-advance-navy-is.html.

3. KLW letter to CJW, 3 Jan 1964.

4. Whitman, Memoranda notebook, Jan. 1964, AHC; KLW letters to CJW, 6 and 7 Jan. 1964; CJW letters to KLW, 2 and 18 Jan. 1964.

5. Cari Romm, "Before There Were Home Pregnancy Tests," *The Atlantic*, 17 June 2015, https://www.theatlantic.com/health/archive/2015/06/history-home-pregnancy-test/396077; "The Side Effects of the Pill," from PBS, *American Experience*, https://www.pbs.org/wgbh/americanexperience/features/pill-side-effects; KLW letter to CJW, 6 Jan. 1964.

6. KLW letter to CJW, 6 Jan. 1964.

7. KLW letters to CJW, 7 Jan. 1964 and 15 and 16 Nov. 1963.

8. KLW letter to CJW, 6 Jan. 1964; *The Cactus* yearbook, UT, 1964; CJW letters to KLW, 11 and 14 Jan. 1964.

9. KLW letter to CJW, 10 Jan. 1964.

10. KLW letter to CJW, 18 Jan. 1964.

11. KLW letters to CJW, 18 and 28 Jan. 1964.

12. KLW letter to CJW, 18 Jan. 1964.

13. As indicated by many entries in the Daily Record of C. J. Whitman, Charlie was both dismissive and suspicious of women generally; when Kathy eventually expressed minor frustrations with roommates, he stated in a letter that he was "glad to know that my Honey is tired of living with women," CJW letter to KLW, 20 Feb. 1964.

14. CJW letter to KLW, 19 Jan. 1964.

15. KLW letter to CJW, 20 Jan. 1964.

16. KLW letter to CJW, 22 Jan. 1964; see also bureau report, "The Second Sexual Revolution," *TIME* magazine, 24 Jan. 1964, pp. 54–59.

17. KLW letter to CJW, 20 Jan. 1964; CJW letter to KLW, 13 Jan. 1964.

18. KLW letter to CJW, 20 Jan. 1964; Whitman, Memoranda notebook, Jan. 1964, AHC.

19. Lesley Gore, "You Don't Own Me," Chart History, *Billboard Hot 100*, accessed 14 Aug. 2022, https://www.billboard.com/artist/lesley-gore.

20. KLW letter to CJW, 23 Jan. 1964.

21. Ibid.

22. KLW letters to CJW, 23 and 25 Jan. 1964; CJW letter to KLW, 25 Jan. 1964.

23. CJW letter to KLW, 20 Feb. 1964.

24. KLW letter to CJW, 25 Jan. 1964.

25. Ibid.

26. KLW letter to CJW, 23 Jan. 1964.

27. KLW letter to CJW, 4 Feb. 1964; KLW letters to family, 30 Jan. and 10 Feb. 1964.

28. See Michael Kimmel on the evolution of gender studies, as a subject within the social sciences, in *The Gendered Society* (Oxford University Press, 2000), 5; KLW letter to CJW, 9 Feb. 1964.

29. KLW letter to CJW, 18 Feb. 1964.

30. CJW letters to KLW, 2, 3, 6, 7, 9, and 11 Feb. 1964.

31. Nat Henderson, "That Was Some Snow," *Austin American-Statesman*, 22 Feb. 1964, p. 1; KLW letters to CJW, 29 and 31 Jan. and 21 Feb. 1964.

32. KLW letter to CJW, 11 Feb. 1964.

33. KLW letter to CJW, 1 Feb. 1964.

34. KLW letters to CJW, 9, 23, and 25 Feb. 1964.

35. KLW letter to CJW, 13 Feb. 1966.

36. KLW letter to Mother and Daddy, 21 Feb. 1964.

37. KLW Valentine card and letter to CJW, both 12 Feb. 1964.

38. KLW letter to CJW, 21 Feb. 1964; see also Eleanor Hamilton, "Sexual Communication," *Modern Bride*, Feb./March 1964, pp. 162–163.

39. KLW letters to CJW, 23 Feb. and 9 March 1964.

40. KLW letter to Mother and Daddy, 3 March 1964.

41. KLW letters to CJW, 3 and 8 March 1964.

42. KLW letter to CJW, 20 March 1964.

43. Daily Record of C. J. Whitman, 22 March 1964, AHC.

Between the Leaves

1. KLW letter to CJW, 5 April 1964; CJW letter to KLW, 28 June 1964.

2. KLW letters to CJW, 2 and 4 April 1964; CJW letter to KLW, 23 April 1964; CJW letter to Leissners, 13 April 1964.

3. KLW letter to CJW, 14 Feb. 1964; Margaret Whitman letter to KLW, 5 April 1964; CJW letter to Leissners, 13 April 1964.

4. FL letter to KLW, 28 April 1964.

5. FL letter to CJW, 29 April 1964; KLW letter to CJW, 25 April 1964.

6. KLW letter to family, 12 May 1964; CJW letters to KLW, 23 and 26 April 1964; CJW letter to Leissners, 17 May 1964.

7. KLW letter to CJW, 6 May 1964.

8. KLW letter to CJW, 23 April 1964.

9. KLW letter to CJW, 11 May 1964; KLW letter to family, 12 May 1964.

10. KLW letter to CJW, 26 May 1964.

11. CJW letters to KLW, 26 April and 16 May 1964.

12. CJW letter to KLW, 20 Feb. 1964.

13. KLW letter to CJW, 1 June 1964.

14. CJW letters to KLW, 26 and 30 April, 6 and 10 May 1964; KLW letter to CJW, 6 May 1964. Stark examines suicidal threats as a tool of manipulation in *Coercive Control*, 253, 264.

15. KLW letter to CJW, 22 May 1964.

16. KLW letter to CJW, 13 June 1964.

17. CJW letters to KLW, 16 and 30 June 1964.

18. KLW letter to CJW, 27 June 1964.

19. KLW letter to CJW, 3 July 1964.

20. KLW letter to CJW, 1 July 1964.

21. Ibid.

22. KLW letter to CJW, 3 July 1964.

23. KLW letter to CJW, 12 July 1964.

24. Ibid.

25. KLW letters to CJW, 20 July and 8 Aug. 1964.

26. CJW letters to KLW, 26 and 27 July 1964.

27. KLW letter to CJW, 6 Aug. 1964.

28. KLW letter to CJW, 8 Aug. 1964.

29. KLW letter to CJW, 27 July 1964.

30. KLW letter to CJW, 3 May 1964; CJW letter to KLW, 6 May 1964.

31. FL letter to KLW, 17 Oct. 1964; KLW letters to CJW, 22 May and 2 Oct. 1964.

32. KLW letter to CJW, 29 July 1964.

33. Daily Record of C. J. Whitman, 23 Feb. 1964, APD Files, AHC; two examples of many in CJW letters to KLW, 3 June and 10 Aug. 1964.

34. KLW letter to CJW, 6 Aug. 1964; CJW letter to KLW, 16 June 1964; Daily Record of C. J. Whitman, 6 March 1964, AHC.

35. KLW letters to CJW, 6 May and 15 and 25 June 1964; CJW letters to KLW, 13 and 15 June and 15 Oct. 1964.

36. KLW letters to CJW, 30 July and 9 Aug. 1964.

37. CJW letters to KLW, 11 and 12 June 1964; CJW card to KLW, 6 Aug. 1964; KLW letters to CJW, 6 and 13 Aug. 1964.

38. CJW letters to KLW, 13 and 18 Aug. 1964.

39. Tom Smith, "Cleo Handed County Multi-Million Tab," *Miami Herald*, 28 Aug. 1964, pp. 1, 2B; see also AP, "Cleo Expected to Arrive Offshore about Dawn Today," *Palm Beach Post*, 27 Aug. 1964, p. 1.

40. For extensive discussion of such aggressive medical treatments at the time, see Patricia Quintilian, "Unnecessary Hysterectomy: The Lack of Informed Consent," *Golden Gate University Law Review* 13, no. 3 (1983).

41. KLW letter to CJW, 11 Dec. 1963.

42. Statement of Whitman family physician, 22 Aug. 1966, p. 3, APD Files, AHC.

43. Kathy's prescription, dated 9 Sept. 1964, is listed on the first page in the Inventory of Medicine Cabinet of Charles Whitman, Supplementary Offense Report, from the APD Files, AHC. The prescribing doctor was George J. Nassef, who had been chief of obstetrics and gynecology at Lake Worth General Hospital in 1963: "Hospital Staff Named," *Palm Beach Post*, 11 Jan. 1963, p. 42; public notice of the lawsuit against Nassef appeared in "Doctor Sued," *Miami Herald*, 29 March 1961, p. 75. (I inquired by email in July 2021 for recorded documents with the Clerk of Circuit Court and Comptroller, Palm Beach County, but their search yielded no results.)

44. "Daisy" ad, preserved from 35mm film in the Tony Schwartz Collection, YouTube, https://www.youtube.com/watch?v=riDypP1KfOU; see also Will Storey, "Revisiting the Daisy Ad Revolution," 24 Oct.

2011, Caucus: The Politics and Government Blog of the Times, https://
thecaucus.blogs.nytimes.com/2011/10/24/revisiting-the-daisy-ad
-revolution.

45. The Tareyton ads featured faces of both men and women, but
the political photographs I was able to locate from the campaign documented only women. For an example, see *TIME*'s cover story, "The Ev
and Barry Show," 10 July 1964, pp. 20–24.

Disturbed Horizons

1. Interview with Linda (Damerau) Cipriano, 16 Oct. 2020; Paul
Tracy, "By Jiminey! Carpet of Crickets and Wind Bring Hint of Fall
Weather," *Austin American-Statesman*, 13 Sept. 1964, p. 1; photo,
"Cringing Coeds Crush Crickets," *Daily Texan*, 27 Sept. 1968, p. 1.

2. KLW letters to CJW, 21, 22, 25, and 27 Sept. 1964.

3. KLW letters to CJW, 21 and 22 Sept. 1964.

4. KLW letters to CJW, 22 and 25 Sept. 1964; CJW letter to KLW,
28 Sept. 1964.

5. KLW letter to CJW, 25 Sept. 1964; KLW letter to Mother, n.d.,
September 1964.

6. KLW letters to CJW, 22 and 25 Sept. 1964.

7. KLW letter to CJW, 28 Sept. 1964.

8. "The Wife Beater and His Wife," *TIME*, 25 Sept. 1964, pp.
81–82.

9. FL letter to KLW, 2 Oct. 1964; KLW letter to Mother, 4 Oct. 1964.

10. KLW letters to CJW, 29 Sept. and 2 Oct. 1964. Stark documents
partner degradation and lack of empathy after medical procedures in
Coercive Control, 259.

11. KLW letter to CJW, 7 Oct. 1964; CJW letter to KLW, 1 Oct. 1964.

12. KLW letter to CJW, 8 Oct. 1964.

13. KLW letters to CJW, 8 and 9 Oct. 1964.

14. KLW letter to family, 14 Oct. 1964.

15. KLW letter to CJW, 13 Oct. 1964.

16. KLW letter to CJW, 14 Oct. 1964.

17. Ibid.

18. Ibid.

19. CJW letter to KLW, 11 Oct. 1964.

20. KLW letter to CJW, 14 Oct. 1964.

21. CJW letters to KLW, 10 and 11 Oct. 1964.

22. CJW letter to KLW, 27 Oct. 1964. Charles Whitman spoke often
about masturbation and what he called wet dreams (once even on an

airplane). He frequently used these accounts to prove that his penis often "los[t] control," emphasizing that, upon their reunion, "that problem will soon be remedied" as his marital "rights" would be restored: see CJW letters to KLW, 6 and 31 May and 3 June 1964. Charlie's intense nighttime anxiety and compulsiveness around sex may suggest a response to past trauma: for research on this phenomenon, see Mark F. Schwartz, Lori D. Galperin, and William H. Masters, "Post Traumatic Stress, Sexual Trauma and Dissociative Disorder: Issues Related to Intimacy and Sexuality," National Criminal Justice Reference Service, 17 March 1995, https://www.ojp.gov/pdffiles1/Photocopy /153416NCJRS.pdf.

23. KLW letter to CJW, 14 Oct. 1964.

24. KLW letters to CJW, 17 and 21 Oct. 1964; KLW letter to family, 22 Oct. 1964.

25. KLW letter to CJW, 21 Oct. 1964.

26. KLW letter to CJW, 17 Oct. 1964; CJW letter to KLW, 18 Oct. 1964.

27. KLW letter to CJW, 4 Oct. 1964.

28. Christina Wolbrecht and J. Kevin Corder, *A Century of Votes for Women: American Elections Since Suffrage* (Cambridge University Press, 2020), 117–119, 123.

29. CJW letters to KLW, 5 and 11 Oct. 1964; Jane (Spotts) Conway, email and narrative about C. A. Whitman, 28 Jan. 2021.

30. Anita Brewer, "Students and Parents Think Alike," *Austin American-Statesman*, 6 Nov. 1964, p. 1.

31. Jack Bell, "All Signs Point to LBJ Win," *Austin American-Statesman*, 2 Nov. 1964, p. 1; KLW letter to family, 14 Oct. 1964; KLW letter to CJW, 22 Oct. 1964.

32. KLW letters to CJW, 1 and 3 Nov. 1964.

33. Emails regarding voter history request, Travis County Tax Office Voter Registration Division, 10 Nov. 2020.

34. KLW letter to CJW, 22 Oct. 1964; CJW letters to KLW, 16 June, 24 and 31 Oct., and 13 Nov. 1964.

35. "The Power Women Have over Men: A Symposium," *Reader's Digest*, Nov. 1964, pp. 71–74; CJW letter to KLW, 27 Oct. 1964.

36. KLW letter to CJW, 1 Nov. 1964.

37. KLW letters to CJW, 6 and 30 Oct. 1964.

38. CJW letters to KLW, 3, 4, 5, and 10 Oct. 1964.

39. Al Williams, "Travis County Smashes Voting Record," *Austin American-Statesman*, 4 Nov. 1964, p. 1.

40. KLW letter to CJW, 30 Oct. 1964; CJW letters to KLW, 2 Nov. and 31 Oct. 1964.

41. KLW letter to CJW, 4 Nov. 1964 (added to letter 3 Nov. 1964).

42. KLW letter to CJW, 4 Nov. 1964.

43. KLW letter to CJW, 5 Nov. 1964; CJW letter to KLW, 2 Nov. 1964.

44. CJW letters to KLW, 4 and 6 Nov. 1964.

45. CJW letter to KLW, 8 Nov. 1964.

46. CJW letters to KLW, 6, 9, and 10 Nov. 1964.

47. KLW letters to CJW, 12 and 17 Nov. 1964; CJW letter to KLW, 14 Nov. 1964.

48. KLW letter to CJW, 17 Nov. 1964.

49. KLW letter to CJW, 12 Nov. 1964.

50. Ibid.

51. KLW letter to CJW, 15 Nov. 1964.

52. KLW letters to CJW, 15, 16, and 17 Nov. 1964; CJW letter to KLW, 13 Nov. 1964.

53. KLW letters to CJW, 17 and 18 Nov. 1964.

54. KLW letter to CJW, 20 Nov. 1964.

55. KLW letter to CJW, 20 and 28 Nov. 1964.

56. Ibid.; CJW letters to KLW, 13 and 16 Nov. 1964.

"Back to Normal Soon"

1. KLW letters to CJW, 5, 9, and 17 Nov. 1964.

2. KLW letters to CJW, 28 Oct. 1964 and 5 Dec. 1963.

3. *Daily Texan*, 4 Dec. 1964, p. 2; CJW Christmas card note to Leissners, 16 Dec. 1964.

4. KLW letter to FL, 22 Jan. 1965.

5. KLW letters to family, 9 and 22 Jan. 1965.

6. KLW letter to family, 27 Jan. 1965.

7. KLW letter to FL, 22 Jan. 1965.

8. KLW letters to family, 9 Jan. and 11 Feb. 1965.

9. KLW letter to family, 25 March 1965.

10. Charles J. Whitman employment history, p. 2, APD Files, AHC; KLW letter to family, 4 April 1965.

11. KLW letters to family, 25 March and 26 April 1965.

12. KLW letter to family, 5 April 1965; see also UT Austin *Cactus* yearbook, 1965, p. 412.

13. CJW letter to Leissners, 13 June 1965.

14. Lloyd Mathews and Tony Proffitt, "Police Charge UT Student in Slaying of Two Girls," *Austin American-Statesman*, 7 Aug. 1965, p. 1; "Blaze Erupts in UT Tower," *Austin American-Statesman*, 10 Aug. 1965, pp. 1, 6.

15. KLW letters to family, 27 June and 31 July 1965.

16. KLW letters to family, 27 June and 12 July 1965; CJW birthday card to KLW, 3 July 1964.

17. CJW and KLW letter to her parents, 13 June 1965.

18. KLW letter to family, 31 July 1965.

19. Here and in the preceding paragraphs, I have adapted observations and analysis from my essay, "But What Would *She* Say? Reframing 'Domestic Terror' in the 1966 UT Austin Shooting," *Pacific Coast Philology* 52, no. 2 (2017): 294–313.

20. KLW letter to family, 28 Aug. 1965.

21. Statement of John and Fran Morgan to Texas Department of Public Service, 2 Aug. 1966, APD Files, AHC.

22. KLW letter to CJW, 22 Sept. 1964.

23. KLW letter to CJW, 8 Sept. 1965.

24. Ibid.

25. KLW letter to CJW, 11 Sept. 1965.

26. KLW letter to family, 27 Sept. 1965.

27. Letter from Pastor B. C. Schmidt, Associate Pastor of First Methodist Church of Austin, to Mr. and Mrs. Leissner, 3 Aug. 1966.

28. KLW letter to family, 14 Nov. 1965; Deffenbaugh summary statement of James Harry Barnfield, 5 Aug. 1966, p. 1, AHC.

29. Teacher portrait of Kathy Leissner Whitman, Sidney Lanier High School, *Viking* yearbook, 1966, p. 15; a sample of CJW letters to KLW, referencing his preferences for hair color: 13 and 30 Jan. 1964 and 7 Dec. 1963.

30. Deffenbaugh summary, Statement of Barnfield, APD files, AHC.

31. Nancy Glass et al., "Non-Fatal Strangulation Is an Important Risk Factor for Homicide of Women," *Journal of Emergency Medicine* 35, no. 3 (Oct. 2008): 329–335, https://www.jem-journal.com/article /S0736-4679(07)00414-3/fulltext; see also Jane Monckton Smith's 2020 "Non-Fatal Strangulation: A Summary Report on Data Collected from SUTDA Survey" (UK), which indicates strangulation as a "high risk marker" of future homicide, SUTDA.org, accessed Oct. 26, 2022, https://sutda.org/wp-content/uploads/Non-fatal-strangulation-Survey -June-2020-.pdf.

Behind the Eyewall

1. Liz Smith, "No Blood, Some Tears, a Sweat of Money," *Sports Illustrated*, 7 March 1966, Vault SI.com, https://vault.si.com/vault/1966 /03/07/no-blood-some-tears-a-sweat-of-money.

2. KLW letter to family, 9 Feb. 1966; J. R. Gonzales, "Dome of the Month: Bullfighting under the Roof," *Houston Chronicle*, 30 April 2012, https://blog.chron.com/bayoucityhistory/2012/04/dome-of-the -month-bullfighting-under-the-roof.

3. KLW letter to family, 9 Feb. 1966.

4. Ibid.

5. KLW letters to family, 15 and 18 Feb. 1966.

6. Statement of John and Fran Morgan to Texas DPS, 2 Aug. 1966, APD files, AHC. In a Valentine's Day letter, 14 Feb. 1964, Whitman used a cover of "privacy" to urge Kathy to be more explicit in her letters.

7. KLW letter to family, 9 Feb. 1966.

8. KLW letter to family, 16 Feb. 1966; see also reference to the insurance policies in a report about the Whitman estate following the murders: "Sniper Charles Whitman's Estate Worth $39,110.37," *Austin American-Statesman*, 5 May 1967.

9. "1966: House Passes Cold-War GI Bill of Rights," *International Herald Tribune*, 7 Feb. 2016 (reprint from *New York Herald Tribune*, European edition, 8 Feb. 1966), https://iht-retrospective.blogs.nytimes .com/2016/02/07/1966-house-passes-cold-war-g-i-bill-of-rights; "Congress Approves 'Cold War GI' Benefits," *CQ Almanac*, 22nd ed. (1966), 313–316, https://library.cqpress.com/cqalmanac/document.php?id= cqal66-1301479.

10. KLW letter to family, 15 Feb. 1966.

11. AP, "Congress Passes Cold War GI Bill," *Daily Texan*, 11 Feb. 1966, p. 1.

12. Maurice Beckham, report of Whitman bank accounts, 2 Aug. 1966, Texas DPS, APD files, AHC.

13. "Today in Music History: 'These Boots Are Made for Walkin,'" Minnesota Public Radio, *The Current*, 22 Jan. 2016, https://www .thecurrent.org/feature/2016/01/21/today-in-music-history-these-boots -are-made-for-walkin.

14. Police records referenced in the FBI files, Cole Report, 17 Aug. 1966, pp. 20–21; see also Lavergne, *Sniper in the Tower*, 55–56.

15. Maurice Beckham, report of Whitman bank accounts, 2 Aug. 1966, Texas DPS, APD files, AHC.

16. Statement of Whitman family physician, 22 Aug. 1966, J. Myers Cole Report, APD files, AHC; Lavergne, *Sniper in the Tower*, 47.

17. Maurice D. Heatly, appointment report of Charles J. Whitman, 29 March 1966, pp. 1–2.

18. Lavergne, *Sniper in the Tower*, 68–69; Pamela Colloff, "96 Minutes," *Texas Monthly*, Aug. 2006, https://www.texasmonthly.com/articles/96-minutes.

19. FBI files, Statement of Joseph G. Leduc, 15 Aug. 1966, APD files, AHC; see also record of military service for Joseph G. Leduc, National Personnel Records Center, National Archives. Leduc does not mention the property default to the FBI—I discovered that myself: see Scott-Coe, *MASS,* 131–138.

20. Nelson Leissner interview, 27 Oct. 2015; see also Scott-Coe, "Listening to Kathy."

21. Nelson Leissner interviews, 27 and 30 Oct. 2015.

22. KLW letters to family, 25 April and 20 June 1966.

23. Ibid. Stark offers a disturbing case study of one man's arbitrary household rules for his girlfriend (including restrictions for her pet) in *Coercive Control*, 317–320.

24. KLW letter to family, 25 April 1966; Lindsey Taylor, "8611 N. MoPac," *Community Impact Newspaper*, 21 April 2014, https://communityimpact.com/news/2014/04/21/8611-n-mopac-2.

25. KLW letter to family, 1 May 1966; AP, "Pioneering Heart Surgeon DeBakey Dead at 99," NBCNews.com, 12 July 2008, http://www.nbcnews.com/id/25649134/print/1/displaymode/1098.

26. KLW letter to family, 1 May 1966.

27. KLW note to Mother, n.d., 1966.

28. Statement of Joseph G. Leduc to FBI, 15 Aug. 1966, APD files, AHC.

29. Beckham, report of Whitman bank accounts, AHC; see also Lavergne, *Sniper in the Tower*, 54.

30. KLW letter to family, 20 June 1966.

31. Statement of Dr. Clyde Lee, Texas University, to Texas DPS, APD files, AHC.

32. KLW letter to family, 20 June 1966; Ray Leissner interview, 22 Nov. 2015.

33. Wilda Campbell interview, 27 March 2021; KLW letter to family, 20 June 1966.

34. Ray Leissner interview, 22 Nov. 2015.

35. KLW letter to family, 11 July 1966.

36. Ibid.

37. Ibid.

38. Record of military service for Joseph G. Leduc, National Personnel Records Center, National Archives; Lavergne, *Sniper in the Tower*, 85–86, 95.

39. Nelson Leissner interview, 20 July 2020.

40. KLW letters to family, 20 June and 11 July 1966.

41. See Stark, *Coercive Control*, 210, 267–270.

42. Rosemary Sobol, "Rare Photos, Interviews Honor 8 Nurses Slain by Richard Speck in 1966," *Chicago Tribune,* 14 June 2016, https://www.chicagotribune.com/news/ct-richard-speck-chicago-mass -murder-victims-20200815-ofyebzxw5jgxrloxvxe4xmezwq-story.html; Ysabel Vitangcol, "I Survived a Notorious Mass Murder and Never Told My Story—Until Now," *Vice*, 21 Feb. 2020, https://www.vice.com/en /article/xgqvjj/richard-speck-murder-nurses-survivor-corazon-amurao -luisa-silverio.

43. Doris Kreuz letter to Mr. and Mrs. Leissner, 11 Aug. 1966, private archive of Nelson Leissner; Supplemental Defense Report from Austin National Bank, 3 Aug. 1966, APD files, AHC; see also Lavergne, *Sniper in the Tower*, 90.

44. Statement of John and Fran Morgan to Texas DPS, 2 Aug. 1962, APD files, AHC, 1–2.

45. Switchboard operators Darleen Koenig and Linda (Damerau) Cipriano interviews, 9 and 16 Oct. 2020 (respectively).

46. See photo caption, "Congress Renamed," *Austin American-Statesman*, 30 July 1966, p. 15.

47. Photos from the scene of her death show that Kathy had pinned her bangs carefully before she went to bed; APD files, AHC.

48. Marje Janacek and Wilda Campbell interviews, 10 Dec. 2015 and 27 March 2021 (respectively).

49. No autopsy was performed for Kathy or for Margaret; former *Daily Texan* editor and reporter Dave McNeely described his memory of a boat ride on Lake Austin in late July with Kathy and Charlie and other friends—his article from the *Houston Chronicle*, 24 July 2016, is cached here: https://www.pressreader.com.

Epilogue

1. Wilda Campbell (roommate of Kathy's cousin Margie Ann Leissner) interview, 27 March 2021.

2. Nelson Leissner interviews, 30 Oct. 2015 and 26 Jan. 2020.

3. Estimates of Carla's death toll vary slightly: I use totals provided

by the National Weather Service and updated for the fiftieth anniversary of Carla in 2011, https://www.weather.gov/crp/hurricanecarla.

4. Nelson Leissner interview, 20 July 2020.

5. CJW letter to Leissners, 1 Aug. 1966.

6. Ibid. I analyzed this artifact at length in the context of Whitman's attitudes towards gender, sexuality, and violence: see Jo Scott-Coe, "Invisible Women, Fairy Tale Death: How Stories of Public Murder Minimize Terror at Home," *American Studies Journal* 62 (2017), https://doi.org/10.18422/62-05.

7. KLW letter to family, 1 July 1963.

8. See Brittany E. Hayes's analysis of women's resistance strategies in coercive and controlling relationships: "Abusive Relationships: An Alternative Framework," *SAGE Open*, July-September 2013, pp. 1–10, https://journals.sagepub.com/doi/pdf/10.1177/2158244013501154.

9. "The Most Dangerous Time," *Guardian Australia Special* (interviews by Melissa Davey), 2 June 2015, https://www.theguardian.com/society/ng-interactive/2015/jun/02/domestic-violence-five-women-tell-their-stories-of-leaving-the-most-dangerous-time; see Walker, *The Battered Woman Syndrome*, 277–317; see also Jana Kasperkevic, interview with survivor and advocate Kit Gruelle, "Private Violence: Up to 75% of Abused Women Are Killed after They Leave Their Partners," *The Guardian*, 20 Oct. 2014, https://www.theguardian.com/money/us-money-blog/2014/oct/20/domestic-private-violence-women-men-abuse-hbo-ray-rice; and Lauren Pelley, "Leaving Is the 'Most Dangerous Time' for Domestic Violence Victims, Experts Say," CBC News Toronto, 8 Dec. 2016, https://www.cbc.ca/news/canada/toronto/domestic-violence-victims-1.3885381.

10. Carolyn B. Ramsey, "The Exit Myth: Family Law, Gender Roles, and Changing Attitudes toward Female Victims of Domestic Violence," *Michigan Journal of Gender and Law* 20, no. 1 (2013): 1, 2, 13. On 25 Sept. 1964, *TIME* magazine published a report that summarized a sampling of such theories—a text I cite earlier in Kathy's narrative; see Joanne Shulmann, "State-by-State Information on Marital Rape Exemption Laws," appendix II in Russell, *Rape in Marriage*, 375–381; Stop Abuse for Everyone (SAFE), "Our History," http://www.safeaustin.org/about-us/our-mission/our-history.

11. Margaret Howard, "Husband-Wife Homicide: An Essay from a Family Law Perspective," *Law and Contemporary Problems* 49, no. 1 (Winter 1986): 65 (note 8 on empirical data), https://scholarship.law.duke.edu/cgi/viewcontent.cgi?article=3825&context=lcp.

12. NCADV, "Domestic Violence," 2020; NCADV, "Domestic

Violence and the Black Community," 2020, https://assets.speakcdn.com /assets/2497/dv_in_the_black_community.pdf; NCADV, "Domestic Violence Against American Indian and Alaska Native Women," 2016, https://assets.speakcdn.com/assets/2497/american_indian_and_alaskan _native_women__dv.pdf; NCADV blog, "Domestic Violence and the LGBTQ Community," 6 June 2018, https://ncadv.org/blog/posts /domestic-violence-and-the-lgbtq-community.

13. David Nevin, "Charlie Whitman: The Eagle Scout Who Grew Up with a Tortured Mind," *LIFE* magazine, 12 Aug. 1966, pp. 28D-29; in a footnote, Gary Lavergne references the Texas DPS summary report wherein Kathy's fear was recorded: see *Sniper in the Tower*, 59 and 62 (note); Special Report of the Grand Jury, 147th Judicial District Court of Travis County, Texas, 5 Aug. 1966; Connally Commission, *Report to the Governor, Medical Aspects of the Charles J. Whitman Catastrophe*, 8 Sept. 1966; see also Scott-Coe, "But What Would *She* Say?," 294–313.

14. US Dept. of Health, Education, and Welfare, Wilbur J. Cohen, Secretary of Public Health Service, and William H. Stewart, Surgeon General, *Vital Statistics of the United States 1966: Volume II: Mortality, Part A* (Washington, DC, 1968), table 1–26: "Deaths from 285 Selected Causes, by Color and Sex: United States and Each State."

15. Supplementary offense report of Sgt. B. Gregory, 5 Aug. 1966, APD files, AHC.

Index

Photos and illustrations are indicated by italicized page numbers.

Feit, Rev. John, 36–37

fidelity, 167, 169, 170, 175, 182, 185–186, 195, 216

finance company, 231–232

firearms, Whitman, Charles, 46, 57, 96, 148, 202, 207, 259; animals and, 44, 132; with fantasies of death and violence, 155, 253; pointed and brandished, 45, 244; rifles, 140, 156, 253. *See also* Tower shooting, at UT Austin

First Methodist Church, Austin, 243–244

First Methodist Church, Needville, 12, 60, 269

Fitzgerald, Jay, 294n24

friendships, with women, 98–99, 116, 123, 166, 176, 249. *See also* social networks

Fuess, Elaine. *See* Brazzell, Elaine

funeral, of Whitman, Kathy Leissner, 269–270

gambling, 46, 47, 130, 132, 136, 140, 144, 148, 151

Garza, Irene, 37

gaslighting, 81, 84, 110, 156, 185–186, 205, 237

gender, xiii, xviii, xix, 302n18, 319n6; IPV and, 273, 274; studies, 172, 309n28

Gendered Society, The (Kimmel), 309n28

Giant (film), 106

Gilbreth, Lillian, 72

Goldwater, Barry, *199*, 200, 214, 215, 218, 220

Goodall Wooten dormitories, UT Austin, 37–38, 43–44, 297n30

Gore, Leslie, 169

Goretti, Maria, 271

grand jury, 274

Great Hurricane (1900), 25

Green, Venus, 304n37

Griswold v. Connecticut (1965), xiv

Guerra, Maria, 36–37

Gunby, David H., 289n1

guns. *See* firearms, Whitman, Charles

hair: bodily autonomy and, 244; color, 115, 121, 125, 137, 145, 156, 244; sex life and, 224; style, 128, 138, 225, 240

Haiti, 111–112, 116, 197

Hamilton, Eleanor, 177

Harry's Place (UT undergraduate library), 133, 144, 184, 217

health, 76, 166, 168, 221–222; medical establishment, patriarchy and, 55, 183, 198, 200, 237; medical procedures and lack of empathy, 99, 203, 206, 244, 312n10; oral, 59, 135, 137, 138. *See also* reproductive health

Heatly, Maurice, 253

help-seeking behaviors. *See* survival strategies

Hispanics, xiv–xv, 19–20, 36–37, 176

Holloway, Cheryl (cousin), 137, 138, 140, 269

Holloway, Frances. *See* Leissner, Frances Holloway

Holloway, Ida Lee "Granny" (grandmother), *77*, 77–78

Holloway, Margie Ann (cousin), 260, 318n1

home loans, Veterans Administration, 251

homemaking: in letters of Leissner, Frances Holloway, 101; Whitman, Kathy Leissner, and, 97, 207, 217, 222, 225, 227, 231, 238, 241, 248, 249

homophobia, 55–56, 79, 170, 302n18

homosexuality, 79, 169–170, 274, 302n15

honeymoon, 59, 60, 64–70, *65*, 72, 125

hooks, bell, xvii

hostage taking, coercive control and, xviii, 303n24

housekeeping: expectations, 59–60, 249; in letters of Whitman, Kathy Leissner, 96–98, 106, 108, 122, 202, 258, 261; at UT Austin, 34

housing, 13, 59–60, 71, 86, 92–95, 119, 133–134, 144, 201–202, 251

Houston Astrodome, bullfights at, 247–248

Houston Chronicle (newspaper), 318n49

Hubel, Sylvia, xii–xiii

Hudson, Rock, 106, 213

Huff-York, Mable, 293n12, 293n13, 293n20

hunting, 14, 43–44, 77, 140, 148, 225, 244. *See also* animals

Hurricane Carla (1961), xi, 4–5, 32, 239,

270, 271; pregnancy, 117, 118, 119, 134, 158, 165, 182, 184, 197, 214, 218; rape myths and, 194; reunion, 185, 225; self-improvement plan, 131–132; sewing machine funds, 120; sex life, 135, 140, 212, 218, 221; sexual coercion, 140, 212, 218, 221; smoking, 134–135; triangulation of communication, 111, 116–120, 236, 270; as trophies, 275; UT Austin and reinstatement failure, 103, 117; violation of boundaries, 218; voting, 214
letters, of Whitman, Kathy Leissner: academic progress at UT Austin, 49–50, 51, 72, 73, 74, 85, 87–89, *88*, 185; to advice column, 18; alcohol, 66, 67, 136, 166, 216, 220; annotations, 16, 165, 182, 188, 230–231, 237, 262; anxiety, 58; arrest of Whitman, Charles, 149–150; autonomy and, 127, 187, 271, 275; baby brother Adam, 207, 208, 217, 225, 226, 230, 260, 262; bargaining, 103; birth control, 55; birthdays, 52, 74, 121, 139, 191, 235–236, 260, 261; body image, 168, 171, 174–175, 176, 189, 192; Boy Scouts, 230; from classmate, 16; cooking, 96–97, 98; death, 250; depression, 158, 162, 237; dieting, 129, 189, 191; economics, 80, 81, 104–105, 121, 135, 230–231; employment, 96–97, 101–107, *108*, 109, 114–115, 120, 126–129, 133, 138, 175–176, 184–186, 190, 204, 206–207, 231–233, 238–242, 248–251, 258–259; exercise, 168, 176; from extended family, 16; family dynamics, 49–53; from female coworkers of Whitman, Charles, 185–186; fidelity, 167, 175, 185, 195; Frosty, 91–92; gambling, 46, 136, 151; gun range, 207; gynecological surgery and recovery, 202–203, 205; hair color, 115, 121, 125, 145; hair style, 128, 225; homemaking, 97, 207, 217, 225, 231, 238, 241, 248, 249; honeymoon, 64–67; housekeeping, 96–98, 106, 108, 122, 202, 258, 261; humor, 18, 97, 121, 129, 187, 192, 225–226; images of, *88*, *108*, *161*, *223*, *263*; as intercessor, 74–75, 85, 119, 208; Jacksonville and first

impression, 94–95; Jazzland, 147, 174; Kappa Delta Pi Honor Society, 233; legacy of, xvii, 276–277; to Leissner, Frances Holloway, 17, 64–67, 72–73, 74–76, 80, 81, 85–86, 87–89, *88*, 92–107, *108*, 109–122, 141–144, 147–148, 157, 176, 184, 205, 208, 228–229, 230–233, 235–237, 238, 243, 248–250, 256–261; life insurance, 250; in "Listening to Kathy," xiv; marital intimacy, 53–54, 59; marriage and relationship, 186–187, 188–190, 205, 206, 209–214, 216, 217, 219–220, 243; married life, 73–75, 85–86; medication, 183, 237, 248; movie recommendations, 106; panic attacks, 191–192; pop culture, 173–174, 187, 190, 193; pregnancy, xix, 158, 163–164, 177, 184, 208; pregnancy scare, 92–93; pregnant women in Jacksonville, 95, 99; rape, 194; reunion, 178–179, 181–182, 192, 225–226; Scocie, 242–243, 257; self-blame, xx, 130, 136–137, 144, 150, 162, 174, 209; sewing, 97, 115, 121, 230, 233, 261; sex and double standard, 194–195; sex life, 175, 178, 182, 189, 192, 211–214, 217, 219, 220, 224, 225–226; sexual coercion, 172–173, 211–212, 217, 220; smoking, 136; solitude, 201, 249; study of, xvii–xviii; style and content changes, 127, 174, 229; as teacher, 204, 217, 222, 232–233, 238–242, 248–249, 258–259; telephone access, 203; with "to" and "too," 221, 262–263, *263*; travel, *88*, 103, *108*, 116, 117, 118, 122, 123, 238, 271; USMC, 95–96, 111–113, 121, 208, 222; UT Austin, 121, 122, 133–134, 138, 144, 166, 171–172, 176, 185, 190, 230, 233, 236; UT Austin Tower, 164–165; voting, 214–215; weather, 173, 258; wedding anniversary, 132, 197; wedding planning, 52–53, 55; weight loss, 192, 209–210, 261; Wharton Junior College, 128, 129, 133; Whitman family dynamics, 70, 91–93, 145, 157, 160, *161*, 162, 169–171, 224–225, 257–258
letters, structural elements: annotations, 16, 139, 165, 168, 182, 188,

169, 251; films, 106, 117, 138, 167, 173–174, 184, 188, 190, 235, 260, 264; novels, 193; records, 187, 212; TV movies, 200; TV shows, 217, 258
pornography, 47, 299n4
"power and control wheel," xix, 239n12
POWs, 303n24
pranks, 44, 46–47, 147, 204, 299n4
pregnancy: future planning, 151, 182, 197; Jacksonville women and, 95, 99; of Leissner, Frances Holloway, 182–184, 203, 205; in letters of Whitman, Charles, 117, 118, 119, 134, 158, 165, 182, 184, 197, 214, 218; in letters of Whitman, Kathy Leissner, xix, 92–93, 95, 99, 158, 163–164, 177, 184, 208; phantom, 162, 163–164, 165; in pop culture, 173–174; scare, 92–93, 119, 199; sperm count and, 177; test, 158, 163–164, 165
prejudice, xiii, 12, 32
premarital exam, 59, 60
Presley, Elvis, 189
priests, in Catholic Church, 67; credible accusations of sexual abuse and, xii; Feit, Rev. John, and, 36–37; Leduc, Rev. Joseph "Gil," and, 42, 44, 52, 61–63, *63*, 133, 254, 259, 261, 301n38, 317n19
privacy, 53, 86, 107, 249, 316n6. *See also* secrecy
Protestants, 61, 104, 243
psychiatry, 81, 82, 83, 302n18
psychological assessment, of Whitman, Kathy Leissner, 222, 224

race: as factor in "hierarchies of victimization," xi; interracial marriage, xiv; IPV and, 274; loss of records due to violence, xvi; 1966 statistics of femicide and, 274; witness testimony and, 37
racial segregation: businesses, 13, 72, 113, *114*, 304n37; churches, 13; education, 13, 20, 23, 31, 32, 34, 172; housing, 13; telephone company, 113, *114*, 304n37
racial threats, 45, 132
racial violence, xviii, 45, 139
racism: activism against, xiv, 34, 72, 139;

anti-miscegenation laws, xiv; discrimination, 296n18; Ku Klux Klan with terrorism and, 139; prejudice, xiii, 32; sexism and, 296n18; stereotypes of danger, 36
Ramsey, Carolyn B., 272
Ransom, Harry H., 133. *See also* Harry's Place
rape: Austin Center for Battered Women and Rape Crisis Center, 273; blaming victims of, 194; Catholic priests with, 36–37; UT Austin with murder and, 235
Rather, Dan, 3, 26
Reader's Digest (magazine), 216–217
Reagan, Ronald, 272
real estate: Leduc with land purchase, 42, 254, 317n19; Leissner, Raymond, with, 182; lots for Leissner ranch-style home, 3, 13–14, 293n14; Whitman, Charles, with, 231
record-keeping, women's: "epistemic smothering" of, xi; examples of, xviii, 9–11, 15–19, 259; theories of interpretation, xvii
Red Cross, 27, 31
religion: Bible class at UT, 141–142; Catholic rituals and, 61; among Leissner family members, 12–13, 37, 60, 61–62; prayer, 83, 100, 137, 143, 144, 149–150, 174, 193; source of concern, 104, 259. *See also* Catholic Church; First Methodist Church, Austin; First Methodist Church, Needville
reproductive health: cramps, 130, 144, 207; cystitis, 147, 198; gynecological surgery and recovery, 198–199, 202–203, 205–206, 209, 214; premarital exam, 59, 60; sterility, 177, 198; stress and, 163; unidentified illness, 197. *See also* birth control; coercive control; pregnancy
reproductive rights activism, xiv
Republican convention (1964), *199*, 200
responsibility: in *Atlas Shrugged*, 193; gender-based, 14–15, 36, 121; individual, 15, 23, 156, 167, 195, 274; mutual, 73–74, 119, 186–187. *See also* social networks
Richards, Ann, xiv

153, *153*; with divorce, 256, 257;
escape from abusive marriage, 252,
253, 255–256, 257; financial support
and, 157; with homophobia, 79;
with isolation, 41; letter to Leissner,
Frances Holloway, from, 70; murder
of, xii, 267, 269, 272, 274; no autopsy
for, 318n49; with police response as
domestic violence victim, 251–252;
relationship with family, 170, 259;
visit with, 262; with Whitman, Kathy
Leissner, and Leissner, Frances Holloway, *234*; wife beating and, 199
Whitman, Patrick (brother-in-law), 41,
62, 66, 84, 91, 138, 224–225; attempt
to enter Navy, 138; with Austin
visit, 79, 80, 81, 83, 85–86; birthday,
257–258; depression and, 67, 79;
homosexuality and, 79, 169–170,
302n15; hunting trip, 77; marriage,
257; politics and, 214; prom and, 182;
relationship with family, 169–170,
253, 258; at St. John Vianney Seminary, 79, 302n15
wife beating, xix, 98, 132, 139, 141, 199,
205, 253. *See also* Intimate Partner
Violence
women: activists, xiv, xv, 34, 273; Alaska
Native, 274; American Indian, 274;
Austin Center for Battered Women
and Rape Crisis Center, 273; Black,
32, 34, 274, 304n37; blaming of, 173,
194, 205; derogatory terms for, 177,
196, 216, 220; in education, 32, 34,
41, 73; with employment discrimination, 103, 109; Engineering Wives

Club, 249; faculty at UT Austin, 34,
41, 73; as family documentarians,
xviii, 9–11, 12, 259; friendships with,
98–99, 116, 123, 166, 176, 249;
Hispanic, xiv–xv, 36–37; IPV and,
xvii, 98, 132, 139, 141, 199, 205,
253, 273, 274; in Jacksonville, 95, 99,
185–186, 195; memory tools of society and exclusion of, xvi; murder of
nursing students, 263; National Wom-
en's Conference, xiii; operators and
Hurricane Carla, 27; patriarchy and,
55, 172, 183, 198, 200, 237; pharmacists in mid-1960s, 172, 294n24;
"The Power Women Have over Men,"
216–217; pregnancy and, 14, 95, 103,
164, 177; record-keeping of, xiii, xvii,
xviii, 9–11, 15–19, 259; at Republican
convention of 1964, *199*, 200; role
of, 72–73; in science, 32, 171–172,
294n24, 296n18; students at UT
Austin, 29, 32, 34–36, 40; in Tareyton
ads, 200, 312n45; UT Austin, security
and, 35–36; white, 32, 113, *114*,
200; Whitman, Charles, and attitude
toward, 186, 194, 195–196, 216, 220,
308n13. *See also* friendships; social
networks
women's movement, xiv
Wonder Fabric Center, 4, 38
WSR-57, 26

Yarborough, Sen. Ralph, 251
Yelderman, Dr. Joe, 13
Yellow Rolls-Royce, The (film), 235